Louise Gillette
(619) 438-1216

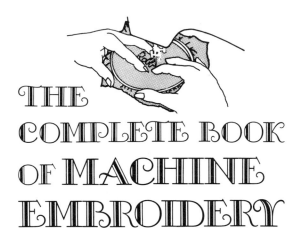

THE
COMPLETE BOOK
OF MACHINE
EMBROIDERY

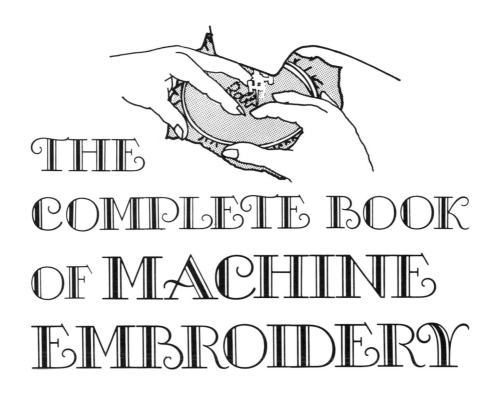

THE COMPLETE BOOK OF MACHINE EMBROIDERY

ROBBIE *and* TONY FANNING

CHILTON BOOK COMPANY   RADNOR, PENNSYLVANIA

Dedication

For my parents,
Pat and Roberta Losey Patterson

R.L.F.

To my brother, John,
whose industry and example have
led me to where I am today.

A.D.F.

Copyright © 1986 by Robbie and Tony Fanning
Previous edition published as *Decorative Machine Stitchery,*
copyright © 1976 by Butterick Publishing
All Rights Reserved
Published in Radnor, Pennsylvania 19089 by Chilton Book Company

Designed by William E. Lickfield
Manufactured in the United States of America
Cover photo by the Fannings

Library of Congress Cataloging in Publication Data
Fanning, Robbie.
   The complete book of machine embroidery.
   (Creative machine arts series)
   Rev. ed. of: Decorative machine stitchery. c1976.
   Bibliography: p. 275
   Includes index.
   1. Machine sewing.   2. Embroidery, Machine.
I. Fanning, Tony.   II. Fanning, Robbie. Decorative
machine stitchery.   III. Title.   IV. Series.
TT13.F36 1986   746.44'028   86–47615
ISBN 0–8019–7648–0 (pbk.)

3 4 5 6 7 8 9 0   5 4 3 2 1 0 9

Contents

Foreword

I inherited Robbie Fanning. When I came to work as editor of *Needle & Thread* magazine, she was writing a regular column. Four years later, her "Commentary" is still going strong— it's one of our readers' favorite features.

I noticed immediately that Robbie is a fine writer, and every editor appreciates that. As I read her columns and came to know her, I realized more: This woman has fun doing what she does; she's marvelously well-read and passes along little gems from that reading without ever seeming pedantic; she will admit that she doesn't know something. The latter characteristic is endearing, but more than that, it frees her to learn. And learn she does. I confess I've come to depend on Robbie's nearness by telephone. Whether it's a source for a product, advice on a fine point of technique, or news about who in our field is doing what, Robbie's right there for me.

If you haven't read anything Robbie's written, you'll be impressed, as I was, by how downright readable she *is*. We've all picked up authoritative, accurate textbooks and read them dutifully to learn what we needed to know. Just as often, though, we've laid the books down again without reading more than a few pages. A certain joy, a certain friendliness, must emerge from the printed word to engage us and carry us along on an adventure. Robbie conveys that joy and friendliness—and lest you think that the subject of machine embroidery doesn't embody adventure, start by reading Chapter 14 of this book. The creative process is real self-discovery, perhaps the highest form of adventure we humans have developed.

Margaret Dittman
Editor, *Needle & Thread*

Preface

The woodworker has a lathe, the potter has a wheel, and I have my sewing machine. This is my tool, my vehicle for expressing a lifelong love of fabric and thread.

Machine embroidery is a simple craft, with only four variations of the basic lock-stitch: either straight stitch or zigzag, either more thread showing on top of the fabric or more underneath. But by playing with different weights and colors of threads; varying the quality of the stitched line (regular vs. free, long stitches vs. short); trying special sewing-machine functions and accessories such as automatic stitches and the tailor-tacking foot; and experimenting with any "fabric" that will pass under the needle, from cotton to window screening, today's machine embroiderer creates marvelous variety—as you will see in the artists' work on these pages.

The first edition of this book, *Decorative Machine Stitchery*, was published ten years ago. *The Complete Book of Machine Embroidery* represents a substantial revision of that earlier text because the world of machine embroidery has changed drastically in the intervening years. Now we have specialized supplies available—more convenient ways to mark designs, to stabilize fabrics, even to hold our fabric taut in a hoop. But the biggest change is the marriage of the computer and the sewing machine.

Ten years ago I said, "And you *don't* have to own a fancy machine that does 400 stitches and walks the dog to do most of the designs in this book. Even the zigzag work can be done on a treadle machine, although obviously it's much more laborious."

Today I would amend that. You still don't have to own a fancy machine to do machine embroidery—but it's even more of a joy to do it on a computer machine. The design engineers of the new machines have incorporated feedback from thousands of home sewers and machine embroiderers into subtle improvements in threading procedures, tension adjustments, presser feet, and much more. I love writing spur-of-the-moment messages in thread. I love being able to make a buttonhole by touching a control button, knowing the machine will then repeat it perfectly as many times as I want. I love being able to *see* how much thread is left in the bobbin. I love the 7 mm width of my zigzag for machine applique. I love being able to combine patterns, elongate them, mirror-image them, play with them. Have I made myself clear? I love my computer machine!

No, you don't need a fancy machine—but if you haven't seen a computer machine, treat yourself to a demonstration. You'll feel as though you've entered the 21st century of sewing machines.

The last ten years have also brought us feedback from readers of the earlier book. You have written us thousands of letters, sharing techniques, alerting us to machine-embroidery artists around the world, asking intelligent questions, pointing out improvements. We have incorporated your suggestions and criticisms into this edition.

In fact, your letters caused us to change our entire presentation. Ten years ago we organized our book in a learn-by-doing sampler of techniques, with a project at the end of each chapter that drew on the knowledge learned in it. I also listed additional ideas after each project. In ten years, you have often commented enthusiastically on the additional ideas, but rarely commented on the designs on the projects. A typical letter would say "The bag was clever, but I made it for my daughter and she loves horses, so I put my own design on it."

Then something Tecla Miceli-Schulz said clicked in my mind. She tells her students to "stitch from the heart or you'll hate doing the work — and it will show." I realized that most of you do not want to be handed someone else's design. You may need help with the base on which to stitch the idea, but you want to develop your own ideas for specific people with specific interests — irises and strawberries for your sisters, a carry-all bag for your mother, a nametag for your father, a koala for your daughter.

Therefore, in Part Two we have included instructions for a dozen "generic gifts" for you, your family, your friends. Most of them can be made fast and many of them help you organize things (thread, supplies, presser feet, etc.). We've given suggestions for how to decorate them and shown you how we worked them for ourselves — but now you can stitch them from your own heart.

Part One contains updated information on techniques, effects, and materials for machine embroidery. (For those of you addicted to machine applique, we present about fifteen different ways to applique, but they are spread over many chapters.) We changed Chapter 10 to include information on lettering, monogramming, and edgings; changed Chapter 13 to a detailed discussion of the sewing machine, one too picky to position earlier in the book, where it might deter first-time machine embroiderers from plunging in; and completely rewrote Chapter 14, on designing.

We also added a potpourri of information in the appendices — the history of machine embroidery, including the table of contents from the old Singer book; how to buy a machine; and other bits of machine-embroidery miscellanea.

A note about our working partnership: we both shared all the work of writing this book, from conception and overall form to photography, writing, and fussing over deadlines. As artist, Tony did most of the drawings and the bulk of the designing. He was the first to question exactly how a stitch is formed on the machine (I'd never bothered to understand) and the first to notice that the feed dogs on the machine go up and down, not back and forth.

But he doesn't stitch. I, Robbie, love machine embroidery. I did all the machine work not credited to someone else. I also did the first draft of writing, so it seemed silly, in explaining how to do a technique, to say "we did this and then we did that." Therefore, the "I" in the book is me.

Our hope is that you will *use* this book — underline in it, write notes in it, paste samples in it — and that because of it, you will learn the full capabilities of your machine. Then you will be able to combine what you've learned with the sense of fun, discovery, and inspiration that we all feel towards our craft.

It would be impossible to list all the people who have helped in the last ten years. But a few must be singled out. This book could not have happened without the priceless input of Jane Warnick, of San Mateo, CA; Jackie Dodson, of LaGrange Park, IL; Judi Cull of Sacramento, CA; Caryl Rae Hancock of Vienna, VA; and Janet Stocker of "Treadleart" in Lomita, CA—thank you.

For depth of research and foreign contacts, we are indebted to Marilyn Green, Palo Alto, CA; Cindy Hickok, London, England; and Margaret Rolfe, Curtin, Australia—thank you.

For twenty years, Don and Rich Douglas of Douglas Fabrics (Palo Alto, CA) have helped educate us about the finer points of sewing machines—thank you.

And finally, our daughter, Kali Koala, has calmly grown up amidst our deadlines and mania. We thank her for saying, "How about I go into my room and read—for a month?"

R.L.F.
A.D.F.

Part I

TECHNIQUES, EFFECTS AND MATERIALS

CHAPTER 1

Introduction to Machine Embroidery

Aside from being beautiful, unique, and sensuous, machine embroidery has one overwhelming factor in its favor: it's fast. How satisfying it is to dream up a colorful, heavily embroidered garment and then actually to complete it in one day. With machine embroidery, large areas of texture and color can be filled in a short time. Ideas can be executed before inspiration fades.

And the scope of possible effects worked on a machine is staggering. Say that you had eight distinct settings for stitch length, going from the tightest stitch to the loosest basting stitch. And say that your zigzag machine had five settings from 0 (or no zigzag) to a wide zigzag. Add to those the various tension settings of upper and bobbin threads and throw in a few thousand variations in color and texture of threads. While you're at it, consider various needle sizes and the million types of fabrics available to us. Feed it to a mathematician and (s)he'll tell you that there are at least 80 septillion possible combinations. And that's for the first stitch!

Fig. 1-3 shows but a few of the 80 septillion. The specific how-to's of each technique are in the chapter texts.

How difficult is machine embroidery? If I can hold a four-year-old on my lap and merely run the foot pedal for her as she free-machine embroiders, you can do it too.

You don't need a fancy zigzag machine to do work similar to most shown in these chapters, except for the specific sections on decorative stitches and zigzag. In fact, graceful machine embroidery is still done on treadle machines (Fig. 1-4). On the other hand, if you're thinking of buying a machine, I would recommend upgrading to one that does have a zigzag and fancy stitches because it increases the versatility of your work. Besides extending your decorative possibilities, it can handle all kinds of knit fabric, from the lightest tricot to the heavy sweater knits, for both garment construction and embellishment.

No matter what your make of machine, though, learn how to take care of it by reading its instruction manual and by consulting a reputable sewing machine dealer. A book such as this can hardly touch the wealth of knowledge of a helpful dealer with years of experience. For example, my favorite dealer instructed me that because one of my machines has a rotary shuttle mechanism, which travels twice as far for each stitch as the rest of the machine, it is vitally important that I keep my bobbin shuttle hook well-oiled. Except for my computer machine, which doesn't need oiling, I oil my machine before every major project, and if it doesn't seem to sew as quietly as usual, I oil that

Fig. 1–1 Free-machined face by four-year-old Kali Koala Fanning (child held in lap by mother, who ran the foot pedal).

hook more often. (I also sing to my machine as I work.)

Dust and lint are the enemies of your machine, especially if you have one of the new computerized machines. Keep a cover over your machine when you aren't using it. Clean its innards every time you sit down to sew, using either the brush that comes with your machine or canned air (available in photography stores). About every eighteen months, either take the machine apart yourself for a thorough vacuuming and cleaning out of gunk, or take it to a dealer. We don't think twice about taking a car in for a periodic tune-up; why not treat your sewing machine with the same respect? With proper care, a good machine can last for years.

Some of the computer machines may be sensitive to magnets. Ask your dealer and be careful about setting magnetized pin cushions near the machine.

Because there is no standard language for machine embroidery, you and I may use different terms for the same part of a machine. Fig. 1-5 shows a generic sewing machine, labeled with the terms I use. Your machine may differ — see your own instruction manual and relabel this picture to fit your machine. We will also start each chapter with a pictorial glossary of the terms used in it.

Judi Cull has students new to machine embroidery write "length" and "width" on press-on address labels. These can be stuck on the machine, yet later removed.

Supplies

What supplies will you need for machine embroidery? Obviously a machine. You will also need a supply of machine needles in the various sizes. Incidentally, buy the needles made for your machine instead of grabbing the nearest packet at the fabric store. One reason the machine may be skipping stitches is that you're using a needle not suited to your machine. Specific needles for specific threads and fabrics will be discussed in Chapter 2, but in general, fit the thread to the type of work or material, and choose the needle to make a hole big enough for the thread. But even the best machine will give shoddy results with a bad needle. If you sew over a lot of pins (a big no-no:

4

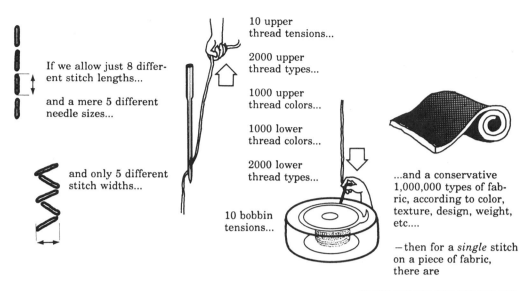

If we allow just 8 different stitch lengths...

and a mere 5 different needle sizes...

and only 5 different stitch widths...

10 upper thread tensions...

2000 upper thread types...

1000 upper thread colors...

1000 lower thread colors...

2000 lower thread types...

10 bobbin tensions...

...and a conservative 1,000,000 types of fabric, according to color, texture, design, weight, etc....

—then for a *single* stitch on a piece of fabric, there are

80,000,000,000,000,000,000,000 possibilities.

Fig. 1–2 Eighty septillion possibilities.

Fig. 1–3 Machine-embroidery possibilities (from center out): eyelet, free-machine embroidery worked from the underside with a heavy thread in the bobbin, automatic stitch, free-machine whip stitch, satin stitch with extra-fine rayon thread, free-machine embroidery on topside with hoop, automatic stitch, free-machine embroidery on net, couching-by-piercing.

5

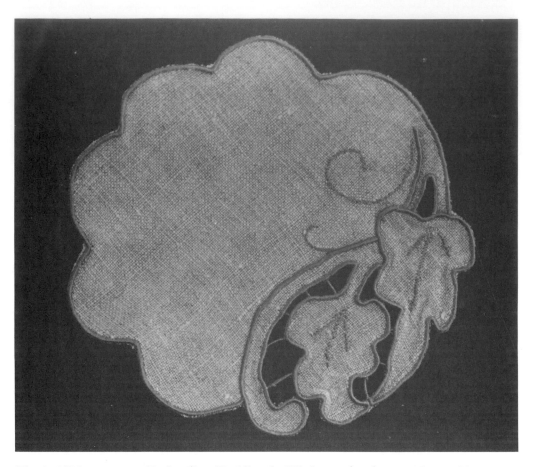

Fig. 1–4 Fifty years ago Evelyn Carulli of Seattle, WA, learned to do cutwork on a Singer treadle. Working on pure linen with fine DMC thread, she carefully moves the hoop back and forth over a thread laid on the surface to achieve the corded satin-stitch edge of this coaster. The patterns are from old Italian needlework magazines.

you can damage your machine and run up a big repair bill or you could injure your eye with flying pin parts) or have been using the same needle for years, put in a new needle for each machine-embroidery project.

Thread is so reasonably priced that you can afford to treat yourself to one spool in at least all the rainbow colors, as well as white, black, and gray. And while you're buying, throw in a few ex-

tra bobbins. The nicest present I've given myself recently is ten extra bobbins—no more unwinding a half-filled bobbin of one color because I need to fill an empty spool in another color.

What threads are appropriate for machine stitchery? Believe it or not, almost any, from the finest embroidery thread to four-ply wool. Some of the thick slubby threads cannot be threaded through a needle and should be

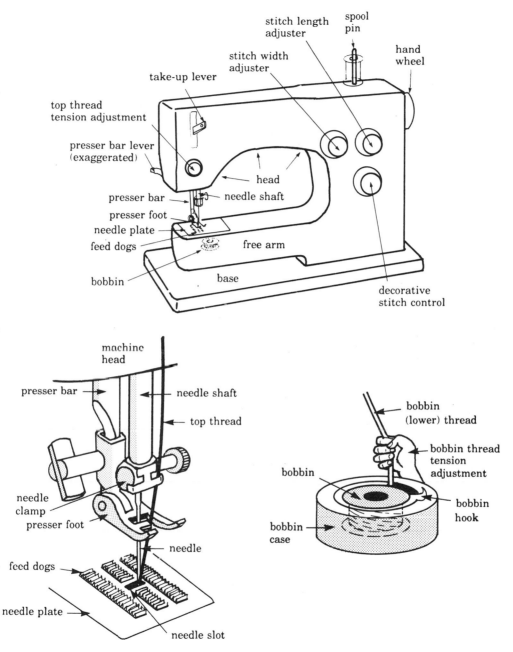

Fig. 1–5 *Sewing machine and its parts. Positions vary, but most modern machines have the same parts.*

wound onto the bobbin and stitched in a special way (see Chapter 6), or laid on the surface and couched down, but any thread that inspires you can probably be incorporated into your work. However, the greater part of your machine embroidery will be done with 100% cotton or rayon thread, so buy a decent supply of it.

Since 20% of the weight of cotton threads is water, after the thread sits around for awhile, it dries out, becomes brittle, and breaks when you sew. Either mist the thread with a plant sprayer, leave the thread outside overnight so dew will soak into the thread (but bring it in before the sun dries it out

again), or store it in the refrigerator.

Your major problem with rayon thread is its slipperiness. If it falls off the spool, it can wind around your upright bobbin spindle and break. Some machines have horizontal spindles or special spool holders that eliminate this problem. Here are four ways to tame rayon (see Fig.1-6): (1) tape a tapestry needle, eye-up, between the spool and the first thread guide on your machine; (2) buy a gadget that transforms your vertical spool shaft to a horizontal one (see Supply Source); (3) put the rayon through the center of the tube, from top to bottom, and draw it out through a notch in the base of the tube (make

Fig. 1–6 Five ways to tame rayon thread: (1) dark spool on top right has notch cut from base (see text); (2) horizontal thread is mounted on a gadget on the vertical spool; (3) a one-inch round of surgical bandage (available from pharmacies) has been slipped over the spool; (4) a tapestry needle is taped next to the thread to act as an extra thread guide; and (5) the third rayon spool stands in a coffee cup of beans.

8

the notch with a file or knife); (4) stand the rayon in a coffee cup behind the machine and surround the thread tube with dried beans, to keep the tube upright. When you sew with rayon, start slowly, so the thread doesn't jerk off the tube.

As for appropriate machine-embroidery fabrics, anything a needle will pass through is fair game, from gauze to leather. Some possibilities come to mind immediately, like cotton fabrics for applique. But splendid machine embroidery is done on see-through plastic, organza, felt, imitation suede, and a host of other unusual fabrics (see Chapters 9-12).

If you were to look at your backing fabric through a microscope, you would realize that heavy machine embroidery on a fabric backing is going to squish the threads of the backing and cause them to pucker. We try to minimize this by backing our fabrics with a stabilizer—in effect, changing, say, a lightweight cotton to a denim. In the past, we've used organza, organdy, muslin, or typing paper. But in the last few years, some marvelous new products for machine embroidery have appeared.

Your choices of fabric stabilizer are: (1) any see-through fabric such as organza or organdy, which remains a part of the stitching; (2) a non-woven interfacing that can be torn away from the stitching (and is generically called "tear-away"); (3) a new product called water-soluble stabilizer, which disappears when doused with cold water; or

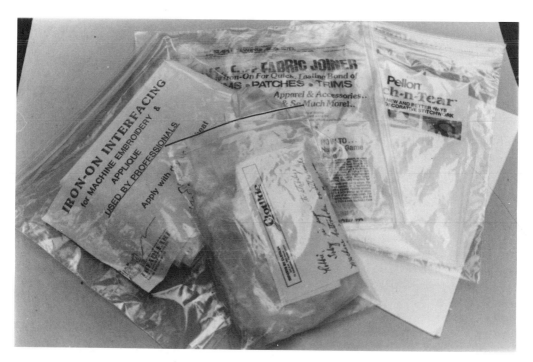

Fig. 1–7 Some choices of stabilizer: iron-on interfacing, water-soluble stabilizer, fusible web, tear-away, and paper. I keep my stabilizers in labeled Ziploc bags.

(4) paper (typing, tissue, or plastic-coated freezer paper), which is torn away when you finish stitching. From now on in this book, I will say "use a stabilizer" and you'll know that the stabilizer can be any of these four choices.

Other supplies you will need are the regular sewing supplies, such as fabric marking devices, sharp scissors, pins, and tape measure, as well as some from the desk drawer — tracing and typing paper, graph paper, ruler, felt-tipped pen. I also keep a pair of tweezers near the machine for pulling out small pieces of stabilizer from the back of machine-embroidered garments and for extracting lint and broken threads from the bobbin case. A needle threader is helpful, too, for guiding thicker threads like buttonhole twist through the machine needle (Fig. 1-8). Put a spot of glue where the wires enter the holder, to prevent them from pulling out.

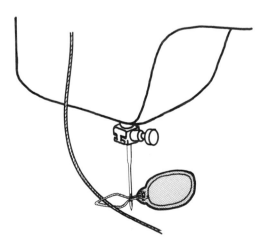

Fig. 1–8 Insert the needle threader from front to back of the machine needle.

You will often use a 6" (15 cm) or 8" (20.5 cm) embroidery hoop. The best hoops are designed especially for machine embroidery, but you can also use a screw-type hand-embroidery hoop. If you do, you may want to wrap its inside ring (the one without the screw or hinge on it) with strips of cotton fabric or bias tape. Secure the end with a spot of glue. When you stretch material in the hoop, particularly the lightweight fabrics such as organza, cotton strips keep the fabric from slipping and puckering (more on this in Chapter 4).

If you plan to do any machine applique, you will need some or all of the new fusing materials. The fastest to use is a glue stick. Read the label to be sure it's a washable glue. Also available is a disappearing basting tape that washes out. A wonderful new invention is an applique pressing sheet that allows you to bond fusible web to the back of fabric. Then you cut out your applique and fuse it to the backing fabric, adding whatever decorative stitching you want to the edge. A variation of this is a paper with fusible web bonded to it. You iron the paper to the back of your applique fabric, peel off the paper, and iron the applique to the backing fabric (Fig. 1-9).

Using a test cloth will greatly increase your chances of success in machine embroidery. For every project, set up a 6" (15 cm) square of the same fabric you're sewing on to be used as the test cloth. On this cloth practice the stitches you intend to use in your embroidery. If the stitches pucker the fabric of your test cloth, loosen the upper and lower tensions until you reach a desirable result, always keeping track of your changes by writing directly on the test cloth with a felt-tipped pen. When you find the best tension settings and the best thread variation for your work,

Fig. 1–9 *With the help of a Teflon pressing sheet, fusible web can be bonded to the back of any fabric.*

you will know how to proceed on the actual item to be embroidered. And if you save this test cloth, pinning it to your pattern or filing it in a sample notebook, you will always be able to duplicate your efforts with a minimum of initial experimenting.

Another item will improve your efforts one hundred percent: an iron. Mother was right; pressing makes the difference between sloppiness and craftsmanship.

One last tip: if your foot pedal slips away as you stitch, put a press-on bathtub applique, available from hardware and grocery stores, on the bottom. The rubber of the applique will keep the pedal from sliding.

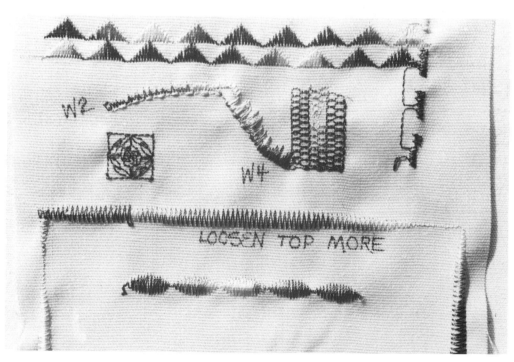

Fig. 1–10 *Typical test cloth.*

Now you know what's possible with machine embroidery: it's not too difficult for you and your machine, and the supplies won't deplete your bank account. Next you need to find out how to transfer a design from a piece of paper to your fabric.

Enlarging Designs

Many times you will want to enlarge a small design into something bigger, so it is useful to know how to blow up a design. If you have access to a modern photocopy machine, you can make enlarged copies easily. You can also take a small design to a blueprint or graphic arts store and they will enlarge it as much as you need.

Even easier, but more expensive, is to buy an opaque projector, which projects your image to any size, depending on how far away from the wall you place the machine. The kind where you set the projector on top of the image to be copied is more useful for blowing up a wide range of original images than is the kind where you set your image on top of the machine.

But if it's midnight and you want to enlarge a design right now, use this easy technique. Lay $^1/_4$" (6 mm) graph paper over a design and trace the design onto it. Decide how much bigger you want the design—twice the size? Three times? Number and letter the squares as shown in Fig. 1-11. Now take a ruler and a fresh sheet of $^1/_4$" (6 mm) graph paper and rule off new squares. For example, if you want your new design twice as big, rule off every other line, both horizontally and vertically. If you want your finished design three times the size, rule off every third line. You will now have squares that are twice or three times the size of your original squares. Number and letter these new squares in exactly the same order as you did the original design. Start with square 1A and draw in the larger square whatever you see in the small square. Do this for each square . . . and surprise!, your design is enlarged.

Once you've enlarged your design to the exact size you want, you can choose one of the eight methods to transfer it onto fabric for machine embroidery.

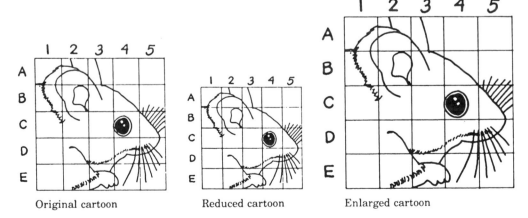

Original cartoon   Reduced cartoon   Enlarged cartoon

Fig. 1–11 Enlarging and reducing designs.

12

Which method you choose depends on either the kind of fabric you've chosen or on whether you will reuse the pattern.

Before we delve into the ways you can transfer designs to your material, we should decide how much of the design to transfer. As is often the case, the rule is "least is best." In general, only the main lines or curves of your design need to be sketched in. At best, only the outlines of large, filled-in areas need to be put onto the transferred design (Fig. 1-12). The old, venerable name for such a line drawing is "cartoon." Long before the Saturday morning TV cartoons, the great painters of the Italian Renaissance were using cartoons to put their preliminary sketches for frescoes upon walls.

On some of your designs, you will also need to indicate direction of stitching. This becomes especially important when you're filling in with zigzag or using decorative stitches with directional designs.

One of the most pleasant advances of recent years is the variety of marking devices. The most convenient is the water-soluble marking pen. It draws a blue or purple line on your fabric that washes out when touched with a Q-tip dipped in cold water. Use a variation, the air-soluble pen, when you will work immediately. Otherwise, the ink vanishes within 48 hours. (Our daughter once wrote my cousin a letter with an air-soluble pen. My cousin wondered why she received a blank piece of paper with faint purple marks.) Store your pens upside-down with the caps on to make them last longer.

Visit a well-equipped sewing or quilting store (or send for the catalogs listed at the end of the book) to acquaint yourself with all the new marking tools available to you—white and blue charcoal pencils, transfer pencils, double-tracing wheels with built-in chalk, etc.

Fig. 1–12 Reduce complicated drawings to simple cartoon form for stitching.

Transferring Designs— Eight Ways

My favorite method of transferring designs is to lay a piece of tracing or tissue paper over the cartoon and to copy it with a black felt-tipped pen. I often use the wrong side of outdated or extra tissue paper from clothing patterns, ignoring any print on the tissue. Wait a minute for the ink of the felt-tipped pen to dry so it won't smudge your fabric, then tape the tissue paper to a window (assuming it's daytime; see Fig. 1-13).

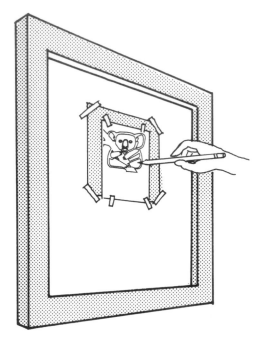

Fig. 1–13 A window can be used to help trace a cartoon.

Tape the fabric over the tissue, centering the design, and trace the design onto the fabric with pencil, water-soluble pen, or tailor's chalk. Caution: If you know the design line will not be completely covered by the sewing machine thread, don't use an ordinary pencil for tracing the design as it does not always wash out. On dark material I use a white pencil and on light material, a blue one. This method of tracing works on a surprising number of fabrics—from the most transparent fabric through mediumweight cottons with even surfaces. It does not work well on linen and other textured fabrics.

At night, use a lighted TV screen on a channel you don't receive. Or go outside, and use the window method by looking into a well-lit room.

In lieu of a lighted window, you can use a make-shift light table. Put a sheet of clear plastic or an old window on a cardboard box (or sawhorses or two chairs or an open drawer or whatever you can improvise), into or under which you've set a bare-bulb lamp. Cover the plastic with plain white paper so the light is diffused. Now tape down the cartoon, put the fabric over it, weight or tape it down, and trace the design (Fig. 1-14).

Best of all, invest in a portable light table (try your local photo, art, or engineering supply stores). I bought a used one from an engineer for $30. I keep it right next to my sewing area and use it constantly. See the Supply List for mail-order sources.

Another way to transfer designs is particularly suited to the machine. This method works well on all fabric except the heavily textured and is especially useful for transferring repeat patterns (Fig. 1-15). Copy the cartoon onto a piece of plastic. A meat tray works, as does acetate from an art store. You can also use typing paper. Sew along the lines of the cartoon with an unthreaded machine, using a Size 9(60) sewing machine needle so that

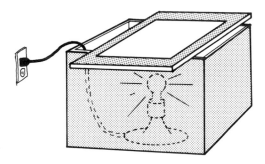

Fig. 1–14 A makeshift light table, made with a cardboard box, picture frame with glass, and a lightbulb.

14

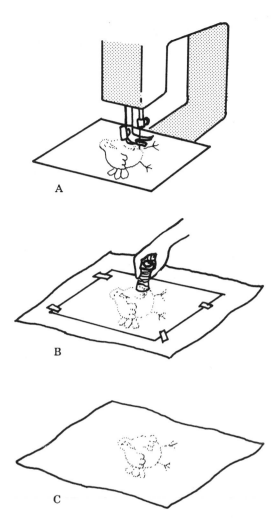

A

B

C

Fig. 1–15 An unthreaded machine and some powder can also be used to transfer designs. A. Without threading the needle, prick holes through paper, following cartoon outlines. B. Rub powder through holes. C. Cartoon is transferred to fabric.

the holes in the plastic or paper are not too big. You can sew with or without the presser foot on. Pin or tape the plastic to your fabric, centering the design wherever you want it, and gently rub

tailor's chalk over the line of holes. I use a rolled-up pad of felt to apply the chalk to the fabric, gently rolling it into the holes of the plastic and taking care not to put too much onto the design at once. If you are using plastic, you can see how well your design is being marked. If you use paper, you will need to check. Pull up one corner of the typing paper from time to time to check whether enough chalk has gone through the holes to mark your design sufficiently. Then carefully lift off the plastic or taped paper and lightly blow off the surplus chalk. If you try to brush it off, the chalk will smudge the fabric.

Since we often put a fabric stabilizer above or underneath fabric to prevent puckering, a third method of transferring designs becomes simple. Put the stabilizer directly over the cartoon and trace with a dark line (Fig. 1-16A). If the item being machine-stitched will ever be washed, use only felt-tipped pens that are guaranteed waterproof (such as canvas-work or needlepoint markers). Now pin-baste the stabilizer to the back of your fabric, with the design against the wrong side of the fabric; otherwise you'll have a mirror image on the topside, which is undesirable for, say, letters and other non-symmetrical designs. Load your bobbin with a thread that is slightly lighter or darker than the color of your fabric. Set your machine for a long stitch (approximately 6 stitches/inch) and machine-baste the design, the stabilizer facing up and the topside of the fabric against the needle plate (Fig. 1-16B). You now have transferred the design to the right side, where it is marked by your bobbin thread. A variation of this method is to trace the design or draw directly onto iron-on interfacing, which is then bonded to the back of your fabric. However,

15

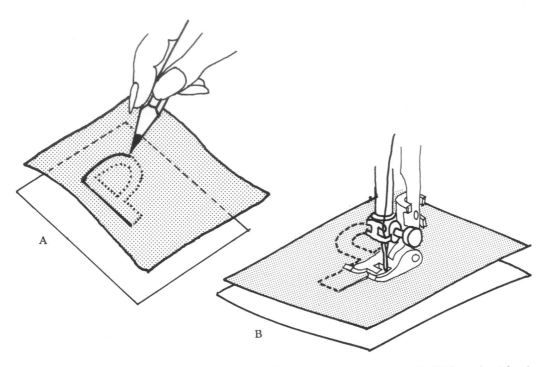

Fig. 1–16 Transfer method using organza. A. Trace cartoon on organza. B. With underside of fabric against right side of organza, machine baste the design. Design will be facing right way on top side of fabric.

the design will be a mirror image on the right side, of course, when you machine-baste through the interfacing.

To transfer a design with dressmaker's carbon paper, available in any fabric store, tape your fabric to a hard surface, like a glass-topped desk or a Formica kitchen counter. Trace the cartoon onto tissue or tracing paper and center it on the fabric, weighing down the top edge with anything handy and heavy. Carefully slip a piece of dressmaker's carbon paper—don't use typing carbon paper because it smudges-- between the tracing and the fabric, and then anchor the bottom edges of the tracing paper over it. Trace the design with an empty ballpoint pen or the handle end of a letter opener. You must

push hard enough to produce a decent line on the fabric, but not so hard as to tear the tissue paper (Fig. 1-17).

Transfer pencils are now available in needlework and sewing stores (see Supply List), taking some of the fuss out of transferring the design. They seem to work better on warm (not hot) materials, so iron both your paper and your fabric with a low dry heat before drawing with the pencil. Lay the warm tissue or tracing paper over the cartoon and copy with a felt-tip pen. Let the ink dry and then turn the tissue paper over and retrace the design on the wrong side with the transfer pencil. Now lay the tissue paper on top of the warm fabric, the transfer pencil side against the fabric, and pin it carefully in place. Use

16

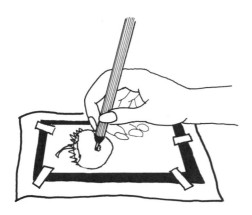

Fig. 1–17 When transferring using dress-maker's carbon, press firmly with a ballpoint pen to transfer the design.

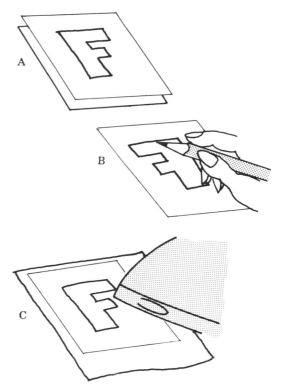

Fig. 1–18 Transfer method using transfer pencil. A. Trace carbon on tracing paper with felt-tip pen. B. Retrace with transfer pencil on underside. C. Iron onto fabric.

a dry iron as hot as your fabric permits (Fig. 1-18). Since the transfer lines sometimes rub off later as you work, as soon as the transfer cools, I like to machine-baste the main lines of the design as a safety precaution. The transfer lines that remain visible on the fabric wash out easily with baby shampoo or when sprayed with hair spray before washing. Since a washing machine is in constant agitation, you don't have to worry about the transfer pencil bleeding. But if you are hand-washing, be sure to agitate the water. If you let the fabric sit, the transfer marks will bleed into the water and then settle elsewhere on the fabric.

Another kind of transfer pen is pressure-sensitive, rather than heat- sensitive. You draw the cartoon on paper, place it against the fabric, and retrace the line with a dry ballpoint pen. The line transfers to the fabric.

Until water-soluble stabilizer appeared, transferring a design to heavily textured fabric was a problem. Transfer pencil, chalk, and carbon lines became lost in the bumps of the fabric, and even machine basting lines were difficult to follow. With water-soluble stabilizer, though, the transfer is easy. However, if you run out of water-soluble stabilizer and need to transfer a design, lay white net over the cartoon and copy the design with a felt-tipped pen. (If you're copying from a library book, lay a protective piece of tissue paper over the design and don't use a felt-tipped pen as it will bleed through the tissue paper; use a crayon instead.) Then lay the net over the fabric and retrace the design lines with a fat-tipped felt-tipped pen (waterproof), which runs through the holes of the net onto

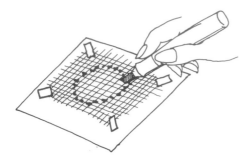

Fig. 1–19 For heavily textured fabrics, trace the design on net. Then draw onto fabric through the net with heavy felt-tip pen.

the fabric (Fig. 1-19). This isn't my favorite method as the results are vague and wavery, but sometimes this is the only method that works.

Another way to copy a design from library books is to use waxed paper and a dressmaker's tracing wheel. Put a towel under the page to be copied and lay ordinary waxed paper from the kitchen over the page. Trace your design with the wheel (Fig. 1-20). You can now use this paper as stabilizer and pattern on the underside of your fabric. Since the paper is milky-colored, though, you won't be able to see your marks if your fabric is also light-colored. If your waxed paper isn't wide enough, simply overlap two pieces and press with a warm iron to fuse them together. The wax won't hurt your iron.

Jackie Dodson, of LaGrange Park, IL, prefers to photocopy designs from her library books. She says color pages

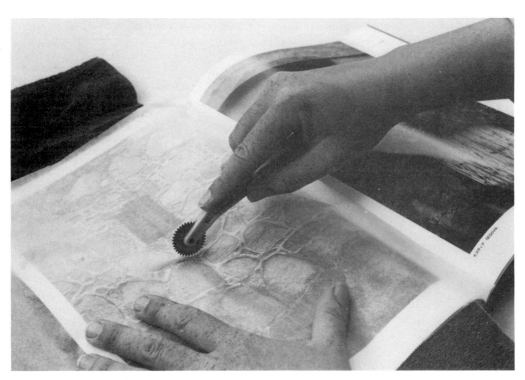

Fig. 1–20 Trace a design with wax paper over a design, padding under the page, and a dressmaker's tracing wheel.

photocopied in black-and-white offer a clearer idea of the major shapes.

The other method I use on heavily textured fabric is to cut the main design shapes out of paper (typing or construction), pin the papers to the fabric, and machine-baste around the outsides of the paper, not catching the edges (Fig. 1-21). Then remove the pins and construction paper. You can use tear-away for this method, too.

Cautions

Now that you know how to transfer designs and are eager to start, it's prudent to remind you of some cautions.

It's important to consider how your machine embroidery will be used and choose appropriate fabrics and threads. I once sent a friend a zigzag message on wool felt, which she decided would make a great patch for her jeans. Wool felt is not washable, which she forgot

Fig. 1–21 For simple shapes, cut the design from construction paper, pin to fabric, and stitch around edges, not catching the paper. Remove pins and paper.

until after her first trip to the laundromat.

Threads, too, must be carefully chosen for ironability and washability. I heard a sad story about a white polyester knit dress with red silk floss topstitching, made for a prestigious fashion show. It was handled and soiled so much before the show that someone tossed it into the washing machine. Those pitiful pink streaks never did come out.

Likewise, if you are using rayon or nylon threads, which cannot withstand a high iron temperature, think twice about stitching on 100% cotton or linen fabric which will need heavy pressing after washing.

Preshrink your fabric, straighten the grain, and test it for colorfastness. All those boring preliminaries prevent that gut-wrenching feeling of spending hours on a garment that is ruined by the first wash.

Also, when working on a garment, to prevent unalterable puckering and shrinking of the fabric, don't cut out the exact pattern shape before machine embroidering. Leave at least a 2" (5.5 cm) border all around. Do the work and then cut out the pattern piece.

Although machine embroidery has its own visual identity and should not attempt to imitate handwork, it does combine harmoniously with all kinds of hand embroidery — stitchery, patchwork, drawn thread, and many more.

If this book touches you at all, by the last chapter you will be eager to develop your own ideas. I would like to stress that there is never only one way to do any of the techniques and procedures described in here. Experiment on your machine and find the way that works best for you.

CHAPTER 2

Straight Stitch

Visual Glossary

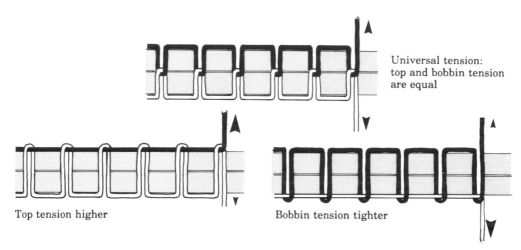

Universal tension: top and bobbin tension are equal

Top tension higher

Bobbin tension tighter

The straight stitch is so versatile that even if you did nothing but straight-stitch machine embroidery, you would have enough ideas and work to keep you busy the rest of your life.

In its simplest form straight stitch looks like the drawn line, as in the scenes on Shirley Fomby's vest (Fig. 2-1). Similarly, you can distort rows of straight stitch to create pattern, as Lois Ericson has done in Fig. 2-2.

Straight stitch is often used to outline a shape (Fig. 2-3). It is also used to emphasize a line with a thicker thread, like buttonhole twist in topstitching.

How a Stitch is Formed

But before going any further, let me ask you an embarrassing question: Do you really know how a stitch is formed on the sewing machine?

Don't laugh — understanding how the machine works explains how it doesn't. And don't be embarrassed — in a continuing private survey, I've discovered that most people do not understand how a stitch is formed, even if they have been sewing on a machine all their lives.

After examining Figs. 2-4 and 2-5, you can see that if, for example, the fabric is not flat against the needle plate at the moment the needle enters the fabric, the shuttle hook on the bobbin will not catch the loop of top thread, and therefore a stitch will be skipped. Remember this, especially when you are doing free machine embroidery.

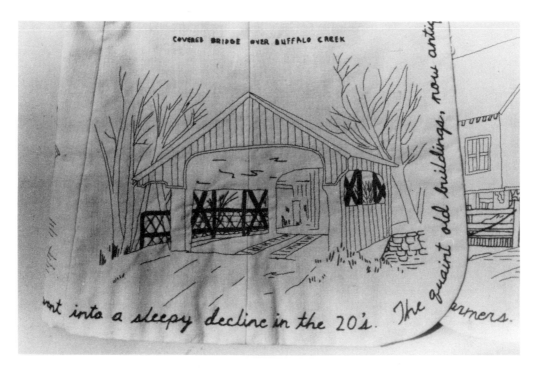

Fig. 2–1 Bottom of a vest by Shirley Fomby of Mundelein, IL, created to honor scenes of Long Grove, IL. The covered bridge over Buffalo Creek is worked in straight stitch with the presser foot on (white muslin with brown thread). The lettering is by hand.

Troubleshooting Stitching Problems

Some of the other stitching bugaboos you might run into, and why they occur, are:

1. The upper thread breaks:
   a. The machine is not threaded properly or the needle is inserted wrong way round or at the wrong height.
   b. Upper tension is too tight.
   c. The thread is dry and brittle; or too thick for either the needle or material; or knotted somewhere between the top spool and the needle.
   d. The needle is bent or blunt.
   e. The presser foot is not lowered.
   f. You are taking the first stitch too fast for the thread being used (e.g., rayon)—start slowly.

2. The lower thread breaks:
   a. Lower tension is too tight.
   b. The thread is unevenly wound on the bobbin or brought up incorrectly.
   c. The hole in the needle plate is old and scarred and needs a light filing with a machinist's file (sewing machine dealer can do this).

3. The needle breaks:
   a. The material has been jerked during sewing, bending the

needle and causing it to hit the presser foot or needle plate.

    b. The upper tension is too tight for the machine.

    c. The needle is mounted incorrectly.

4. Stitches are uneven or skipped:

    a. The bobbin innards are linty and clogged.

    b. Needles being used are not made expressly for machine.

    c. The needle has a scooped-out part (called a scarf) too shallow for the thread or stitching method being used — use a Yellow Band or Stretch needle.

    d. The machine is incorrectly threaded.

    e. The fabric was not touching the needle plate at the moment the stitch was formed.

5. The material puckers:

    a. Thread is too thick for the material — use a stabilizer.

    b. Upper and/or lower tensions are too tight.

    c. Stitches are too long.

    d. Fabric was jerked away from needle at end of stitching, gathering fabric, rather than pulled gently to the side, pinching ends of threads.

    e. Fabric needs added body to withstand heavy stitching (especially in zigzag stitching) — use stabilizer.

Any other machine irregularities, such as poor timing or sluggishness, should be checked by a dealer.

I won't fill your ear with the details of which needle and thread to use with which fabric. If I start listing them here, you'll just yawn and say "Oh, that" and you won't learn anything at all. So right now I'll tell you the barest minimum and when in the future you need more specific information, you can turn to the Needle and Thread Chart at the back of the book or to Chapter 13, Know Your Tools. Incidentally, American, Japanese, and European needles have different numbering systems, which is why I always give two numbers — e.g., Size 14(90) means Size 14 for American machines and Size 90 for European and Japanese machines.

Thread

As for thread, we now have a cornucopia of choices — cotton, rayon, polyes-

Fig. 2–2 Close-up of vest by Lois Ericson of Tahoe City, CA, the author of Fabrics . . . Reconstructed *(see Bibliography). Straight stitch channels create counterpoint to the lines of the dyed fabric.*

Fig. 2–3 Burgundy and pink tabard by Nancy Gano of San Jose, CA, quilted by lines of straight stitch following designs drawn onto the fabric with an indelible laundry marker. The front is folded under to show the quilting lines on the underside of the back.

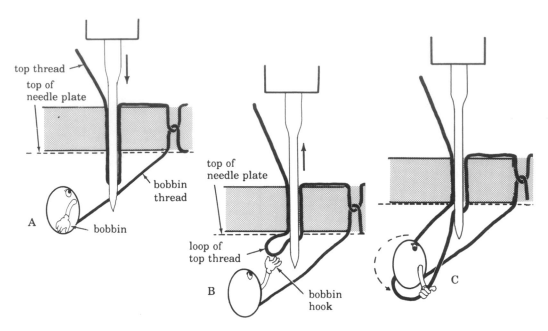

Fig. 2–4 How a stitch is formed. A. Top thread meets the bobbin. B. A tiny loop is formed by top thread. C. Bobbin grabs the loop and locks the stitch below the fabric.

ter, silk, metallics, cotton-wrapped polyester. Since the numbering system used for threads is not uniform throughout the world—e.g., an American size 50 thread is thicker than a European size 50—I will avoid confusion by describing threads as extra-fine, ordinary, and heavy, rather than by size number. See the Supply List for brand names under each category.

I use *ordinary* cotton-covered polyester for garment construction, but hardly at all for machine embroidery, as the outer fiber tends to shred, causing the thread to knot and break. But I do use *extra-fine* cotton-covered polyester for satin stitch. Since new threads are being introduced all the time, don't reject any thread without giving it a thorough workout. Experiment with loosening top tension and using a larger

sized needle if your thread breaks while playing with it.

Fabric stores now carry European, Indian, Thai, and Japanese threads of 100% cotton, rayon, silk, or polyester that are extra-fine and that produce, in particular, remarkable free-machine embroidery. Check the Supply List at the end of the book for mail-order sources and ask your favorite fabric store to stock a full range of colors.

In most cases you will use a size 12(80) or size 14(90) needle with ordinary sewing-machine thread, but remember that *you choose the thread to suit the fabric and the needle to suit the thread.* On organza, for example, you would choose extra-fine cotton, rayon, or silk sewing-machine thread matched with a size 10(70) needle. Remember that the purpose of the needle is to

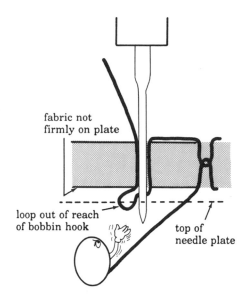

fabric not
firmly on plate

loop out of reach
of bobbin hook

top of
needle plate

Fig. 2–5 How a stitch is skipped: If the fabric is not flat against the needle plate, the loop lifts out of reach of the bobbin hook and a stitch is skipped.

make a hole in the fabric big enough for that diameter of thread. If the hole isn't big enough, the thread is cut by the edges of fabric surrounding it. If you backed your organza with stabilizer, you are working with a heavier fabric than plain organza alone; therefore, you may need the next larger size of needle.

Preparing Fabric/ Preventing Puckering

You're impatient to start sewing, aren't you? But before you can do even an inch of straight stitch, your fabric must be prepared. If your fabric will later be washed, preshrink it now by wetting the fabric and drying it in a hot dryer (except for permanent press fabrics — use a cool to warm dryer). If you're making something that will be

washed, be sure your threads are colorfast (silk floss, for example, is not guaranteed colorfast). Iron fabrics with wrinkles.

Some fabrics will need extra body to keep the stitches from puckering the material. Medium- and heavyweight woven fabrics may not need any help (always make a test cloth), but the lighter weight cottons and almost all knit fabrics need to be stiffened by a stabilizer (your choices were listed in Chapter 1).

Which stabilizer is best? The answer varies. When you enter the world of the machine-embroidery subcult, you enter a busy, happy hive of opinionated quirks. One person uses only paper as stabilizer and that paper *must* be *Women's Wear Daily* because it's the correct weight and the ink doesn't rub off.

"Paper!" screams another aficionado in horror. "I can't stand that clackety-clack sound and it dulls the needle. Only tear-away for me, thank you. And I *don't* put the stabilizer in the hoop — only the fabric."

Use what you like and what you can afford. (Jackie Dodson says she once found a Chinese newspaper behind embroidery on a T-shirt from Taiwan.) Most often you will use tear-away stabilizer, which comes in light and crisp weights. You can also use water-soluble stabilizer, which disappears when wet.

But if you run out of either, don't despair. There are other ways to prevent puckering. Putting a piece of typing paper between the fabric and the needle plate helps. The paper is then gently torn away after stitching (Fig. 2-6). The paper trapped by the stitches disappears with the first wash.

The weight of paper you choose depends on how heavy the stitching will

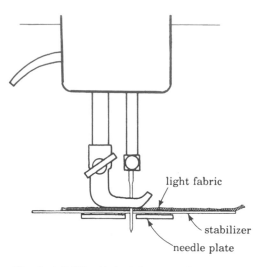

light fabric

stabilizer

needle plate

Fig. 2–6 Stiffen light fabrics with stabilizer.

be, whether or not you're using a hoop, or whether the embroidered article will be washed before use. Use typing-weight paper if you don't use a hoop. Choose tissue paper if you use a hoop and want the embroidery to have a soft feel even if it isn't washed. (You can always put the fabric in a hoop and pin the stabilizer underneath it.) If you have a large piece of fabric to stitch in long rows, tear the typing paper in long strips or use adding machine tape. If you have large areas to stitch, use shelf paper. A third kind of paper to use is plastic-coated freezer paper from the grocery store, which is ironed onto the underside of your fabric and acts like a square hoop. Remove it by ironing again, which loosens it, and tear it off.

Other ways to prevent puckering include spray-on starch ironed into the fabric to give extra body for intricate stitching.

More often I back fabrics with a piece of organza, organdy, or lightweight iron-on interfacing. You can even draw your design on the organza or interfac-

ing and decorate the piece from the wrong side, as described in Chapter 1.

For all garments to be home-sewn and embroidered, be sure to do the embellishing *before* you cut out the contours of the pattern piece, for two reasons: (1) you can use a hoop even near the edge of the piece; and (2) if any puckering occurs, you can sometimes make adjustments in cutting out the piece, whereas if you had cut the piece first and then stitched it, the puckering would be unalterable (Fig. 2-7).

To do this, first cut off the excess tissue paper around the pattern piece, anchor it with weights or pins, and trace around with pencil or tailor's chalk. Remove the pattern piece and machine-baste the lines you drew, so you can see them on the underside and so that bias edges are not stretched. Cut a large rectangle around the garment, allowing at least two inches (5.5 cm) of extra fabric all the way around. Transfer your design to the appropriate place on the garment piece and do the stitching. Then press on the wrong side, so you won't flatten the stitching. Put the original pattern piece over the fabric. Draw new outlines if the fabric has shrunk slightly because of the embroidery. Then cut out the actual contours of the garment piece.

Top and Bobbin Tensions

Before you try a straight stitch on your fabric, run a line of it on your test cloth: set up a small rectangle of the same fabric you're sewing on and try a line of straight stitch on it. Does it pucker the fabric? Are you happy with the stitch tension? What does it look like if you tighten the top tension? Loosen the top tension? Tighten the bobbin tension? Loosen it? If you have never manipulated your tension settings, this is the time to experiment,

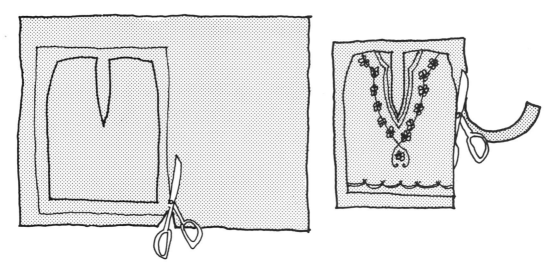

Fig. 2–7 Embellish garment before cutting out: First cut a large rectangle around the pattern piece; embellish the garment piece before cutting the contours.

because the rest of the book constantly involves adjusting the settings. Don't worry if your machine can only, say, manipulate top tension. Work within your machine's limits–but find out what they are by playing.

Most machines have a midway point for both upper and lower tension settings. When both indicators are set at these midway points and you have the same thread in top and bobbin, you have what I call a *universal tension setting*. If you do not know how to loosen your bobbin tension, consult the instruction manual for your sewing machine or ask your dealer.

The bobbin tension of some machines is preset in the factory. Therefore, the instruction manual will tell you not to fiddle with bobbin tension. If you want to explore the full range of effects possible with machine embroidery, ignore the manufacturer's warning. Put a dot of nail polish on the bobbin to mark the factory setting. Specific details on what to do are in Chapter 4. For now, merely

manipulate top tension and play with different weights of thread in the top and bobbin; remember that the heavier thread tends to pull the lighter thread to its side of the fabric.

If no tension setting seems to keep the fabric from puckering, put a piece of stabilizer (interfacing, tear-away, paper, or organza) under the test cloth and try again. As you change the tension settings for the test cloth, write them down directly on the cloth.

Threadless Practice

The first time I ever sewed on a machine, I was given a sheet of printed straight lines and spirals, both curved and squared. Using an unthreaded machine, I sewed slowly and carefully along the lines. It taught me to take my time and to watch the stitch that was being formed, at the same time looking ahead to where the needle would enter the fabric next. I learned to vary the speed at which I sewed, slowing for curves, turns, and intricate places, and speeding up on the long lines of straight stitch (Fig. 2-8). If you have not had much practice sewing on the machine, you might want to copy your cartoons onto typing paper and then practice stitching the main lines with an unthreaded machine. If you're satisfied with your work, you could then use the paper to transfer the design to fabric, via the tailor's chalk method (see Chapter 1).

If you have a European or Japanese machine, take the time to make a stitch-length sample (Figure 2-9). This will tell you how many stitches per inch each setting makes.

Avoiding Headaches

Remember to save yourself headaches by holding the threads together behind the presser foot as you begin to sew. Otherwise, the fabric is sometimes dragged through the needle plate into the bobbin-case area, and valuable

time and psychic energy is lost in unsnarling the mess (Fig. 2-10). And do yourself a favor: anytime you hear the machine making horrible noises, stop sewing and investigate. Don't keep sewing, hoping the noise will go away. Usually the culprit is a thread in the wrong place.

When you spend hours at the machine, your comfort depends on your posture and the way you hold your arms and fingers. If you slump, and at the same time flap your elbows in the air like pelican wings, you will have a backache and be exhausted in a short time. Hold yourself erect, with a straight spine and tight abdominals. Lean forward from your hips. Rest your elbows on the sewing surface and place your fingers as shown (Figure 2-11). Experiment to find the ideal height for your machine. I like my portable machine about three feet above the floor. When I perch on a stool, my machine

Fig. 2–8 Practice stitching control on these simple patterns.

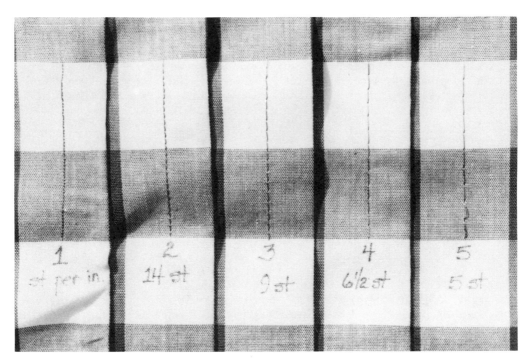

Fig. 2–9 If you're sewing on a European or Japanese machine, make yourself a stitch-length sample. If you use 1" gingham, you can easily measure how many stitches per inch.

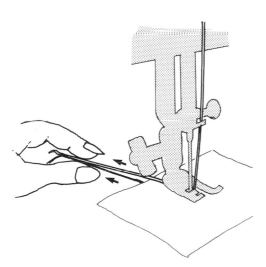

Fig. 2–10 Hold threads together behind presser foot as you begin to sew.

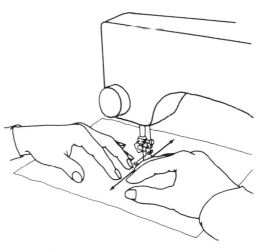

Fig. 2–11 Place your fingers in front of the presser foot on either side of the stitching line.

embroidery is about chest-high, up where I can see it. I don't have to hunch over at all.

I don't wear glasses, however. If you do, you may need to change the distance between your eyes and your work—or change your glasses. Barbara Lee Smith of Oak Park, IL, also likes her machine on a high worktable (she puts her foot pedal on a box so that she can still use the knee-lift on her machine). She found that her eyes were about 13" from her work and that she needed half-frame glasses just for machine embroidering. Eye tests are usually given from about 16", which may not reveal the problems you have in seeing work closer than that.

Straight-Stitch Applique

At last, you may begin the machine embroidery. One good use of straight stitch is for applique, and there are at least four good ways to do it (Fig. 2-12).

Method 1: Cut out your shapes with a $\frac{1}{4}$" (6 mm) seam allowance and then straight stitch along the seam line, so that when you clip the curves and press the seam allowance under, the edge is crisp and neat. Pin the shape to its backing, using a glue stick on the back of the applique or lots of pins to keep the fabric from shifting while stitching, and sew $\frac{1}{8}$" (3 mm) away from the turned edge (Fig. 2-13). If you do a lot of this, check the feet that came with your machine and check with your dealer— there may be a special foot that helps guide the fabric evenly (e.g., blind hemmer, topstitching foot, etc.).

By holding your fingers as shown in Fig. 2-11, you will prevent the fabric from puckering. When you reach sharp turns in the shape, stop the machine with the needle in the fabric, lift the presser-bar lever, and turn the fabric slightly so that the presser foot is aimed in the right direction. If you force the fabric under the presser foot at turns, you may stretch the material on the bias, which results in unsightly bulges (Fig. 2-14).

Method 2: A second method for straight-stitch applique is to cut the applique shape with a $\frac{1}{4}$" (6 mm) seam allowance. The same shape is cut from lightweight fabric. Seam the two shapes right sides together all around the edges. Clip curves. Cut a slash in the middle of the lightweight fabric. Pull the applique fabric right side out through the slash. Press edges. Sew ap-

Fig. 2-12 Straight-stitch applique four ways: (1) turn under edges $\frac{1}{4}$" and topstitch near edge; (2) hidden applique (see text); (3) cut applique with no seam allowance, top-stitch $\frac{1}{4}$" from edge, and deliberately fray edges; (4) sew back and forth over tiny scraps, cut out the applique, and sew it to the backing (the Peggy Moulton method).

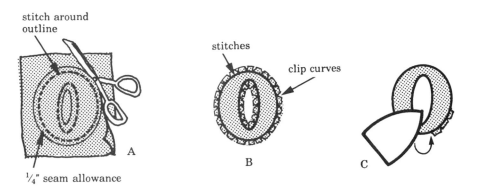

stitch around outline

¼" seam allowance

stitches

clip curves

A   B   C

Fig. 2–13 Making an applique. A. Add a ¼" seam allowance around your pattern. B. Clip curves. C. Press seam allowance under before you applique.

plique shape to backing fabric with straight stitches. This handy method is called "hidden applique". (Be careful on light-colored fabric — sometimes the slash shows through the applique.)

Method 3: In the third method, the edges are left deliberately frayed as

part of the design. Cut applique shape with no seam allowance. Topstitch ¼" (6 mm) in from the edge. Use a pin to fray the edges.

Method 4: And finally, a method I learned from Peggy Moulton, who is clever at using ordinary scraps in inno-

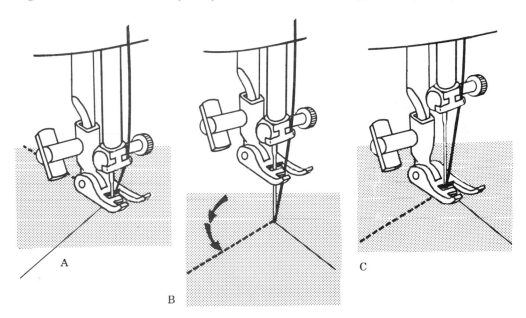

A   B   C

Fig. 2–14 Turning a corner correctly. A. When you reach a sharp turn. . . B. Stop with needle in fabric, raise presser foot lever, and turn fabric. C. Lower presser foot and continue stitching.

vative ways: lay small scraps of fabric on a foundation (old sheet, muslin, etc.). Sew back and forth with close rows of straight stitch. Bond iron-on interfacing or fusible web to the back of the fabric and cut out your applique shape. Topstitch it to the backing.

If you are not bonding the back of your applique and your piece will receive heavy wear (such as washable clothing), you must be concerned about matching grain lines. Try to cut out your applique shapes so that when they are pinned to the backing, the grain lines of both the applique and backing are lined up. For example, I once made an appliqued butterfly, fluttering at an angle on the backing fabric. Instead of cutting out the butterfly on the straight grain of the applique fabric, I cut it on the bias so that when I pinned it at an angle on the backing, the grains would line up, as indicated by the arrows in Fig. 2–15.

How do you handle enormous applique shapes, say for a bedspread or wall hanging? First of all, work on a flat surface when you are pinning the appliques to the backing, so everything will lie flat. Pin liberally or fuse by web, gluestick, or disappearing basting tape, so the fabric won't shift as you sew. Keep your hands to the sides of the fab-

ric, using your fingers as guides, as shown in Fig. 2–11. You can backstitch the first and last stitches, but I prefer to pull the ends to the back and tie off in knots. When you have a large number of ends to finish, however, you may want to pull them to the back and put a spot of fabric glue on them, which will hold through repeated washings.

Crosshatching

Crosshatching is an easy way to fill in large areas with color or texture. It is done by laying intersecting lines of straight stitching on top of each other in a grid. The following description of how to crosshatch is accurate, but it makes an easy maneuver sound complex. Study the pictures and try not to be boggled by the text.

Stitch down a line. At the bottom, leave the needle in the fabric, raise the presser-bar lever, turn the fabric 90 degrees, and lower the presser-bar lever. Take one or two stitches. Repeat the procedure by leaving the needle in the fabric, raising the presser-bar lever, turning another 90 degrees, lowering the presser-bar lever, and stitching another long line of stitches. Use your presser foot as a spacing guide between rows of stitches. It's hard to declare how far the second line should be away from the first line because the length of your

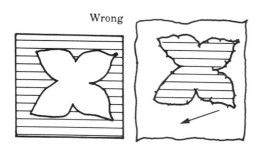 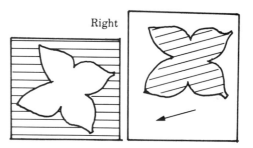

Fig. 2–15 To avoid puckering, make sure to cut out the applique so its grain will match the grain (arrows) of the backing fabric.

32

stitches at the bottom of each row determines how far away you will be from the first row of stitching. Maintain this spacing to keep your lines parallel. When you have finished a rectangle of parallel stitches, turn the fabric 90 degrees and stitch rows of straight stitch, perpendicular to the previous rows (Figs. 2-16 and 2-17).

It is annoying to run out of bobbin thread halfway through crosshatching a project, so start with a full bobbin. Since you won't see the bobbin thread, use up old spools and odd colors of thread. The finer the thread, the more you can get on the bobbin, the less often you will have to change the bobbin.

Crosshatching can also be done in an irregular manner by using the back-stitch lever on a machine (Fig. 2-18).

Since we use a straight-stitch crosshatching for texture, choose a thread that has some sheen to catch the light. If you do row upon row of stitching with 100% cotton, the effect will be lost and you might as well use checked fabric. But if you use polyester, thin silk, or

Fig. 2–16 Fill in areas with crosshatching. Begin by stitching parallel lines, pivoting 90 degrees at each end.

rayon thread and perhaps play with the color changes of variegated thread, you create the vibrant feeling characteristic of all embroidery.

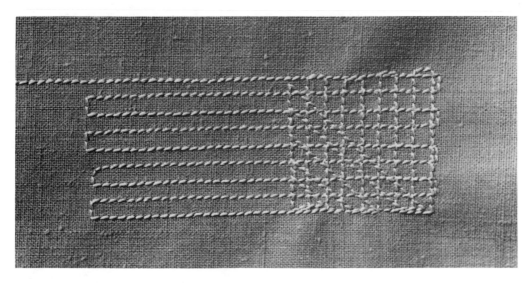

Fig. 2–17 Cross each line with perpendicular lines of crosshatching.

Fig. 2–18 Use the backstitch lever or dial on your machine to fill in areas with irregular crosshatching.

A hint: I once tried filling in small shapes, such as initials and little flowerpots, with crosshatching. With all the irregular turns and twists in the shapes, I nearly pulled my hair out from frustration. Then I realized that it would be easier to make a large rectangle of crosshatching, with long lines of stitching. After bonding a piece of iron-on interfacing or fusible web to the back of this rectangle, I cut out my small shapes and appliqued them by machine to a backing. The bonding kept the edges from fraying (Fig. 2-19).

This method works particularly well for lettering. If you design the letters to touch each other, you can applique them in one operation, as if they were script.

Some people like to use cello-tape instead of pins to hold applique to a backing, stitching right through the tape and later pulling it off. I cannot recommend cello-taping these letters to the

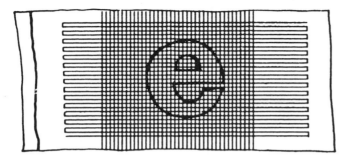

Fig. 2–19 Crosshatch fabric first. Bond to iron-on interfacing. Then cut out your applique.

backing when the edge is so vulnerable to fraying. When you pull the tape off, it destroys your bonded edge. But cellotape works well for nonwovens like leather and vinyl.

Quilting

Quilting with the presser foot on is best done for items with straight lines or broad, sweeping curves. Otherwise, the fabric begins to creep and before long, puckers will be caught on the front and back of the piece. (If your machine has adjustable presser foot tension, use it; also see Chapter 12 for quilting with the darning foot. For a more thorough discussion of machine quilting, consult our book, *The Complete Book of Machine Quilting*, listed in the bibliography.) I once quilted an enormous piece of striped fabric for a king-sized bedspread. I worked on a pingpong table to support the fabric and loosened both top and bottom tensions slightly to accommodate the extra thickness of top, batting, and bottom. I also stitched on top of adding machine tape to keep the fabric from creeping.

Today I heartily recommend using a walking foot when machine quilting with the presser foot on (Fig. 2-20). It keeps all the layers from creeping. Ask your machine dealer to show you the

proper walking foot for your machine. You may have to use a foot made for another brand of machine.

Trapunto is the name of another form of quilting in selected areas. Back a fabric with organza or muslin and straight stitch around a shape on the topside of the fabric. Turn the fabric over and slit only the organza. Stuff batting, felt, or yarn (depending on whether the article is washable or not) into the opening and pad the area evenly. Don't overstuff it or the fabric will pucker. Either cover the slash with iron-on interfacing or sew up the slash in the organza by hand, using a whipstitch or a catchstitch (Fig. 2-21).

Additional Ideas

* Copy the decorative design on an old sewing machine. Blow it up slightly and simplify it for applique. Using non-frayable but washable fabric such as knits, applique the shapes with straight stitch to the Sewing Machine Cover in Part Two.
* Using the hidden applique method, applique bright-colored garden tool shapes to a ten-pocket tote for gardeners.
* On a length of fabric, draw a mother quail from the side and enough babies behind her to make a door towel

Fig. 2–20 My favorite tool for machine quilting; the walking foot. It prevents the layers from creeping, causing unwanted puckers.

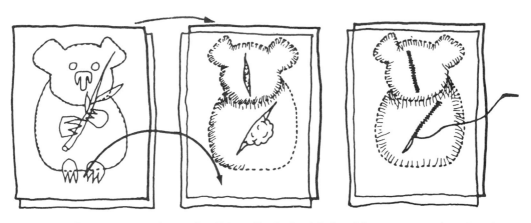

Fig. 2–21 Trapunto is a form of quilting. Back the fabric with organza and outline large shapes with straight stitch. From the back, slash the organza just enough to stuff the shapes slightly. Then sew up the slashes by hand and finish details with hand embroidery.

to place at the bottom of a door to keep cold air out. Quilt the features and outlines with straight stitch.

* Crosshatch a large area of fabric with silk or rayon thread in basketweave patterns. Bond fusible webbing to the back of the entire piece. Then cut out basket shapes and applique to a backing. Fill the baskets with fabric flowers, using the petal shape from Part Two.

* Crosshatch in icy blue and cut out the word "January," appliqueing it to a canvas rectangle that is the beginning of a fabric calendar, and that will also serve as a sampler of the techniques you're learning. Watch the Additional Ideas section at the end of each chapter for the coming months of the fabric calendar.

CHAPTER 3

Simple Zigzag and Applique

Visual Glossary

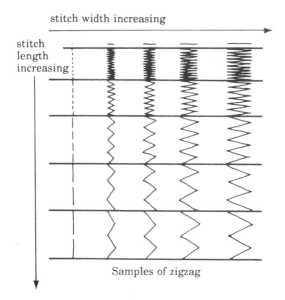

stitch width increasing

stitch length increasing

Samples of zigzag

Those of us fortunate enough to have a zigzag sewing machine know the joys and potential of garment construction with this comparatively new invention (only available since the 1930s) — sewing lingerie and bathing suits, overcasting seams, making knit outfits. But the possibilities of simple zigzag in machine embroidery have been relatively unexplored.

Feathering, Beading, and Filling

By playing with the bobbin and upper tensions, and by changing both the stitch length and width, we can achieve a variety of intriguing yet easy-to-do effects.

For example, look at the differences between ordinary zigzag on medium-weight cotton at normal tension settings and zigzag with the upper tensions tightened to its highest setting (Fig. 3-2.) Below these samples are differences in length of stitch and in loosening of the bobbin tension. Doesn't this variation resemble cretan stitch in hand embroidery and wouldn't it make a lovely border?

Another effect possible with simple zigzag is called beading, which means to bring the bottom thread to the surface by tightening upper tension and to work the zigzag closely together in a satin stitch. If a contrasting color of thread is wound into the bobbin, interesting color play can highlight your work. Some machines have a special way to achieve beading, but for most machines, you will have to experiment on a test cloth to find the upper and lower tension settings that bring the

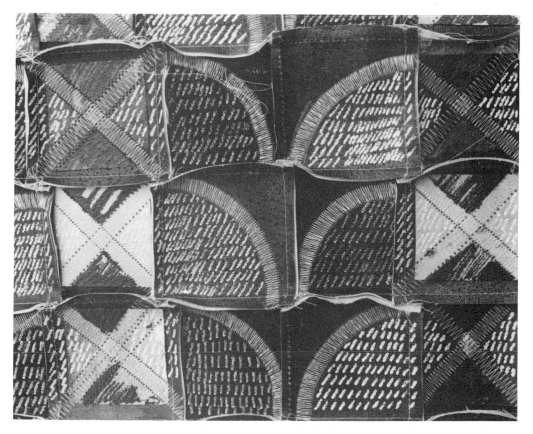

Fig. 3–1 Ellen Zahorec, Brevard, NC. Detail of "Shroud for Strip and Dot," 4' × 8'. Machine zigzag and paint on canvas. Photo by Alex Hughes, courtesy of the artist.

bobbin thread precisely to the surface and not beyond. Remember that every time you stop your machine, the bobbin thread is brought *farther* to the surface than it would in the normal process of stitching, so that when you start up again, the bobbin thread pops up to the middle of your zigzag instead of behaving itself on the side. Remedy this by planning beading in a straight or widely curving line in order to sew an entire line without stopping the machine.

Remember, too, that if you use a heavier thread on top than in the bob-bin, the bobbin thread will be pulled up more.

We mentioned crosshatching in Chapter 2 and this same technique can be done in zigzag. Be careful that your tension is not too tight or the fabric will pucker. You may also want to use a stabilizer. If you need to cover large areas fast, zigzag crosshatching does the job (Fig. 3-3).

Another way to fill in a large area is called swirl stitch (Fig. 3-4). When the stitches change directions, as in this technique, use thread that catches the

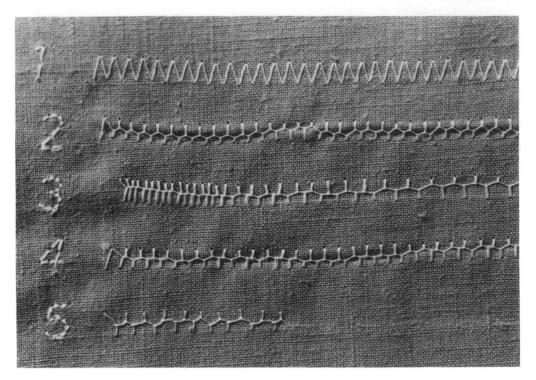

Fig. 3–2 Differences in tension settings: (1) normal zigzag; (2) highest top tension; (3) loosened bobbin with variations in spacing of stitches; (4) machine-worked cretan stitch; (5) hand-worked cretan stitch.

light, like rayon or silk. Put the fabric in a hoop and release the pressure. Leave the regular presser foot on and the feed dogs up. Now run the machine fast while you twirl the hoop from right to left and back. Try not to overlap stitches.

Satin Stitch

The most used form of zigzag is tightly packed into a satin stitch. And it is here that you begin to appreciate the subtleties of matching all elements of presser foot, technique, fabric, thread, and needle.

An applique foot has a wedge scooped out of the underside, allowing the foot

to ride smoothly over the satin stitches just formed (Fig. 3-5). It is easier to control the stitches being formed if you remove the connecting bar on the foot in front of the needle, transforming your foot into an open-toed applique foot. For a plastic foot, merely cut the bar off with strong scissors and file the edge with an emery board. For a metal foot, place the foot in a vise and remove the bar with a hacksaw, filing the edge with a metal file. You can also buy an open-toed applique foot (see Supply List). Since the removal of the connecting bar leaves an area in front of the needle without pressure, some fabrics may tend to lift when the needle lifts.

40

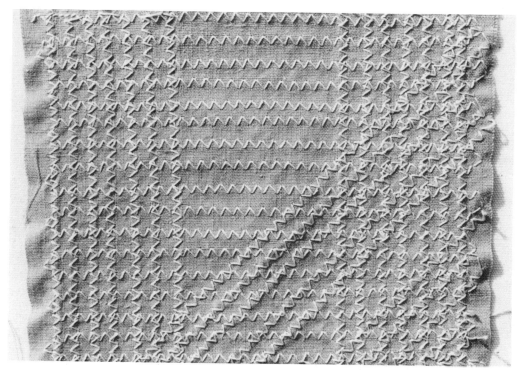

Fig. 3-3 Three rows of zigzag crosshatching. Inspired by Graphic Games, *by Victor Baumgartner (see Bibliography – Good Books on Pattern).*

Counteract this by placing one hand in a V-shape on either side of the foot (Fig. 3-6). This also prevents tunneling.

Satin stitch pulls the foundation fabric tremendously. If you are using any fabric lighter than denim, be sure to loosen top tension and to back the fabric with stabilizer or your fabric will be pulled into an unwanted tunnel.

To form satin stitch, you must experiment with decreasing stitch length, which packs the zigzags together, and increasing width, which determines how wide your satin stitch will be. When you find the position on your stitch length dial or lever that gives you an acceptable satin stitch, mark the position with your pen or pencil so

that you can find this hallowed place again – even $\frac{1}{16}$" (1.5 mm) variation in setting makes a difference. If you can't find a way to write on your machine, put a tiny press-on label or tape above the width dial and write on that.

The trick is to find the place that pulls your fabric through the presser foot without either destroying the solid line of zigzag stitching, or letting threads pile up so much that the presser foot cannot climb over the mess. Again, practice on your test cloth. Sew rapidly but not recklessly because your thread will break.

For years I have been frustrated with the coarseness and sloppiness of my satin stitches, but I finally learned the

41

Fig. 3–4 Swirl stitch, worked by Jane Warnick. Run the machine rapidly while twirling the hoop. Gold Natesh fine (rayon) on red raw silk.

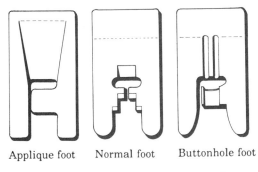

Applique foot   Normal foot   Buttonhole foot

Fig. 3–5 Undersides of three presser feet.

secret to the perfect machine satin stitch: use extra-fine thread. It's the same in hand embroidery. Two strands of embroidery floss make a fine satin stitch, while all six strands make a lumpy one. If your favorite fabric store does not carry extra-fine thread, see the Supply List at the end of the book. But don't take my word as gospel. Experiment for yourself. Experiment also with loosening top tension slightly, which makes the stitch form a slight mound (Fig. 3-7).

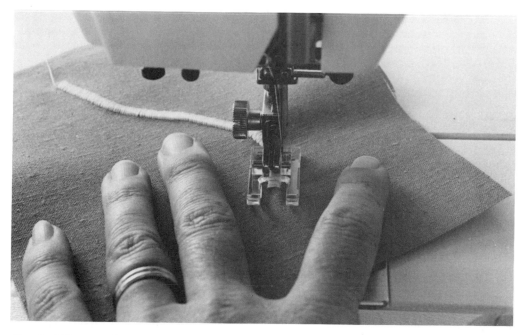

Fig. 3–6 Prevent the fabric from lifting by placing your fingers in a V in front of the satin stitch.

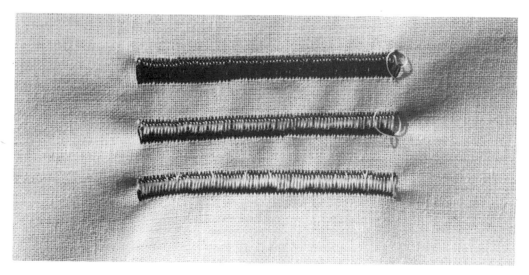

Fig. 3–7 Underside of satin stitch, with light-colored thread in the bobbin and dark through the needle. Top row: top tension has been loosened too much and the dark top thread obscures the light bobbin thread. Bottom row: top tension has not been loosened enough and the fabric tends to tunnel. Middle row: top tension has been loosened enough to form a slight mound on the topside of the fabric, making a pleasing satin stitch.

What thread you use in the bobbin depends on your machine and the fabric you're using. Some machines object fiercely if you use two different weights in top and bobbin. Others are docile, no matter what you use. I like cotton-covered polyester in the bobbin, because it pulls the extra-fine thread to its side, and makes a plump satin stitch, but this would be too heavy for lightweight fabrics. Again, you must experiment. No matter what thread you use, start with a full bobbin, so you won't run out half-way.

As for width of satin stitch, I usually select the second or third widest setting on my machine, a personal quirk. Somehow a satin stitch in the widest settings never looks neat enough for me. But I don't make banners or architectural hangings. For those, the scale of the new 7 mm-wide satin stitches may be more appropriate. Again, experiment and form your own opinion.

You've matched presser foot (applique) to technique (satin stitch) to fabric (heavyweight, if only because you added stabilizer) to thread (extra-fine). Now you must choose the appropriate needle. If you are decorating with satin stitch on one layer of fabric, use a 9/10(70) needle. If you are machine appliqueing and thus dealing with two or more layers of fabric, use a larger sized needle — 12(80) or 14(90).

Turning satin stitch corners takes some practice before you reach perfection. As you come to the end of a zigzag line, keep your needle on the outside edge of your stitching as you turn — e.g., if the line of stitching turns left, your needle will stop in the fabric at the right-hand corner. Lift the presser foot, turn the fabric counterclockwise 90 degrees, put down the presser foot, and merrily stitch, watching carefully that the foot is not catching on the extra lay-er of thread at the corner (Fig. 3-8). This is where the wedge in the applique foot does its work. It easily climbs over the stitch pile-up at the corner.

Variations on corners are (1) to leave them open, which is only appropriate on decorative lines of satin stitch, not on applique; or (2) to miter them by tapering in and out of the corner (Fig. 3-9).

You will also need to practice turning inside and outside angles and curves, and forming points (see Fig. 3-10).

Experiment with blocks of satin stitches in borders, as Jane Warnick has done in Fig. 3-11. She also tried variegated thread, changing direction when thread color changed.

Cutwork

Once you are comfortable with satin stitch on your machine, try cutting out areas of your design and satin stitching the cut edges. This is called cutwork (Fig. 3-12). I prefer to work two layers of satin stitch and if possible, I work in a hoop so the material won't stretch. Traditional cutwork is worked on finely woven linen and linen blends. I also use the same color of extra-fine machine-embroidery thread on top and bobbin.

First satin stitch in a narrow width around the motif. Then, without removing the hoop, cut out the center of the design close to the stitching. For additional support, pin water-soluble stabilizer underneath the fabric. Then satin stitch again with the next largest width. If you want to make bars (or "brides") across the cut-out area, lay narrow cords across the opening after the first stitching. Satin stitch over the cords. Then trim cord ends and satin stitch the outer shape. This will hide the cord ends. Finally, dissolve the water-soluble stabilizer.

44

Fig. 3–8 To turn satin-stitch corners, keep the needle on the outside edge as you pivot the material. The underside of this clear applique foot has a wedge scooped out, helping it to pass smoothly over the previous satin stitches.

Vari-Width Zigzag

The last effect we will explore with simple zigzag is called vari-width zigzag or tapering, which means to change the stitch-width lever from the narrowest setting (0, or a straight line) to the widest and back again after a few stitches. Some machines have a dial or special lever arrangement to allow slipping back and forth from the 0 setting

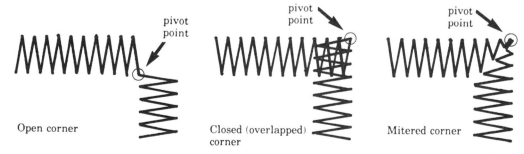

Fig. 3–9 Open, closed, and mitered corners.

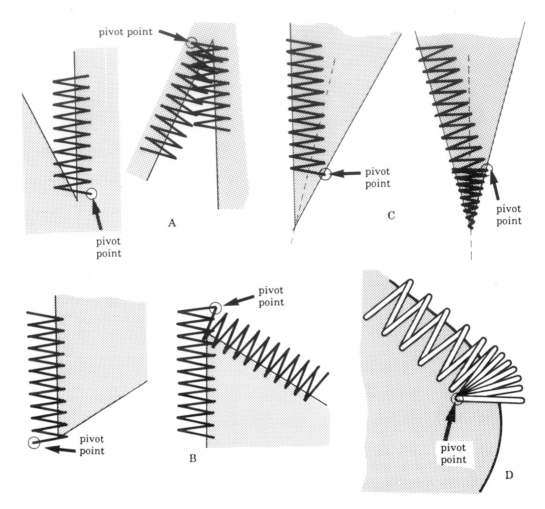

Fig. 3–10 Embroidering corners, points, and curves. A. Applique stitching on inside corners. B. Stitching outside corners. C. To taper a point, stitch down one side until the right side of a stitch falls just outside the applique. Then pivot slightly and stitch down the center of the point, reducing the stitch width as you go. D. To applique a curve, stitch into same hole as you pivot fabric.

to the widest. Changing these settings at regular intervals produces a variety of line (Fig. 3-13). To ensure regularity without spending an hour measuring and marking intervals, machine-baste a straight line (longest stitch length setting) and cover up every other basting stitch with wide vari-width zigzag.

46

Start and end satin stitch with your machine set at 0 width and 0 length. Take a few stitches in one place to lock the stitches. When you later cut the threads, cut the top threads first. Then give a gentle yank to the bobbin threads and the top thread will be pulled to the back.

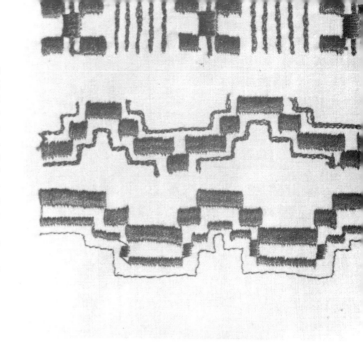

How to handle goofs? Practicing on the test cloth prevents 90% of them, but if you make a mistake, rip stitches from the underside to a corner or intersection. Remove excess threads on the topside (I use tweezers). Begin anew with your needle on the outside corner of the turn, holding the two threads securely in your hands, and with the stitch-width lever set to 0. Take a few stitches to lock the threads but don't allow the material to move. Reset the stitch-width lever to whatever your setting was and continue stitching as before. The new stitches will lock the ends of the old ones.

Save your test cloth; you never know when you will need it again and it can save you hours of experimenting. Label it with the settings you used and enter it in your sample book or pin it to this book.

Fig. 3–11 Satin-stitch blocks in a border, worked by Jane Warnick and inspired by Boussert's Folk Art of Europe.

Fig. 3–12 Detail of brown Ultrasuede tunic by Myrna Wacknov of Foster City, CA. After lines of satin stitch are worked in variegated thread, areas are cut out.

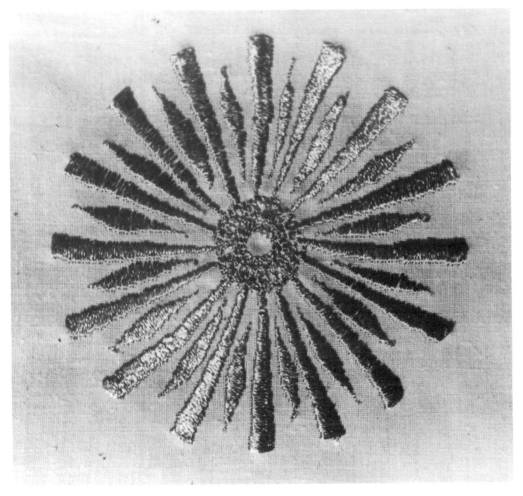

Fig. 3–13 Tapered zigzag worked with Natesh fine (rayon) by Jane Warnick. The change in dark/light is caused by how the light catches the rayon. Jane cautions you to stabilize the center when working circles because the stitching stretches outward, creating a bulge in the center.

Satin-Stitch Applique

There are at least five ways to machine applique with satin stitch. Which way is best? Machine embroiderers are vehement about their preferred method. One person insists on stabilizing the background fabric with such-and-such a product and abhors using scrap paper; another person abhors the feeling of the background stabilizer and insists that straight stitching first is the secret. Try the following five methods on a test cloth to see which you prefer; your way is the best way.

For all methods of machine applique, be sure the bulk of the satin stitches are on the applique fabric. Otherwise frayed edges of the applique will peek

48

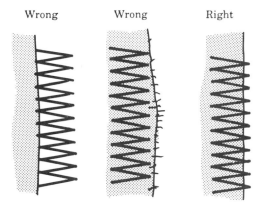

Wrong   Wrong   Right

Fig. 3–14 When doing satin-stitch applique, stitch close to the edge, and overlap it slightly. Otherwise the edge will pull loose or fray.

out or will escape from the stitching and possibly pull out. If you can decenter your needle to the right, you can more accurately place the needle at the exact edge of the applique. Using an open-toed applique foot also helps control where the stitches land (Fig. 3-14). Most stray threads can be pulled out with tweezers.

Fig. 3–15 Wende Cragg, Fairfax, CA, "Ode to Ming," 36" × 21". Velveteen applique. Wende uses spray glue to fuse appliques to a foundation. She uses any thread on hand for the applique, especially Molnlycke and Dual Duty. Sometimes she has trouble with the needle breaking at the edges, where she inserts piping, but she solved the problem by using a needle larger than size 12(80).

Fig. 3–16 One block of "Basket Sampler" quilt (83" × 101") by Karen Bray of Walnut Creek, CA. See text for Karen's method and see Bibliography for her book, Machine Applique.

Method 1: Cut out the shape to be appliqued with no seam allowance. Run a glue stick around the under edge, spray washable glue on the back, or use the Teflon pressing sheet to fuse webbing under the shape. Glue or fuse the applique on the foundation. Strengthen the foundation fabric by pinning stabilizer underneath, to be torn off after stitching. Or if the applique is small, place the background fabric in an embroidery hoop, taking off the foot to slip the hoop under the needle and then replacing the foot. (See Chapter 4 for directions on how to put on an embroidery hoop for machine work). Satin stitch around the edges. *Advantages:* Easy, quick, long-lasting. *Disadvantages:* With glue only, difficult fabrics may fray and creep, small points and shapes move under the presser foot.

Method 2 (Karen Bray's method; see Bibliography): Trace the shape of the design onto the applique fabric. Cut a large square or rectangle around the applique design so that 1 to 2 inches (5 cm) remains all around the design. Pin the applique fabric to the design fabric. Straight stitch around the lines of the

50

design, using 10 to 12 stitches/inch, and trim the applique fabric close to the stitching (applique scissors make this easy). Now satin stitch around the applique shape. Karen does not use any stabilizer or paper beneath her applique and yet they are pucker-free. (Fig. 3-16) *Advantages:* It works and is pucker-free; backing fabric behind the applique can be removed if you want to hand-quilt single layer only. *Disadvantages:* Extra fabric is required for each applique — would be wasteful and expensive for some fabrics and not usable on small scraps; straight stitch is extra step that takes more time.

Method 3 (Barbara Lee Pascone's method; see Bibliography): First stabilize a square of the applique fabric by fusing an iron-on interfacing to the back of it. Remember to use a damp press cloth for the strongest bond. You can dampen with a plant mister. Transfer the design to the applique fabric via heat transfer pencil, light table, or whichever method you prefer. Cut out the applique shape and pin it to the background fabric. Pin a piece of stabilizer underneath everything (fabric stabilizer, because Barbara believes paper dulls the machine needle). Satin stitch. Optional: Cut away extra stabilizer on back. *Advantages:* The fused applique will not fray or pucker, nor will the stabilized background; small bits of fabric can be used in this way without fear of movement; light-colored fabrics become more opaque so the color of the backing doesn't show through. *Disadvantages:* Fusing tends to erase the very tactile quality we love in fabrics, making everything flat and even; for quilts, the fusing method can make the appliques too stiff.

Method 4: European instructions for satin-stitch applique start with mark-

ing the pattern on the back of the foundation fabric. Pin a square of applique fabric bigger than the applique shape to the topside of the foundation fabric, matching grains. Underside up, stitch the applique shape with a narrow zigzag (not satin stitch). Turn it over and trim the applique fabric close to the stitching. Now satin stitch the applique shape from the topside. For extra insurance against puckering, put stabilizer under the foundation fabric, to be torn

Fig. 3-17 Judy Haroutunian of Fabricraft (Cardiff by the Sea, CA) uses Barbara Lee Pascone's method of machine applique: fuse iron-on interfacing to the back of the applique before satin stitching. Detail of child's dress, made for the Fairfield Processing fashion show at the Houston Quilt Market.

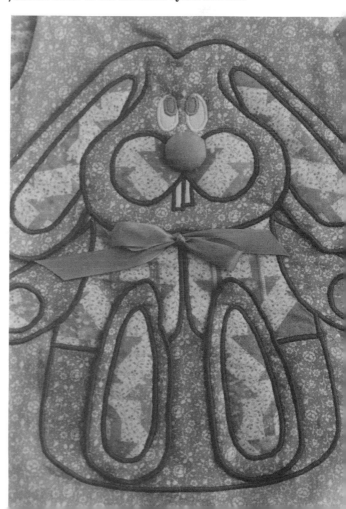

Fig. 3–18 Marilyn Allen of Duluth, MN, uses the European method of machine applique, which is especially useful on pile fabric. Marilyn designs machine-applique patterns for The Crafty Critter (see Supply List).

away after stitching. *Advantages:* All pattern transfers go on the underside of the foundation fabric, so you don't have to worry about transfer marks being seen; the method is neat and pucker-free and is especially useful when using fur-like fabrics for applique. *Disadvantages:* Some people are uneasy about not being able to see what's happening to the applique fabric until after the preliminary step; when the applique is complicated, with many layers, you may become confused about which fabric to stitch first.

Method 5: Layered satin stitch, sometimes called reverse applique, is worked by stacking three or more layers of the same-sized fabric together and machine- or pin-basting the edges. The design is satin-stitched from the topside and then layers of fabric are carefully cut away to expose the other colors underneath. Small swatches of fabric can be inserted by straight-stitching a shape, cutting away the top layer(s), and pinning a square of the special fabric larger than its final size in place on top. Turn the fabric over and straight-stitch or zigzag (with a narrow stitch) the design shape again. From the topside, trim away excess applique fabric close to the stitching (Fig. 3-19). Satin stitch, making sure you cover the two previous rows of straight stitches.

Depending on what fabrics you use, this method can be made to look like Cuna Indian molas, Persian Resht applique (an insertion technique), lace or transparent insertion, or stained glass. For the latter, on a small scale, as long as the proportion of the width of the satin stitch to the size of the design shapes is the same as full-sized stained glass, you can use dark thread (black, brown, gray) to achieve a stained-glass look to layered satin-stitch applique. In other words, you must scale down the colored glass shapes and work small. But if you wish to work larger, you

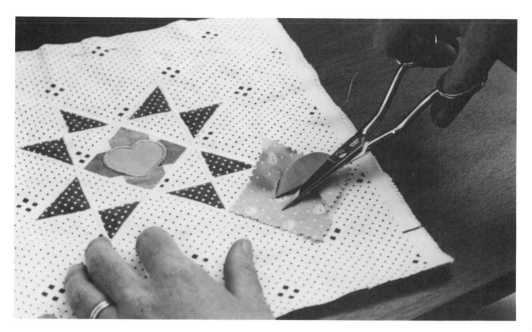

Fig. 3–19 Layered satin stitch is achieved by stacking layers of fabric, satin stitching shapes, and then cutting down to reveal various layers. Gingher duck-billed applique scissors make the job easier.

must either combine rows of satin stitching, use black ribbon or bias tape, or layer black fabric on top, to be satin-stitched and cut away, exposing the colors underneath. *Advantages:* The satin stitch is strong and faster than turning under the edge and handstitching; it adds interest and texture to the design. *Disadvantages:* If the fabrics used are slippery or have a nap (velvet, corduroy), they will move around unless you take precautions; straight stitch the design line before cutting away fabrics for satin stitching.

Whichever method you choose, remember that you can give dimension to your appliques, either by pushing a bit of batting under them before you close the shape with satin stitches, or by coaxing the fabric into small tucks be-

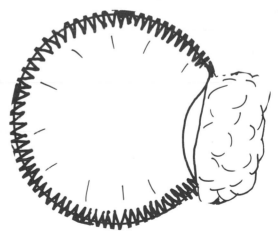

Fig. 3-20 Three-dimensional appliques can be achieved by stuffing with a little batting before closing the edge and/or by coaxing small tucks in the applique before stitching.

fore securing it to the background (Fig. 3-20).

You can also make your appliques completely three-dimensional by cutting them out, as Barbara Lee Pascone has done in Fig. 3-21. Barbara recommends making a six-layer sandwich for 3-D images: from top down, fabric, batting, two layers of heavyweight interfacing, batting, and backing (Fig. 3-22). She pins on both sides of the outline and straight stitches around the image. She quilts any details inside the image.

Then she cuts out the piece and satin stitches around. After trimming any loose fibers sticking out, she satin stitches a final time, making sure the needle enters the fabric on the left at the same place it did on its first trip around (decentering the needle to the left helps).

When Barbara wants an intentional wobble on the edge, as for flowers, she does not use inner layers of interfacing. After satin stitching, she stretches the edge gently to make it ripple.

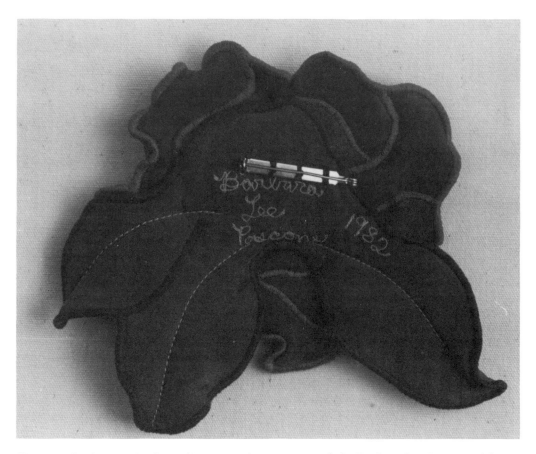

Fig. 3-21 Back view of a three-dimensional name tag made by Barbara Lee Pascone of Camarillo, CA, author of Successful Machine Applique *(see Bibliography under Barbara Lee). The front of the name tag is pictured in Fig. 8-1.*

54

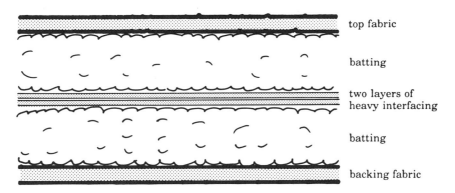

top fabric

batting

two layers of
heavy interfacing

batting

backing fabric

*Fig. 3–22 Another way to make 3-D appliques: cut them out from a six-layer
sandwich.*

One final warning before we close this chapter: machine applique is addictive.

Additional Ideas

* Make a chocolate-lover's quilt using Nina's Quilt Module in Part Two, appliqueing kisses, bars, brownies, fudge, and other goodies.
* Decorate the front openings of His and Hers Caftans with undulating rows of satin stitch, using variegated thread on top and a contrasting color in the bobbin. Bead the edges of the satin stitch. Put satin-stitch spots in the centers of each wave of the undulation.

* Combine open zigzag with rows of rickrack on a ready-made shirt.
* Make a rajah's stuffed elephant with sumptuous satin-stitched blankets and heavily machine-embroidered ears (do the work first before cutting out the animal).
* Make a pink satin-stitched "February" beaded with red bobbin thread. Crosshatch a rectangle with red rayon thread, bond iron-on interfacing to the back, cut out hearts, and applique them around February on your fabric calendar. (See Chapter 2—Additional Ideas, if you don't understand.)

CHAPTER 4

Simple Free-Machine Embroidery

Visual Glossary

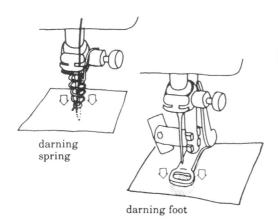

darning spring

darning foot

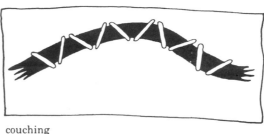

couching

"Fun" and "liberating" are the two words I've heard most often about free-machine embroidery. Free-machine embroidery is done after removing the presser foot, lowering or covering the feed dogs, and moving the fabric freely in any direction while stitching.

People who are not comfortable drawing with a pencil usually blossom with free-machine embroidery, achieving spontaneous effects they'd never dreamed they could.

Preparation

Since preparation of each machine is slightly different, the best way to find out what works on your machine is to read its instruction book and to talk to your sewing machine dealer. Follow the same instructions as for darning. You need to know whether you can lower the feed dogs on your machine, where the bobbin tension screw is and how to tighten or loosen it, and how to bypass the bobbin tension altogether.

Fig. 4-2 is a brief chart of the major brands and how to adapt them to free-machine embroidery. If your brand is not listed here, look in the yellow pages of your telephone directory for the address of your nearest dealer.

Since you'll be using a hoop, you may also want to extend the amount of working space around the needle. If you have a flat-bed extension, use it. If not, you can rig one by stacking up books around the free arm to the level of the needle plate.

Remember that there is more than one way to adapt your machine to free-machine embroidery. The only way to find out what works best for you is to experiment. When I started with free-machine embroidery, everyone told me that you had to lower the feed dogs. For a while I was paralyzed because there's no way to do that on the machine I was using. Then I realized that darning is similar to free-machine embroidery, so I put the darning plate over my feed dogs, and the darning foot on instead of the presser foot. Naturally I didn't follow my own advice about practicing on a test cloth. I plunged in to work on a huge banner for my mother. To my utter frustration, about every two minutes the darning plate popped off and if I didn't notice it immediately, the needle soon struck loose metal and broke. Later, my favorite sewing machine dealer calmly pointed out that the stitch length dial *must* be set at 0 or the feed dogs move back and forth, dislodging the darning plate. (I never finished the banner either.)

Meanwhile, before I discovered this secret, I was so spitting mad at the darning plate that I took it off permanently—and found out that it didn't make any difference whether the feed dogs were lowered, covered, or otherwise hidden. As long as I put on the darning foot—which holds the fabric down during the formation of each stitch and thereby prevents skipped stitches, broken thread, and snapped needles—I could freely stitch. Others with different brands of machines have told me the same. Depending on how heavy the stitching is, they often don't bother to lower the feed dogs at all; removing the presser foot, releasing the pressure, and holding the fabric taut in the vicinity of the needle (with hoop, fingers, darning foot, etc.) works perfectly well. So experiment on your machine and have fun while you learn.

Fig. 4 1 Barbara Smith, Oak Park, IL, "After Tempe," 6½' × 3'. Whip stitch on dyed silk. Collection of D.O.S. Designs. Photo courtesy of the artist.

CHART OF MAJOR BRANDS

	feed dogs	bypassing bobbin tension
Bernina	drop	thread through hole in bobbin case without going through tension spring
Brother	drop	loosen only; cannot bypass
Elna	cover	thread through hole in back of case
JC Penney	drop	thread through hole in bobbin case
Kenmore (Sears)	drop	thread through hole in bobbin case
Necchi	drop	loosen only; cannot bypass
Nelco	varies	varies
New Home	drop	do not put bobbin thread through tension—just drop in
Pfaff	drop	loosen only; cannot bypass
Riccar	drop	thread through tiny wire spring
Singer	cover	do not put bobbin thread through tension spring—just drop in
Viking/Husqvarna	drop	thread through large square hole in bobbin case
White	drop	thread through wire spring

Fig. 4–2 Major Sewing Machine Brands.

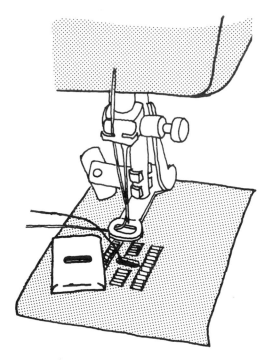

Fig. 4–3 Prepare for free-machine embroidery as you would for darning: cover or lower the feed dogs and put on the darning foot or spring.

It is extremely important to choose the correct size needle and appropriate thread for the fabric you are practicing on, so consult the Needle and Thread Chart at the end of the book. Remember that the function of the needle is to make a hole large enough for the thread. Briefly, you can free-machine embroider on almost any fabric, although tightly woven fabrics are sometimes more difficult to work on and knits tend to stretch. You can always back these fabrics with stabilizer (typing paper, tear-away, lightweight interfacing, or water-soluble stabilizer) before putting them in the hoop.

Practice free-machine embroidery on some mediumweight cotton fabric with two different colors of the same weight thread on top and bobbin, so that you can easily judge whether your bobbin thread is loose or tight. Use a spring-type machine-embroidery hoop.

If you don't have one, use an ordinary 6" (15 cm) or 8" (20.5 cm) wood or plastic embroidery hoop, but put it on backwards—that is, the top part of the hoop with the screw goes on the bottom; next comes the fabric; and last goes the bottom of the hoop (Fig. 4-4). Push the inner ring $\frac{1}{8}$" (3 mm) below the outer ring for a snug fit. The fabric should be tight as a drum. It also helps to wrap the rings of the embroidery hoop with strips of cotton fabric, bias binding, or electrical tape to keep the fabric from slipping. In a pinch, you can pleat the edge of the fabric between the inner and outer hoops, to make your fabric tight.

Some wooden hoops are adapted for machine embroidery by an indentation on the wood and a slim height, both factors allowing easy slipping of the hoop under the needle. However these hoops are hard to find (check the Supply List at the end of the book). You can file a half-moon on the upper and lower edge of your embroidery hoop if it's too thick to go under the needle. You can also tip the hoop on its side and slide it carefully under the needle—or merely take off the needle while sliding the hoop under the presser-bar lever, and then put the needle back on.

You *can* free-machine embroider with no foot on the machine (with the fabric in a hoop), but if ever you were destined to sew together your fingers, this would be the time. To be on the safe, unpainful side, I recommend using the darning foot for free-machine embroidery while you're learning. The darning foot acts like a tiny hoop around the needle, pressing the fabric against the needle plate at the moment a stitch is being formed, but lifting with the needle so that you can maneuver the fabric in any direction. (Some machines use a darning spring rather than a foot.) If your darning foot is plastic or metal, you may want to cut out the front part of it, so you can see better. (See Chapter 3 for instructions on altering the applique foot.)

Free-Machine Embroidery

Check your set-up against mine: I have mediumweight cotton fabric in a 6" (16 cm)-diameter machine-embroidery hoop; a size 12(80) needle, and ordinary 100% cotton sewing machine thread (two different colors in top and bottom); stitch length set at 0; darning foot on; zigzag needle plate. (You lower your feed dogs if possible, or cover them. I prefer to ignore them. Also release the pressure, if your machine has that feature.) Because I will be moving the hoop vigorously, I've put the extensions on my free-arm to make a large flat working surface.

All right, your machine is ready, your fabric stretched in the hoop, and you're ready to experiment. Setting the needle at its highest point, slide the hoop under the needle. My hoop is only $\frac{3}{8}$" (1 cm) thick; if yours is deeper, you may need to take off the darning foot first, slide the hoop under the needle, and then put on the darning foot. And don't forget to lower the presser-foot lever. This lever controls upper tension—

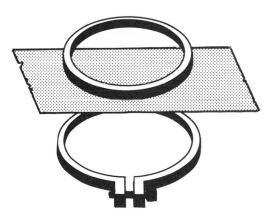

Fig. 4–4 *The outer part of the embroidery hoop goes* underneath *the fabric.*

Fig. 4–5 "Miriam's tooth fairy pillow," 4½" × 3½", by Mimi Ahern of San Jose, CA. Free-machine embroidery on pocket with hand smocking on the reverse.

and I could kick myself every time I have forgotten to depress the lever, only to rip out unwanted loops in the upper thread. (Jane Warnick has the new Brother computer machine that talks. If she forgets, it reminds her "Please put the presser-bar lever down.")

Your machine may be different from mine, however. On some models, the machine actually stitches better if you do not lower the presser-bar lever but instead tighten the top tension to eliminate big loops on the underside. Start by experimenting with the directions I give you. Then if your machine balks, experiment with changing one element at a time, until you find out what works for your machine.

First, *always*, you need to lock the initial stitch. Hold the thread in your left hand, hand-turn the wheel to make one stitch, and draw up the bobbin thread. Holding the two threads firmly, take about three stitches in the same hole (Fig. 4-6). You have now locked that first stitch and can cut off the two threads. Be careful not to cut the wrong threads, which I've (grumble, snarl) done a million times. Sometimes I wait to cut the threads until I've stitched several inches away from them.

Now try writing your name in thread. Place your hands firmly around the hoop, keeping your index and middle fingers near the needle (but without impaling them, if you're not using a darning foot). Do this, because at the

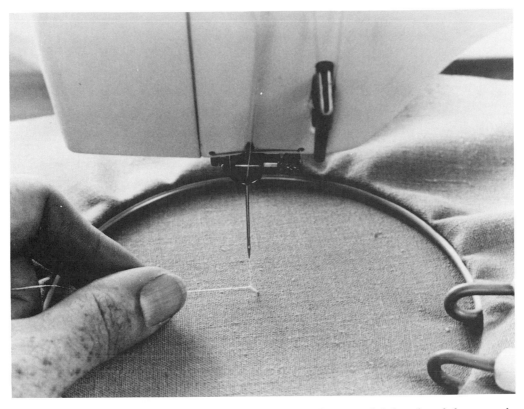

Fig. 4–6 To lock the initial stitch, hold the upper thread in your left hand and draw up the bobbin thread. Take three or four stitches in the same place and cut off ends.

moment the needle enters the fabric, the material *must* be pressed against the needle plate or a stitch cannot be formed. I keep my pinkies and thumbs outside the hoop and move the whole affair with all my fingers pressing firmly but not tensely against the cloth (Fig. 4-7). Remember, *you* move the fabric, since there are no regular presser feet or feed dogs to guide it. Exciting, isn't it!

Oh, your needle just broke? That's because you're moving the fabric too fast, taking giant, jerky stitches and thereby bending the needle so that it does not enter the hole in the needle plate, striking metal instead. Slow down a little and try not to jerk the hoop around—so what if you take two stitches in the same place. Of course, if you take too many stitches in the same place, the thread may also break.

Try every movement you can dream up—forwards, backwards, sidewards, loops, spirals, squares, ogees (what?). If you stitch lots of little "e's" as a fill-in stitch, it's called granite stitch. Try running the machine fast and slow (if you can switch your machine to slow speed, try that too.) At some point you will be backing up—and bang, run into the side of the hoop. What to do? Turn

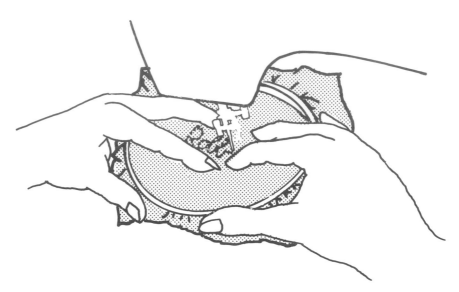

Fig. 4–7 *Use your middle fingers to press the fabric against the needle plate and your thumbs and pinkies to guide the hoop.*

Fig. 4–8 *Amy Chamberlin of Upper Marlboro, MD, has developed a clever way of portrait painting with the machine. She sandwiches a color photocopy between layers of organza and fills in the color with granite stitch and many changes of thread color. Photo courtesy of Janet Stocker.*

the hoop, of course; you can write your name upside-down or backwards in free-machine embroidery.

If at any time the top thread loops underneath the fabric, stop stitching and rethread your machine. If that doesn't work, tighten top tension until the loops disappear.

Now let's try some special effects. By manipulating bobbin and thread tensions and by changing the weight of cloth stitched on, a whole range of textural effects can be achieved. For example, by loosening the bobbin tension and not changing the upper tension at all, we can make the top thread lie on the surface in an even line similar to couching in hand embroidery. I like to use this effect with gold sewing machine thread (Fig. 4-9). Practice changing the speed of the machine, to see how it changes the look of the top and bobbin threads.

Whip Stitch

It is also possible to bypass the tension spring completely, allowing you to use heavy thread in the bobbin and to

Fig. 4–9 By loosening bobbin tension, the gold thread lies on the surface as if it were couched. On the left is a medium-weight cotton fabric; on the right is a soft wool, into which the gold thread sinks. Use a large-eyed needle with metallic threads to prevent the thread from fraying.

bring the bobbin thread up to the surface in large loops, called a whip stitch. The heavy thread may be six-stranded embroidery floss, linen carpet warp, handspun wool, etc. — how to handle these is covered in Chapter 6. Whip stitch is an easy way to give subtle texture to your work and it's twice as effective if you use two different colors on

top and bottom (Fig. 4-10). Because it puckers the lighter fabrics badly, always use a hoop for this stitch.

Bypassing bobbin tension is different on each machine; again, check the chart in Fig. 4-2 or your sewing-machine manual. Bobbin cases have either one or two screws. When there are two, the one on the left usually holds

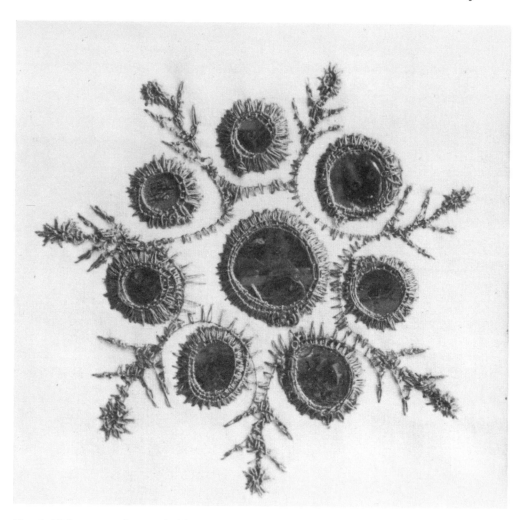

Fig. 4–10 Loosen or bypass bobbin tension and tighten top tension to work a whip stitch. It also helps to use a heavier thread on top, to bring the bobbin to the surface in loops. Sample worked by Jane Warnick.

the whole thing together, and the one on the right is the tension screw (Fig. 4-11). Turn it clockwise to tighten bobbin tension and counterclockwise to loosen. (Lucille Graham says "Right is tight" to remember which is which. This also applies to tension dials and most screws.) If you must loosen a screw to release the bobbin tension, place a piece of felt or a box under the bobbin case on the table to prevent the screw from falling out, bouncing off the table, and secreting itself in your shag rug. One of the machines has a hole in the (stationary) bobbin case through which I pass the end of the thread if I want to bypass bobbin tension.

If you have never played with bobbin tension and are worried that you cannot return the tension to normal, ask your dealer or a machine-embroidery teacher to show you what normal tension is on your bobbin. Or test it yourself by hanging a two-ounce weight on the bobbin thread (my heavy-duty Olfa cutter weighs two ounces) loaded into the bobbin case. Hold the case and let the weight dangle (Fig. 4-12). It should not slip. If it does, tighten the bobbin screw until the weight hangs. When you jerk the thread, it should slip down a little and then hang without slipping; if it does not slip when jerked, the bobbin tension may be too tight. When you find the location of normal tension, mark it with a tiny spot of white paint, typing correction fluid (temporary), or nail polish.

Those of you with factory preset bobbin tension should consider buying a second bobbin case, to be marked with nail polish and used only for machine embroidery. The cases for some machines are expensive but will enable

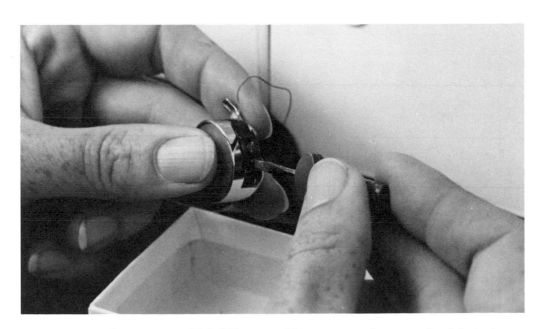

Fig. 4–11 If you have a removable bobbin case with two screws, the one on the right is the tension screw. Turn it to the left to loosen it.

65

Fig. 4–12 It's easy to reset your bobbin case for normal sewing. Hang a two-ounce weight on the bobbin thread and tighten the screw until the weight does not slip. My Olfa heavyweight cutter weighs two ounces.

you to greatly extend your range of possible effects.

To whip stitch, tighten your upper tension (9 or the tightest position works best for me), and loosen or bypass bobbin tension. Your fabric is still in a hoop, the stitch length at 0, and feed dogs down or covered. I don't use a darning foot because the loops are drawn up farther on the surface without it. Be sure to start with a full bobbin because this technique uses lots of thread.

Working whip stitch in spirals and loops pulls the bobbin thread into a pleasing flower-like form (and the back is nice too) (Fig. 4-13). I've found making the spirals and loops counterclockwise works better for me. When you are first practicing, if your bobbin thread only breaks once, you receive an A+. (When it doesn't break at all, you graduate with honors.) Why does the thread break? See Chapter 2 for a detailed discussion, but briefly you are probably moving the frame too fast or using too small of a needle (try the Blue Stretch or Yellow Band special-purpose nee-

Fig. 4–13 Begin the whip stitch in the center of the flower and spiral out to a petal. Stitch each petal in counterclockwise loops.

dles). You will have more loops on each petal if you move the frame slowly, and more spikes if you move it fast.

If your bobbin thread refuses to come up to the surface in loops big enough for your taste, experiment with changing the weights of thread in top and bobbin. Remember that the heavier or stronger thread tends to pull the lighter to its side. Therefore, an extra-fine machine-embroidery thread in the bobbin will be more easily pulled to the surface if you use an ordinary thread in the top. Likewise, if you want a thicker thread to be pulled to the surface, you may want to use an even heavier or stronger thread on top, such as buttonhole twist or nylon invisible thread. Since these loops are fairly subtle, you may want to use a thread in the bobbin that catches the light more than cotton, such as rayon, silk, or polyester.

In designing your own work, either clump your flowers or plan to lock off the threads at the beginning and end of each flower, as a trail of whip stitch on the surface of your fabric from one flower to the next can look busy and messy. Also, whip stitch does not cover printed fabric solidly, so design accordingly. You do not need to clip threads for each flower until you're finished working. Simply lock the last stitches of the flower, turn the handwheel so the needle is in its highest position, pull out some thread above the needle, and move the hoop to the next flower, which you start by locking stitches. Later, you can clip all the excess surface threads (I don't bother to clip those on the underside).

Another way to work whip stitch is in straight lines, moving the hoop slowly but running the machine fast (see Fig. 4-14).

Fig. 4–14 Wilcke Smith's first piece of machine embroidery (collection of Robbie Fanning), "Spirit Space," 10" × 6¾". The figure is worked by hand and comes out of the pocket. The squiggly lines are worked in whip stitch, running the machine fast and moving the hoop slowly. Pinks, oranges, burgundies on black wool. Wilcke lives in Albuquerque, NM.

The more you practice free-machine embroidery, the easier it becomes. As you accumulate experience, you will develop a stitch style as distinctive as your handwriting—some people run the machine fast and move the hoop slowly; others stitch slower and move the hoop faster.

When you feel comfortable with free-machine embroidery, you may want to dispense with the darning foot as long as your fabric is held taut by a hoop. If you keep your fingers around the hoop and not near the needle, you won't impale yourself. This makes it easier to change thread colors often.

As you draw your fabric away from the needle to cut off threads for tying, be careful: if you do not pinch the last stitch taken and pull the fabric gently to the side of the needle, the threads may draw up and pucker the fabric (Fig. 4-15).

Last, reset your tension settings to universal and your stitch length to its normal setting.

Additional Ideas

* Buy or construct an over-sized shirt, leaving the underarm and sleeve seams open. Decorate the sleeves and yoke with free-machine embroidered drawings of the universe with Halley's Comet passing through. Date it "1986," sew up the side and sleeve seams, and save it for your grandchildren.
* Blow up to 4" tall and trace alphabet letters from Part Two onto the back side of sandpaper. Prepare 12 Nina's Quilt Modules from Part Two. Take your supplies and machine to a pediatric ward of a hospital. Let a child pick out the letters of his or her name. Trace around each letter on a

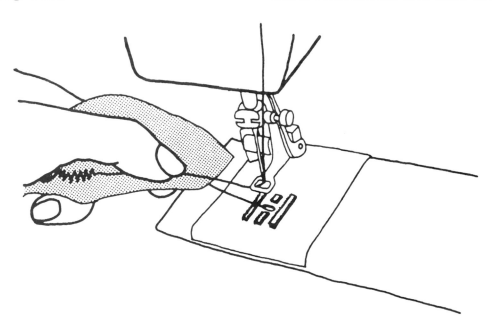

Fig. 4–15 To prevent puckering, pinch the last stitch taken as you pull the fabric to the side.

quilt module, and free-machine quilt everything in the center block but the letter, so it will stand out. Connect the modules three across and four down and give the lap quilt to the child.

* Take a bag of solid-colored fabrics out into your garden. Study the colors of the garden. Then cut out simple circles and rectangles to represent the dominant colors in your garden. Back in the workroom, lay the fabrics on a backing. With whip stitch, free-machine embroider details of the flowers over the fabrics — stamens, outlines, stalks, leaves.

* Make fabric placecards by free-machine embroidering guests' names on non-frayable fabric (like felt or interfacing), cutting out with pinking shears, and fusing to colored cardboard.

* Fill in the letters of "March" for your fabric calendar with free-machine scribbling in rainbow colors. Outline them in bold couched thread. (See Chapter 2—Additional Ideas, if you're confused.)

CHAPTER 5

Advanced Free-Machine Embroidery

Visual Glossary

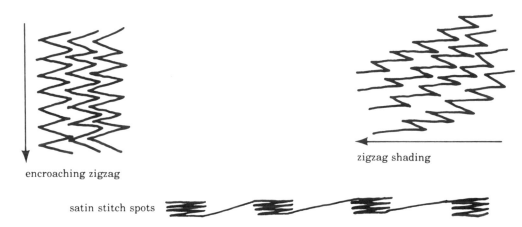

encroaching zigzag

zigzag shading

satin stitch spots

In this chapter, we will further explore the possibilities of free-machine embroidery, working with and without a hoop and with zigzag. You might as well stash your normal presser foot for the rest of the chapter, as we will keep the darning foot on the whole time.

Preparation

Whenever possible, use a hoop in free-machine embroidery—your work will be neater and more professional looking. But it is important to know how to stitch without a hoop. Why would you want to work without a hoop? Sometimes the design is long and continuous, so that constantly moving the hoop is tedious. Sometimes you have no choice: perhaps the fabric is delicate and will be marred by the impressions left by a hoop, or your piece of fabric is not large enough for a hoop. For example, I once made a spur-of-the-moment present of one machine-embroidered long-stemmed rose, stitched on a long rectangle of fabric too skinny to put into a hoop (Fig. 5-2).

For such times, you must learn to use your fingers as a complement to the darning foot, holding the fabric against the needle plate each time the needle enters the fabric. When you are working without a hoop, hold your hands so that the fabric is pressed against the needle plate (Fig. 5-3).

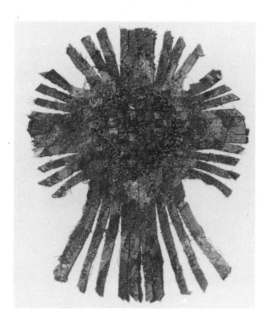

You can see that if you held your fingers under the fabric, you might lift the fabric away from the needle plate, so that stitches are not formed. When you are not working with a hoop, it is important to sew slowly and smoothly in order to give yourself plenty of time to readjust your grasp on the fabric. If you can switch your machine to slow speed, try it. To keep a large piece of cloth from unrolling each time you change grasps, roll up the excess fabric and secure it with clothespins or large safety pins.

Your preparations for free-machine embroidery without a hoop are the same as for with a hoop: stitch length 0, stitch width whatever you want, covered or lowered feed dogs (optional), darning foot on. You will need a flat surface to support the fabric, so if you have a portable free-arm machine, add whatever is needed to make it flat (e.g., the carrying case of one of my machines

Fig. 5–1A Peggy Moulton, Orinda, CA, "Fascination," 8" × 10". Machine applique cut up and plaited, with pin heads as part of the center design.

Fig. 5–1B Detail

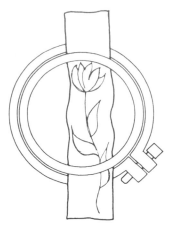

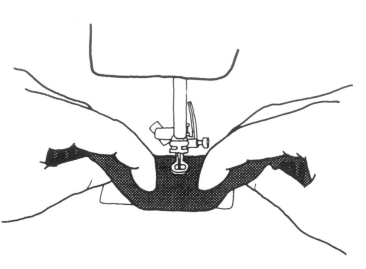

Fig. 5–2 When the fabric is too small for the hoop, learn to free-machine embroider without a hoop, using a darning foot and pressing the fabric flat with your fingers.

Fig. 5–3 Gather the material in your hands, pressing the fabric against the needle plate near the needle.

becomes a flat sewing surface when added to the free arm). You can order a flat-bed extension for most machines (see your dealer or the Supply List) or have a carpenter make you one. You can also buy special portable tables with surfaces that raise and lower.

Check tensions by stitching on a test cloth before attempting a finished article. To prevent puckers, I almost automatically loosen top tension for all free-machine embroidery and back with a stabilizer.

Always, always, bring up the bobbin thread (see Chapter 4), lower the presser foot, and take about three stitches in one place to lock the first stitch. Cut off thread ends.

Two of my machines have variable-speed features. I like to put them on slow for free-machine stitching without a hoop. When you see curves, corners, or spirals approaching the needle, slow down and use your fingers to hold the

material against the plate for each stitch — these situations will pucker your fabric if you are not careful.

After you finish the design, always press it to remove any tendency to pucker. Jane Warnick made a special pressing pad of four layers of wool (Fig. 5-4). You can also use a thick towel. Remember to match your iron setting to the most sensitive material you've used — rayon threads, for example, need a low heat. To protect your work from pressing errors, use a press cloth between the iron and the fabric. Or take Jackie Dodson's suggestion: use a Teflon sole plate on your iron so that nothing will be scorched.

Knowing how to free-machine embroider without a hoop comes in handy on large items, like quilts. Often you will need help simply to maneuver the enormous bulk of fabric under the needle. I know an artist who has developed an efficient quilt-moving machine: four

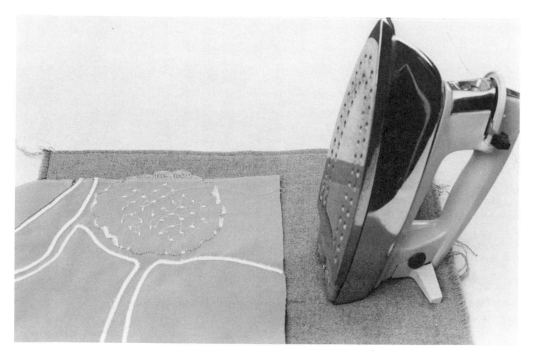

Fig. 5–4 Jane Warnick's pressing pad of four layers of soft wool. It prevents the texture in machine embroidery from being flattened.

children, who support the corners of the quilt, and run from side to side in a hilarious choreography as their mother stitches and screams commands.

Now that you've practiced working without a hoop, let's explore some more effects possible with free-machine embroidery.

Couching and Yarn Work

All you people with straight-stitch machines, don't despair at your zigzagless world—there is an easy way to fill in areas of color that does not require a zigzag. Draw your design on the right side of the fabric and back the whole thing with stabilizer. Stretch the fabric in a hoop. Set up the machine for free-machine embroidery—darning foot, feed dogs covered or down, pres-

sure released, 0 stitch length, universal tension, cotton sewing machine thread in upper and lower.

Now take a piece of any thick thread (crochet cotton, needlepoint yarn, knitting wool, embroidery floss) and lay it on the outline of the design. Lower the presser-bar lever and hand-turn the wheel until the needle is piercing the thick thread and the bobbin thread is brought up. Lock the stitch and cut off the thread ends. Stitch right through the thick thread in small stitches, until the design is solidly filled (Fig. 5-5). You can also stitch back and forth in a manner similar to the long-and-short stitches of hand embroidery (Fig. 5-6). If your sewing-machine thread color matches the thick thread, stitches will be practically invisible.

When you are done stitching, remove the fabric from under the needle. Then thread a tapestry needle with the ends of thick thread still on the surface. Pull these threads to the underside of the fabric and cut them off $1/4$" (6 mm) from the fabric surface. The ends need no further treatment as your straight stitches have already secured them.

A variation of this couching-by-piercing can be done using invisible nylon thread in the top (see Supply List) and ordinary sewing-machine thread in the bobbin. Instead of piercing all of the heavy thread (rug yarn, floss, etc.), only selected parts are held down by the invisible thread, which adds a beautiful texture to your work. Choose a heavy-weight backing fabric (such as are found at upholstery and drapery stores) so you won't need a hoop. Set up the machine for free-machine embroidery. You will lay down two parallel lines of nylon thread, stitching at the same time by sewing back and forth between

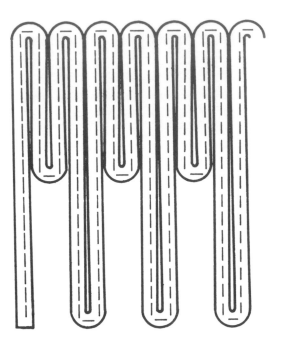

Fig. 5–6 *Machine-stitch right through the thick thread to create a pattern like the long and short stitches of hand embroidery.*

Fig. 5–5 Couching-by-piercing is an easy way to achieve large areas of color texture fast. Here yarn is being spiralled into a flower form.

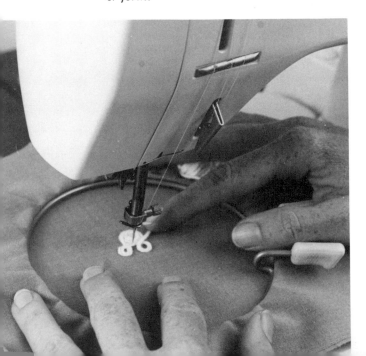

the lines, but will only pierce the yarn on each parallel line. The procedure, starting at the bottom of the lines and moving up, follows (refer to Fig. 5-7):

1. Draw two parallel lines on your backing fabric. Start in the middle interval at the bottom by bringing up the bobbin thread and locking the first stitch.

2. Lay the end of a long piece of yarn on the surface of the fabric from the middle to the left side. Stitch down across the end of the yarn to secure it, and then stitch along the underside of the yarn to the left parallel line without piercing the yarn. Stop the needle in the fabric at the parallel line and carefully stitch up over the yarn on the parallel line.

3. Stitch across the right parallel line without piercing the yarn already laid

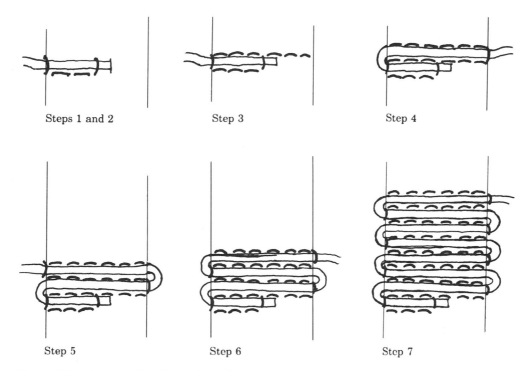

Steps 1 and 2   Step 3   Step 4

Step 5   Step 6   Step 7

Fig. 5–7 Making parallel lines of couching.

down. Stop the needle in the fabric at the parallel line.

4. Now pull the yarn across the interval directly *behind* the darning foot and needle. Stitch up over the yarn on the parallel line.

5. Stitch across the interval to the left parallel line, stopping the needle in the fabric on the line. Pull the yarn straight across the interval and stitch up over it.

6. Repeat until finished.

7. Lock and cut off sewing machine threads. Leave a 3" (7.5 cm) tail on the yarn, which is threaded into a tapestry needle, pulled to the back, and cut off.

This method of securing yarn to a surface can also be used in isolated motifs like flower heads (Fig. 5-8). Use a small crochet hook or the screwdriver that came with your machine to manipulate the loops. If the item is not a washable garment, the loops at the outside edge can be cut and fuzzed for added texture. Any article that has been stitched with invisible nylon thread should be ironed on the underside with a wool-warm iron.

Free-Machine Applique

Another good application of free-machine embroidery, even when you don't have a zigzag machine, is free-form applique. See Fig. 5-9 for five ways to secure edges.

All of these forms of straight stitch are fun, but when you combine free-machine embroidery with a zigzag machine, the possibilities become infinite (Fig. 5-10).

Zigzag Fill-In

The technique of filling an area with solid machine satin stitch is called encroaching zigzag. It's one of my favorite techniques, for while it looks difficult to others, it is easy and fast to work. You often see it used on the front of garments made in India and Mexico.

For the best results in encroaching zigzag, use an extra-fine cotton or rayon sewing machine thread (see Supply List) in both the top and bobbin. For

Fig. 5–9 Five ways to secure edges in free-machine applique: (1) circle a shape until it is secured (if the center puckers, pad it); (2) radiate out from a central point; (3) stitch back and forth until the shape is covered; (4) blend the edges of the shape with the background by stitching back and forth over the edge; (5) echo the shape and its neighbors with lines of free-machine embroidery.

those of us with machines that can't drop the feed dogs, this is the one situation in which you may want to cover your feed dogs, because the buildup of threads on the back occasionally snags on the teeth of the feed dogs. (Since I don't like using the cover for my feed dogs, I put two rows of masking tape over them.) Otherwise, set up the machine for free-machine embroidery as usual: darning foot on, zigzag needle plate, stitch length at 0, stitch width at whatever you like. Since zigzag tends to pull at the fibers of the fabric, I always back my material with a stabilizer. Again, whenever possible, use a hoop to keep the material stretched tight.

To fill in a shape with solid encroaching zigzag, run the machine at a rapid rate, but move the fabric slowly and smoothly. You can either lay down lines of satin stitch that snuggle up to each other, or you can put a third row of satin stitch on top of the first two rows (Fig. 5-11). It is sometimes easier to follow a stitching line if the needle is decentered to the left or right, so you can be sure the needle is entering the fabric exactly where you want it to.

Another way to fill a shape is by subtly shading with zigzag stitches in more of a sidewards motion of the hoop than the up-and-down parallel movements of encroaching zigzag (Fig. 5-12). For this shading, I loosen top tension and tighten bobbin tension slightly, using extra-fine thread in the top and bobbin. But don't limit yourself—experiment with all kinds of thread in the top. The same design worked in cotton thread has a different feeling from one worked in silk or rayon. Remember, though, to match needle to the thread. For extra-fine cotton, I use a size 9/10(70) needle, but the eye of this needle is not big enough for extra-fine rayon thread.

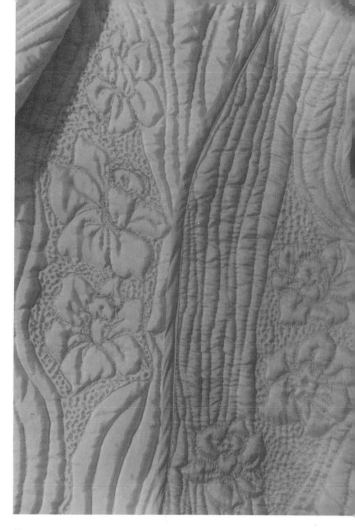

Fig. 5–10 Silk vest by Betty Mason of Lincoln City, OR. The flowers are surrounded by freely worked zigzag stitch, which resembles hand quilting.

Switch to a size 12(80) (see Chapter 13 for more information on needle sizes).

Stitch as though you were climbing stairs, carefully layering your zigzag stitches (Fig. 5-13). Fill from the widest parts to the narrowest, lapping each row over the previous row. Keep the stitches parallel, turning the hoop gently to fill the shape as you stitch. The movement of the hoop is back and

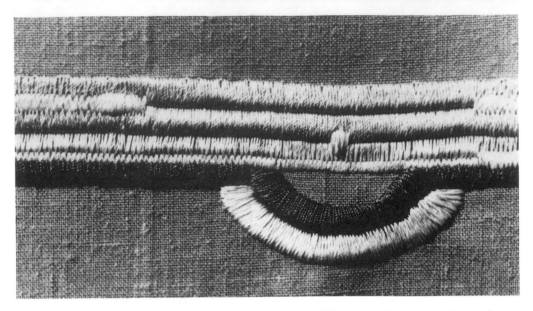

Fig. 5–11 Encroaching zigzag fills an area with color. Work a third row of satin stitches on top, if you wish. Thread: Sulky Size 30 (rayon).

Fig. 5–12 Sidewards zigzag used to fill a flower shape, worked on the Necchi Logica computer machine. Photo by Marlin E. Frakes.

Wrong   Right

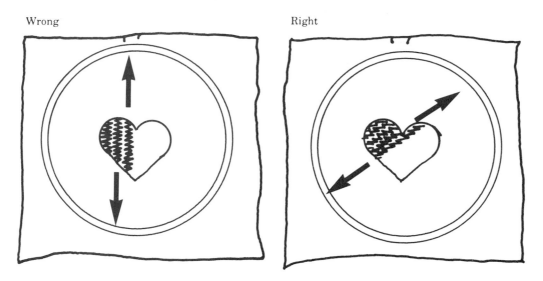

Fig. 5–13 *When filling in with zigzag, work diagonally like going up a stairway, and overlap the rows slightly.*

Fig. 5–14 *Marlene Andrey of San Jose, CA, makes machine-quilted greeting cards.*

forth, edging slowly forward to fill in the shape. If you miss a spot, go back and fill it in. Don't be afraid to experiment: what happens if you run the machine fast and move the hoop slowly? Vice versa? Find out on your test cloth.

Once you have learned the technique of free-machine embroidery, both straight stitch and zigzag, with and without a hoop, your imagination will soar. You'll lie awake at night, scheming: "What if I tried this?" "Why can't I get this effect by trying that?"

Shisha

Caryl Rae Hancock, of Vienna, VA, dreamed up a clever way of attaching shisha mirrors by machine. She realized that she could embroider a separate piece of fabric with a hole cut out of

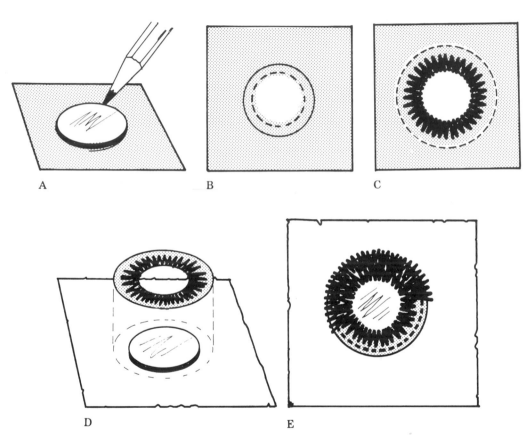

Fig. 5–15 Caryl Rae Hancock of Vienna, VA, invented a clever way to attach shisha by machine. A. Trace around the shisha mirror on a piece of organza. B. Stitch about ⅛" inside the traced line; then cut away fabric inside the stitched line. C. Satin-stitch around the hole, then cut out, leaving bare organza around the outside. D. Position the shisha mirror on background fabric and cap it with the satin-stitched doughnut of organza. E. Straight-stitch around the outer edge of the organza to fasten the mirror. Then finish the outer edge with satin stitch.

80

*Margaret Cusack, Brooklyn, NY, ad for Peek Freans. Machine applique.
Photo courtesy of the artist.*

Wilcke Smith, Albuquerque, NM, "Witch of Moon Canyon," 24" × 18". Whip stitch background, hand embroidery. Photo courtesy of the artist.

Jackie Dodson, La Grange Park, IL, detail, "Loon Lake," 31" × 25". Net and organza overlays, free-machine embroidery. Photo by R. A. Fanning.

Annemieke Mein, Sale, Victoria, Australia, "Mating Mythical Moths," 117 cm × 77 cm × 15 cm. Dyed, stuffed, free-machine embroidery. Photo courtesy of the artist.

Heather Dorrough, Paddington, NSW, Australia, detail, Parliament House commission, 38' × 9' (12 panels). Machine embroidery on lightweight canvas with applique and dyeing. Photo courtesy of Crafts Council of Australia.

Madge Huntington, New York City, detail, "Gaia." Fabric collage and machine applique. Photo courtesy of the artist.

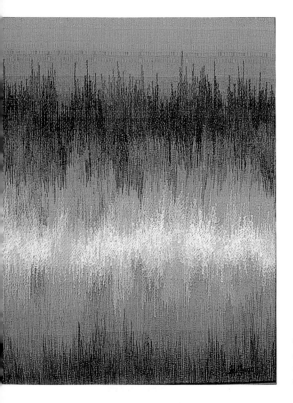

Joy Clucas, Castle Gardens, Colchester, England, "Shimmer," 3' × 2'3". Free-machine straight stitch. Photo courtesy of the artist.

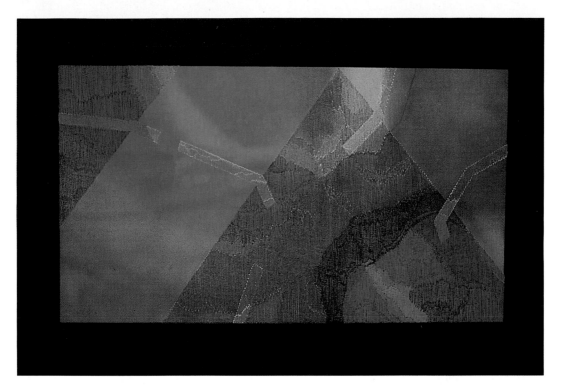

Barbara Lee Smith, Oak Park, IL, "The Slices Celebrate," 23½" × 41". Dyed silk with whip stitch. Photo courtesy of the artist.

Detail, "The Slices Celebrate." Photo courtesy of the artist.

B. J. Adams, Washington, DC, "Utsuroi," 86" × 47" (5 parts). Fabric manipulation and satin stitch. Photo courtesy of the artist.

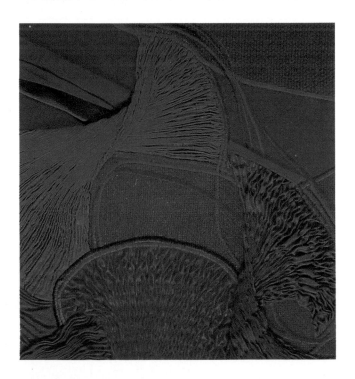

Detail, "Utsuroi." Photo courtesy of the artist.

Marina Brown, New York City, in her wedding dress. Free-machine embroidery with straight stitch only. Photo by Lee Rogers.

Nancy Freeman, Alameda, Ca., "Orinda Theater." Machine applique. Photo courtesy of the artist.

Verina Warren, Stanton-in-Peak, Derbyshire, England, "Bright Meadows Woven with Flowers of Gold," approximately 14" × 12". Silk dyed and worked with whip stitch. Photo courtesy of the artist.

Detail, "Bright Meadows." Photo courtesy of the artist.

Merry Bean, Arlington, VA, detail, three-panel screen. Ultrasuede designs completely outlined in antique gold tricot lame, as described in Chapter 8. Photo courtesy of the artist.

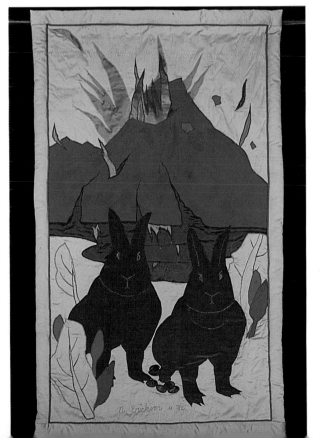

Nancy Erickson, Missoula, MT, "Guardians of Fiery Mountain," 49" × 83". Painted velvet, satin, and cotton with machine applique. Photo courtesy of the artist.

Elizabeth Gurrier, Hampton, NH, detail, "A.C.E. #20." Unbleached muslin painted with Createx colors, machine and hand quilting. Photo courtesy of the artist.

Bonnie Abbott, Pittsburgh, detail, "Picasso to Anemone," 27" × 16" × 14". Glass and fiber sculpture of a fish tank in collaboration with John Sietz, glass sculptor. Direct dye on cotton with free machining, whip stitch, automatic stitches. Photo courtesy of the artist.

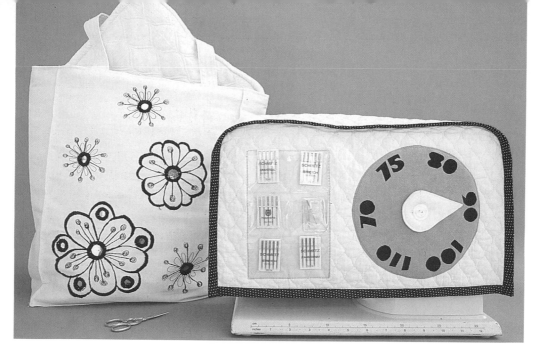

Jane's tote with pillow; sewing-machine cover.

Dotty's sewing duffel (collection of Roberta Patterson); portable book cover.

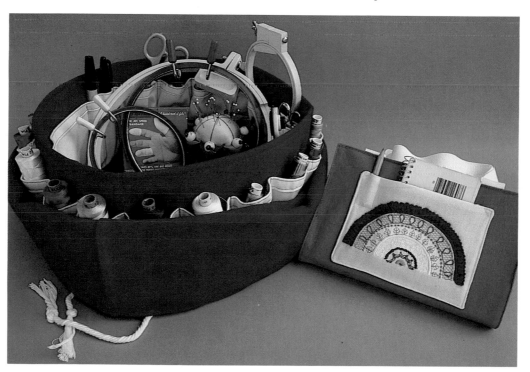

A simple thank you (collection of Don and Rich Douglas); get-well envelope; traveler's sewing kit (collection of Mary Losey).

Top view of the flop box; Robbie Fanning, Menlo Park, CA, "Please Don't Rain on my Parade, and I Won't Shine on Yours," 6" × 10". Silk, organza, free-machine embroidery, beads.

it and place it over the mirror to hold it in place.

To work Caryl's method, start by putting a piece of organza in a hoop. Trace around your shisha mirror with a water-soluble pen. Free-machine embroider in a straight stitch slightly inside the drawn line, going around the circle three times to strengthen it before cutting. Remove the hoop from under the needle, but don't remove the hoop from the organza. Cut out the center circle. Change your machine setting to free-machine zigzag and overcast the edges of the circle with satin stitch. Then stitch in a sidewards zigzag outward from the center, turning the hoop, until you have covered $1/2$" (13 mm) all around. Now remove the organza from the hoop and cut around the outside, close to your zigzag stitching. Glue the shisha mirror to a backing fabric. If you wish, put the backing fabric in a hoop. Place the embroidered organza over the mirror and pin it in place. Free-machine straight stitch around the mirror, through the zigzag stitches. This secures the organza to the backing and holds the mirror in place. Hide the edges of the organza by extending the zigzag stitches onto the backing (Fig. 5-15).

Once Caryl blasted the path to a new way of thinking, others began to refine

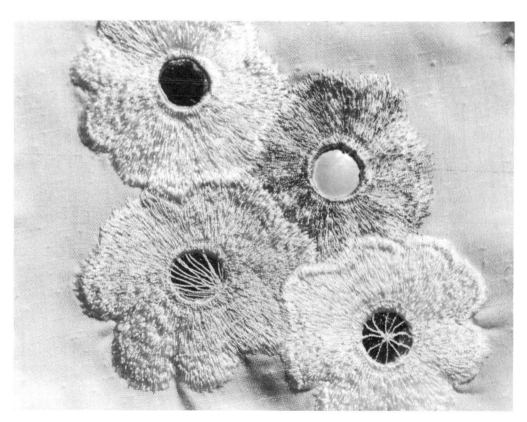

Fig. 5–16 Shisha embroidery using technique developed by Caryl Rae Hancock.

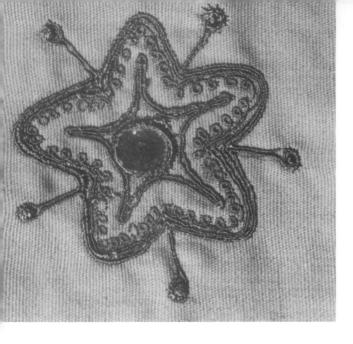

Fig. 5–17 Jane Warnick discovered another way to attach shisha by machine: whip stitch worked in circles around the mirror pull up to hold the mirror in place.

her method. For example, Jane Warnick realized she could attach shisha by working a whip stitch around the mirror. The top thread pulls up over the edge of the mirror to hold it (Fig. 5-17).

Jane Warnick developed another variation of Caryl's method after breaking a mirror on the tote bag shown in Part Two. In order to replace it, she had to cut into the bag from the inside. "Eureka!" she thought. "Why not cut holes directly in the bag and do

Fig. 5–18 Next, Jane Warnick refined Caryl Rae Hancock's method by cutting holes and working the embellishment on fabric (right sample), then attaching the shisha from behind (left). See the finished tote in Part Two.

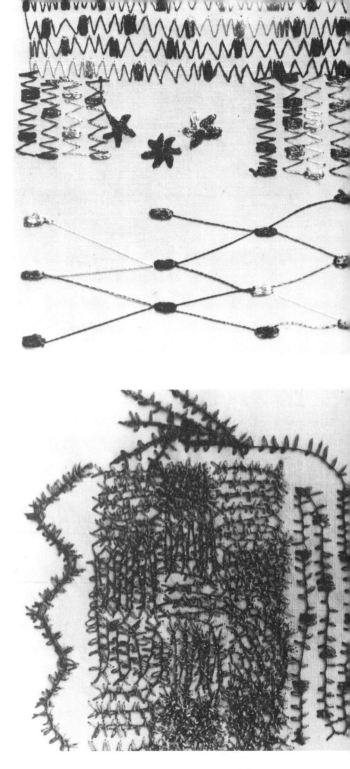

Fig. 5–19 Satin stitch blobs, some flowers, some connected by zigzag, some separated by one giant stitch. Sample worked by Jane Warnick.

the embroidery, without the extra piece of organza? Then I can glue the shisha to an extra piece of fabric and insert it from the back." (See Fig. 5-18.) Since her bag is lined, the insertions do not show. She attaches the extra piece of fabric with the mirror glued to it to the bag with a narrow round of zigzag around the mirror.

What method will you dream up?

The idea of doing the embroidery on a separate piece of fabric and then applying it to the final piece and hiding the edges with more embroidery is a good one. Should you goof, it is easy to redo the small piece of fabric and you won't have ruined the larger.

Textures

Zigzag can be used for texture as well as for filling in shapes. For a French knot effect, work solid zigzag in small spots, with about ten stitches per knot. If the spots are grouped, one small stitch can be taken between them, without the need to tie off the ends of each spot. If you have a vari-width zigzag dial, satin-stitch spots can be made by carefully changing the zigzag width from 0 to the widest stitch and back to 0 (or program your computer machine to lock off automatically at beginning and end). For added texture, cut some of the spots with a seam ripper to make tiny tufts of thread. However, don't use this technique on items to be washed unless you bond the back of the satin-stitch spots with iron-on interfacing to keep the threads from pulling out. If you

Fig. 5–20 Jane Warnick's zigzag whip stitch.

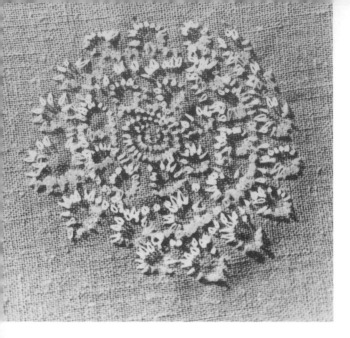

Fig. 5–21 If you fuse iron-on interfacing to the back, you can remove the top thread of whip stitch to leave loops on the surface.

work four to five satin stitches around a center, you have a small star or flower shape (Fig. 5-19).

Another way to gain texture is to work whip stitch with a zigzag. Remember whip stitch? (See Chapter 4.) Tighten your top tension and completely loosen or bypass the bobbin tension. Be sure the fabric is stretched in a hoop, because whip stitch is particularly pucker-producing. Lock the first stitch and work straight rows. The bobbin loops look like little leaves or thorns (Fig. 5-20).

Bring up the bobbin thread and lower the presser-bar lever, but *don't* lock the first stitch. Hold the threads securely as you start a line of whip stitch. When you finish, raise the presser foot and pull the hoop gently to the side away from the needle. Cut off the threads, leaving ends a few inches long. Remove the hoop and press the fabric from the back. Now bond iron-on interfacing to the back. Turn the fabric to the right side, and with tweezers or a blunt tapestry needle, gently pull out the top thread, as if you were removing a basting thread. Lovely loops of thread are left (Fig. 5-21).

Some people work their zigzag embroidery and then cut it out to make a three-dimensional form (Fig. 5-22).

This chapter is probably the most important in the book. With these techniques, you are set free to explore your

Fig. 5–22 Detail of three-dimensional flowers on vest by Janet Stocker of Treadleart (see Supply List). Petals are worked separately with sidewards zigzag, then tucked and stitched into place on the vest.

machine's capabilities to the fullest—using heavy threads, automatic stitches, and machine accessories on the full spectrum of materials available to us, from net to leather, from the simplest cotton to those fabrics you make yourself. In the next chapters, you'll see what other machine enthusiasts have invented and will be flooded with ideas of your own.

Additional Ideas

* Make a new-baby quilt that looks like an oversized envelope. Free- machine quilt the baby's name and address. Put his or her birthdate in the postmark circle. Use sidewards zigzag to paint a stamp.

* Create a furry ram ornament for your Christmas tree. Coil two cords into horns and cover them with satin stitch. Attach them to a body of rug yarn with a felt ram's face.
* Embellish small circles drawn on fabric with detached whip stitch (bond the back) and satin-stitch spots. Cut out the circles and gather them over buttons.
* Cover Betty's Box (Part Two) with a mass of shisha flowers. Put seeds inside and give to a friend.
* Draw "April" on your fabric calendar, surrounded by Easter eggs, a basket, and a bunny, all worked in solid encroaching zigzag in pastel colors. (See Chapter 2—Additional Ideas, if you missed out.)

CHAPTER 6

Heavy Threads in Bobbin

Visual Glossary

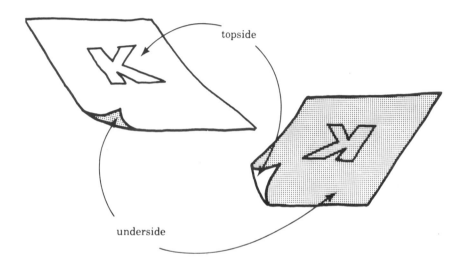

topside

underside

Now that you have mastered free-machine embroidery with and without a hoop, you are ready to branch out into one of the most spectacular forms of decorative machine embroidery—laying thick threads onto the surface of your work to create texture. But how to thread that fat fiber through the needle? The secret: you *don't* thread it through the needle. Instead you load it into the bobbin case and stitch with the underside of your garment up (Fig. 6-2).

How thick can the thread be? The thickest I've tried is four-ply knitting yarn, but since not much can be wound onto the bobbin at a time and the bob-

bin must be reloaded several times per project, I've been too lazy to experiment further. Otherwise, I've wound up to six strands of embroidery floss, pearl cotton, linen warp, slubby yarns, raffia, and my own combinations of yarns (a strand of gold with a strand of crochet cotton, for example).

Preparation

These thick threads will break if they are passed through the ordinary bobbin tension spring, so you must determine how to bypass bobbin tension on your machine. Look at the chart in Chapter 4 to find your machine's adaptation. Remember that if you must loosen a

86

Fig. 6–1 Jude Russell of Portland, OR, "Evil Tree Spirit," 2½' × 3'. Bobbin wound with heavy thread.

screw to release the bobbin tension, place a piece of felt or a box lid under the bobbin case on the table to prevent the screw from falling out, bouncing off the table, and hiding itself in far corners (Fig. 6-3).

To wind thick threads onto your bobbin, set up your machine for winding bobbins the way you normally would (i.e., disengage the flywheel and put the empty bobbin wherever it goes for winding). If the thread comes on a small cardboard tube and isn't too thick, you can place the tube on the upper thread holder, wind the thread around one thread guide into the empty bobbin, and slowly fill the bobbin, keeping one hand on the spool of thread to keep it from flying off, and one on the thread near the bobbin to help it feed evenly. If the spool of thread is large, put a pencil through the center of the spool and hold it in your right hand. Put the end of the thread through the

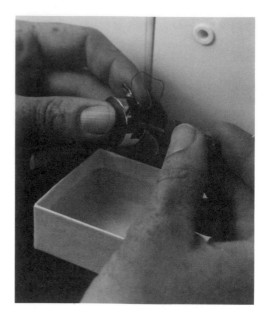

Fig. 6–3 To prevent losing the tension screw, put a box or felt under bobbin case as you manipulate the screw.

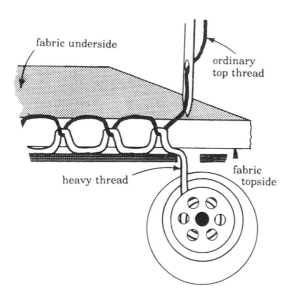

Fig. 6–2 Laying heavy thread on surface is done by working from the underside.

hole in your bobbin, as you would to wind ordinary machine thread. Hand-turn the bobbin several times until the thread end is secured and then use the fingers of your left hand to guide the thread evenly onto the bobbin (Fig. 6-4). Don't drive the machine too fast or the thread may jump the bobbin and wind itself into a horrible mess around the bobbin shaft. For some threads (embroidery floss, thick wool, etc.), you will have to hand-wind the bobbins. Be careful not to pull too tightly as you patiently, evenly, wind on the thread. Also, don't wind the bobbins too full or they will not fit into the bobbin case.

If you have a brand that winds the bobbin in the machine, use a size 16(100) needle. The large eye will accommodate such heavy threads as metallic, crochet cotton, and darning wools. Use the secondary spool holder

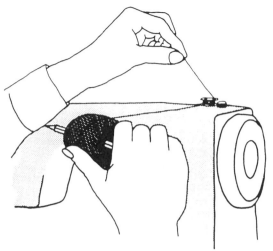

Fig. 6–4 To wind thick threads onto the bobbin, put a pencil through the center of the spool and guide the thread evenly with your fingers.

bobbin tension and to loosen the upper tension; however, doing so produced an unpleasant, irregular, wavy effect when what I wanted was a straight couched line (perhaps another time I may use that wavy effect to advantage). I ended up using a normal bobbin tension setting and a tight upper tension.

Fig. 6–5 Pendant by Joan Schulze, Sunnyvale, CA, 2¾" diameter. Heavy threads in bobbin, whip stitch, satin stitch. Photo courtesy of the artist.

to hold the heavy-thread cones, balls, or spools. You can hand-wind heavier threads and loosen bobbin tension on your extra purchased bobbin case, but you cannot bypass bobbin tension on these machines.

Since your heavy bobbin thread cannot pass easily through ordinary cottons and other medium-to-tightly-woven fabrics, the upper tension should be loosened somewhat (still loosening or bypassing bobbin tension and working from the underside), allowing the bobbin thread to lie flat on the surface of the material, similar to couching in hand embroidery.

I cannot emphasize enough the importance of a test cloth in using thick threads. In a Mexican-style peasant blouse I once made, I used a heavy 100% polyester buttonhole twist found in many fabric stores. It was definitely too thick to pass through the needle, so I assumed that I would need to bypass

Of course, when I put the lines of blue thread onto the yoke of the blouse, I was stitching through both the fabric and the interfacing, so my test cloth was also a piece of fabric with interfacing. But when I stitched three lines of blue onto the sleeve, I had to set up a new test cloth, double-folded to simulate the hem in the sleeve--and it's a good thing I did, because the tension that was right for fabric with interfacing was all wrong for doubled fabric. Thus, every time your fabric conditions change, check the tension settings on your test cloth.

Couching

For ordinary straight stitch with the presser foot on, you need only load the bobbin with the thick thread, loosen or bypass bobbin tension, loosen the upper tension slightly, and stitch from the underside, exactly as you would for everyday seam sewing. Fanatics stitch in the same direction for every row of thread, including basting, to prevent puckering. At any rate, do keep track as you work, checking to see that all is going well. Since you're working from the underside, you are apt to make more mistakes than you would if you could see what was happening to your threads.

Be sure you hold both top and bobbin threads as you take the first few stitches. Otherwise, you can end up with an incredible snafu in the bobbin case.

Try stitching with a zigzag and heavy threads in the bobbin, which creates a strong line, especially effective in decorating clothing (Fig. 6-7). Be cer-

Fig. 6–6 Tecla Miceli-Schulz of Brea, CA, put gold thread in the bobbin for the central grid on this blouse. The neck was gathered by elastic in the bobbin; then #5 pearl cotton was loaded into the bobbin and used in a decorative stitch over the gathering lines. Tecla has devised a pad of technique sheets to keep track of machine settings (see Supply List).

Fig. 6–7 Crochet cotton in the bobbin was worked in a zigzag stitch in the center of these wings, surrounded by automatic stitches and free-machine quilting.

tain to double-check a satin stitch on your test cloth--the heavy thread will fill in and you won't need as short a stitch length as you use for extra-fine thread in satin stitch.

Naturally you can load thick thread in the bobbin, work from the underside of the fabric, and do free-machine embroidery with a darning foot and no hoop (Fig. 6-8). Don't worry too much about regularity when you are curling, looping, and spiraling around the material. Part of the charm of this kind of machine stitchery is its spontaneity and free formation.

Cable Stitch

By using ordinary thread on the upper and a size 14 or 16(90-100) needle, again working from the underside with heavy thread and bypassing bobbin tension, a heavily textured effect called cable stitch can be made. The large needle also allows you to pull up and lock the first stitch. Move the work slowly so that the bobbin thread has a chance to build loops (Fig. 6-9).

I am not offering specific directions to loosen or tighten top tension because it varies according to the type and weight of thread you use. Experiment on a test cloth and remember that of the top and bobbin thread weights, the heavier thread will pull the lighter thread; therefore, if you want the bobbin thread to loop, don't use a top thread heavier than it. The character of the bobbin thread will also affect the look

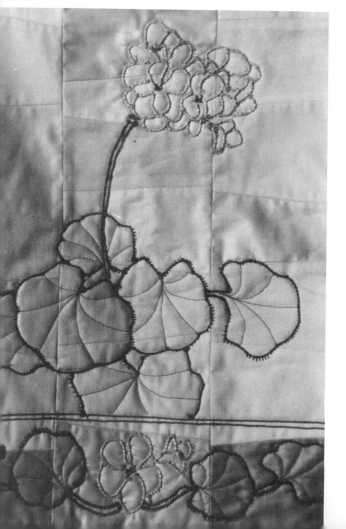

Fig. 6–8 Detail of "Geranium Vest" by Maggie Turner of Portland, OR. Pearl cotton is loaded into the bobbin and stitched underside up.

of the cable stitch—for example, embroidery floss loops more than linen.

A simple yet exquisite effect can be produced by winding thick gold thread (available in most fabric stores in many weights) onto the bobbin, setting up the machine for free-machine embroidery, bypassing bobbin tension, working from the underside, and making spirals and curlicues on the borders of luxurious fabrics like velvet, velveteen, crepe (which should be backed by typing paper while working), silk, and satin (Fig. 6-10).

If using metallic threads, be careful to wash with cold water, and don't rub it or use chemicals. If you want any garment machine-washable, you should not incorporate wool, silk floss, or other nonwashable threads into the design. Plan on dry-cleaning instead.

Elastic

Another textural effect comes from hand-winding elastic on the bobbin (be careful not to stretch it). Use a soft fabric like satin or tricot knit. Put the fabric in a hoop and stitch in a meander or figure 8 pattern. When you release the fabric from the hoop, it will pop into soft puffs (Fig. 6-11). These can be inserted into bodices, sleeves, or even in quilt blocks (I saw such a quilt, made in the late 1800s). Joan Michaels-Paque discovered that if you stitch in a triangular or square path, the fabric stands up in tiny pyramids.

Starting and ending these thick threads on garments can be messy. I recommend pulling the fat thread through to the back and tying off, but sometimes knots do not hold well, so tie a double knot and secure it with fabric glue.

Fabrics

What materials are appropriate for embellishment from the underside?

Fig. 6–9 *Mukluks by dj bennett of Lake Forest, IL, author of* Machine Embroidery with Style *(see Bibliography). The boots were inspired by a trip to Alberta. dj tried to suggest beadwork with cable stitch and leather applique.*

Fig. 6–10 *Metallic threads are sometimes difficult in free-machine embroidery when worked from the topside. But loaded into the bobbin and stitched underside up, they are cooperative. Gold Kanagawa thread on velvet.*

Fig. 6–11 Elastic thread in the bobbin, Dual Duty (cotton-covered polyester) on top, worked in straight-stitch free-machine embroidery in circles and figure eights on silk satin. When the hoop is taken off, the circles gather into soft puffs. Sample by Jane Warnick.

Cotton, wool, knits — almost any are easy to work with except those with high naps like fake fur or exaggerated puckers like seersucker or the Indian-look fabrics. Remember that if you want to do free-machine embroidery with a heavy thread in the bobbin and without a hoop, either your fabric must be heavy enough not to pucker, or it must be backed with stabilizer.

Of course, if your fabric is loosely woven, like burlap or hopsacking, you can set up the machine for free-machine embroidery, bypass bobbin tension, work from the *topside,* and bring those unusual fibers to the surface of your work in trailing loops or whip stitch spirals (see Chapter 4). Whenever possible, though, I would use a hoop

Fig. 6–12 Janet Kuemmerlein, Prairie Village, KS, commission for All Saints Episcopal Church in Atlanta, GA, 14' × 8'. Applique and yarns couched by machine.

when doing whip stitch, as it tends to pull the fabric badly.

Of course, you can always lay heavy threads onto the surface of your fabric and free-machine stitch over them with regular thread, setting your machine up for free-machine embroidery without a hoop, using the darning foot, as we discussed in Chapter 5. You can either stitch freely back and forth over the heavy thread, use your zigzag or decorative stitches, or be fancy with spirals and loops.

Carolyn Hall coils heavy threads into baskets using a presser foot with zigzag to join the edges of the fiber (Fig. 6-13).

You can also completely cover a cord or thick yarn with satin stitch, twisting soft yarns to keep them from being flattened. In this case, loosen top tension and use a cording foot.

What styles of clothing are amenable to decoration with thick yarns? If you are stitching in straight lines from the underside, the contours of almost any pattern can be followed; but if you are working free-machine embroidery without a hoop from the underside, it is easier to work near the edge of the garment, so that you can more easily grasp and maneuver the material—look for yokes, cummerbunds, borders, small purses, headbands, etc., to decorate.

Additional Ideas

* Load 1/8" (3 mm) silk ribbon in the bobbin. Stitching from the underside, decorate the neck, armscye, wrist, and bottom edge of a tunic with 2"-wide (5 cm) bands of zigzag stitches.
* Using crochet cotton in the bobbin, stitch flowers in the centers of squares of gingham fabric. Finish the edges and join the squares with machine fagoting (technique described in Chapter 7).
* Make a cover for a wastebasket, working some straight lines of heavy

Fig. 6–13 Machine-sewn basket by Carolyn Vosburg Hall of Birmingham, MI, author of The Sewing Machine Craft Book *(see Bibliography).*

thread from the underside, connected by free-form shapes worked in cable stitch.
* Line a vest with a plaid fabric. Load the bobbin with metallic thread and, stitching with the underside up, follow the lines on the plaid. The metallic thread on the outside will echo the lines of the plaid lining.
* Wind crochet cotton in crocus colors onto bobbins and fill in the letters of "May" for your fabric calendar, working from the underside. (Still confused? See Chapter 2—Additional Ideas.)

CHAPTER 7

Automatic Stitches

Visual Glossary

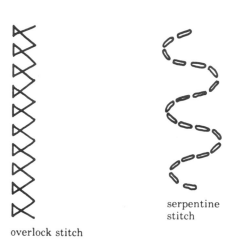

overlock stitch

serpentine
stitch

carpet fork

The ability of some machines to make automatic stitches greatly extends the range of machine embroidery. And yet the potential offered by automatic stitches has not been fully explored by most stitchers. As a friend said recently, "There has to be more to it than little duckies on children's clothes."

Yes, there is definitely more, especially when you begin to combine and manipulate automatic stitches. This is where the new computer machines shine. You can program them to combine stitches, elongate them, flip them, distort them.

But first, here are some general guidelines to keep in mind as you explore automatic stitches:

- If ever you needed a test cloth, this is the time. I have seen a tunic top with the front panel worked in solid decorative stitches—but the panel was badly rippled, destroying the beauty of the stitches, probably because the seamstress had not loosened the tensions and backed the piece with stabilizer. Try out each stitch you plan to use on a test cloth of exactly the same material as your garment.
- Strengthen your fabric. When I am working a long row of stitches, I almost always back my material with stabilizer, often using adding-machine tape or typing paper, gently tearing it off later.
- Use a special-purpose needle (Stretch or Yellow Band) or a topstitching nee-

Fig. 7–1B Detail, "Lavender and Old Lace."

Fig. 7–1A Joan Arnaud, Cranston, RI, "Lavender and Old Lace."

dle. During the formation of automatic stitches, the thread saws back and forth through the needle much more often than for normal sewing. Special-purpose needles have highly polished eyes, while topstitching needles have larger eyes than ordinary needles.

- Be sure to watch the formation of the stitch in the slot of the presser foot, instead of watching the stitching line in front of the foot. This is particularly important when you are following a curving line. Better yet, use an open-toed applique foot (see Chapter 3). In addition to allowing you to see stitches as they form, the foot's wedge on the underside helps it pass easily over previous rows of stitching.

- Whenever possible, work the automatic stitches before cutting out pattern pieces.
- Make a fabric book of your decorative stitches in different weights of thread (see Part Two). If the stitch is locked up inside your machine, you won't use it. If you see it worked in thread, you'll be tempted to explore its potential.

Topstitching

The most obvious use of your decorative stitches is in the replacement of topstitching. Again, if you are planning extensive machine stitchery on homemade clothing, do the work first before cutting out the garment. Cut off the excess tissue paper around your pattern piece and pin or weight it on the fabric. As a guideline, draw or machine baste around the edge of the pattern directly onto the fabric and then remove the pattern piece. I also machine baste along the seam line as an added guideline, since automatic stitches used as topstitching are generally spaced one presser-foot width away from the *seam* line — not the line you have drawn to indicate the edge of the fabric.

The choice of thread for decorative topstitching is dependent on your background fabric. As a loose rule, I like to match the type of thread to the type of fabric — cotton thread with cotton fabric, wool thread with wool fabric, etc. Occasionally, when working decorative stitches with extra-fine thread, you will need a heavier line to make the pattern show up better, so use two threads and a larger-sized needle or a topstitching needle, which has a bigger eye. Either use two spools of the same thread or wind a bobbin full of the thread and put it on the second spool holder (if your machine doesn't have two, use the bobbin-winding shaft or tape a plastic straw to your machine). Thread both the regular spool thread and the second thread separately through all the thread guides and tension springs, as usual. If your needle shaft has guides for two threads, put one on each side; otherwise, thread the two threads together.

You may need the help of a needle threader to coax both threads through the needle. Insert the needle threader from the back of the hole to the front, slide the threads through the gap in the needle threader wire, and pull the threader to the back again, which pulls the two threads through the needle easily (Fig. 7-2).

Now do your automatic stitches on a test cloth, loosening tensions if neces-

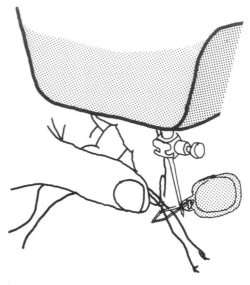

Fig. 7–2 Threading two threads: Insert the needle threader from back to front through the needle eye, thread the two ends through the wires and pull the threader back through the eye.

sary, and you will find that the double thread works well. You can even use two colors of thread and achieve an unusual color mix. I have used blue and yellow thread together; this looks green from a distance and like a blue-yellow tweed up close.

Heavy Threads

As we discussed in Chapter 6, any thick thread can be wound into the bobbin and laid on the surface of your garment by working with the underside up. This is true for the automatic stitches, too. Attractive results can be had, for example, by winding crochet cotton (size #20, suggests Jackie Dodson), metal thread, darning wool, or soft one-ply yarns (the kind used to knit baby sweaters) onto the bobbin, to become decorative stitches on the topside by working with the underside up.

98

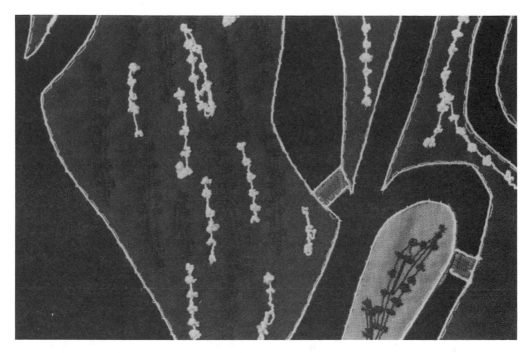

Fig. 7–3 Close-up, Jude Russell's "Evil Spirit" (see Fig. 6–1 for full view). Heavy threads in bobbin worked in automatic star stitch.

Use ordinary cotton sewing-machine thread on top and adjust tensions, loosening bobbin and tightening top tensions, so that the thick thread lies on the surface of the fabric.

Even with this method of working the underside up, I still use a stabilizer (tear-away or, more often, a piece of adding-machine tape or typing paper), cello-taping the paper onto the underside of the fabric and drawing the line of stitching directly on the paper. Afterward, the paper is gently pulled off, using tweezers to remove any stubborn pieces.

Don't forget that many kinds of ribbon, cord, or braid can be attached to a background with automatic stitches (Fig. 7-4). I like to work the ribbon separately. Stitch down the center of the ribbon and then apply it to the background by stitching the edges with more colorful rows of decorative stitches (see Fig. 7-3).

Corners

When you are working a line of decorative stitches around a rectangle, such as a pocket, your motifs should match perfectly at the corner. To accomplish this, you must make two preparations.

First, stitch six repeat motifs on a test cloth. As you sew, count exactly how many stitches form each pattern, so that you can stop the machine at the exact finish of the sixth pattern. (Judi Cull suggests familiarizing yourself with the formation of the stitch by trying it on paper with an unthreaded needle. Watch where the stitches are in re-

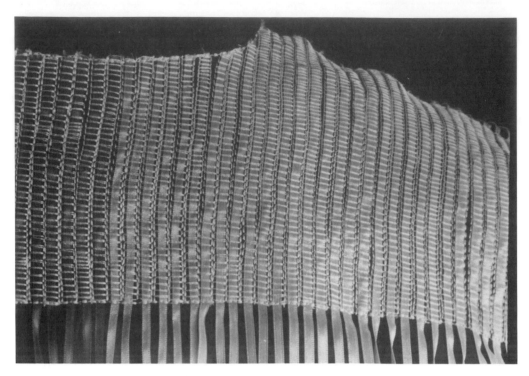

Fig. 7–4 Yoke on blouse worked by Debbie Casteel of Aardvark Adventures (see Supply List). The ribbons are held down by an automatic stitch similar to blanket stitch in hand embroidery.

lation to the foot.) The computer machines make all of this a snap. You can program the machine to stop sewing after each motif is complete.

Second, lay the test cloth on the stitching line of the article, with the finish of the sixth pattern exactly at the corner. Mark with pins backwards from the corner where each pattern must fall, using the test cloth as a guide (Fig. 7-5).

Begin stitching a motif on the article exactly at the beginning of your marks. As you stitch, watch the slot in the embroidery foot. If at the beginning of a motif the needle does not enter the fabric exactly where you've marked, push the fabric gently with your fingers. The

result will be a slightly longer pattern, but the next pattern will be perfect, and the corners will be perfect. Your fingers remain to the sides of each pattern, moving down to the next patterns, one by one. At the corner, sew the motif slowly so you have absolute control over the machine. You may want to hand-turn the wheel for the last stitch of the motif. Leave the needle in the fabric after the last stitch, raise the presser-bar lever, turn the fabric counterclockwise 90 degrees, lower the presser-bar lever, and begin the next line of stitching. Aren't you clever!

If your line of automatic stitching curves around a corner, don't try to change the direction of stitching in the

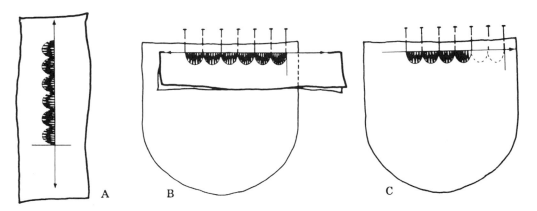

Fig. 7–5 *Working decorative stitches around corners. A. Stitch six motifs on a test cloth, counting exactly how many stitches form one motif. B. Lay the test cloth on the stitching line of the pocket and mark backward from the corner with pins. Mark all corners this way. C. Sew the decorative stitches, making sure each motif begins and ends at the pins. At the corner, leave the needle in the fabric and pivot the material. Continue stitching all the way around.*

middle of a motif. Imagine the curve to be made of small straight lines. Sew one motif on a straight line, watching carefully through the slot of the presser foot. At the end of the motif, leave the needle in the fabric, raise the presser-bar lever, move the fabric until you can see the line of stitching in the slot, lower the presser-bar lever, and stitch another straight line of motif. Continue stitching one motif at a time (Fig. 7-6).

Patterns

Once you start experimenting with your automatic stitches, you quickly become hooked on their endless possibilities. Many of the stitches are not mirror images, as they are formed on either side of the needle. Therefore, by turning around 180 degrees at the end of a line of decorative stitches and stitching a second row, you can create beautiful patterns. Look at the difference in effect of staggering one stitch in three ways (Fig. 7-7).

The patterns, of course, must fit together perfectly. A motif that is out of

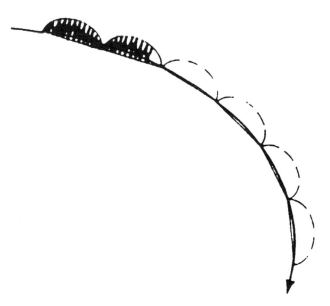

Fig. 7–6 *To work decorative stitches around curves, think of the curved line as a series of short straight lines. Do not curve in the middle of a motif or you will ruin its formation.*

101

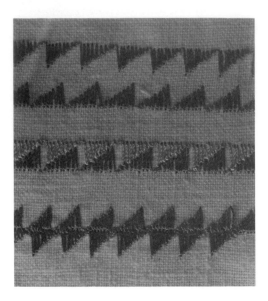

Fig. 7–7 Pay attention to the spaces around your lines of automatic stitches. Here are the effects of staggering one stitch three ways.

line or not symmetrical is disturbing to the eye. Sew slowly and watch through the slot in the presser foot to be sure the beginning of a motif on the second line of stitching is perfectly matched to its counterpart on the first line of stitching. If it is not, push or hold back the fabric slightly with your fingers to elongate or shorten the pattern.

In addition to repeating one pattern, you can build new designs by combining rows of automatic stitches. Experiment on a test cloth to weed out the combinations that don't mix well. And pay attention to the dark-light value of your colors. If you stitch rows of automatic stitches on a light background, make sure they are all mid-gray or dark in value, so they'll show up; a row that is too light will tend to disappear and destroy the pattern you're building. Roughly, the pure colors fall into these categories: (1) *light:* white, yellow, yellow-orange, green-yellow; *medium:* orange, orange-red, blue-green, green; *dark:* black, red, red-purple, purple, purple-blue, blue.

Knowing how to handle squared corners for combination automatic stitches is important. I like to use three methods. First and easiest is to stitch the patterns on a separate band of material or a grosgrain ribbon. If the edges of the fabric are raw, turn them under $1/4$" (6 mm). When you are done, fold the band, right sides together, and mark a 45-degree angle from one corner (I use a plastic right angle purchased at a stationery store). Straight stitch along the marked line, and then cut $1/8$" (3 mm) from this seam. Open out the band and press the seam open. Now applique the squared corner to the article, either with a straight stitch or with another decorative stitch (Fig. 7-8).

The second method is simply to suggest a corner, as shown in the upper right in Fig. 7-9. First mark each corner with three parallel lines diagonal to the corner. I machine baste these guidelines so I can see them easily. Work the automatic patterns starting at the two outside diagonal lines, stitching from the corners outward. Afterward, embroider one of the motifs on the remaining center diagonal line at the corner.

The third method involves stitching around corners and takes more practice. Not all decorative stitches adapt easily to this, so try them on a test cloth first. Draw a diagonal line at each corner. On the line of stitching, mark six motifs away from the corner in each direction, as you did in Fig. 7-5 above. As you near a corner, make certain the motifs are falling in the correct places. Compensate if necessary by pushing or pulling the fabric slightly with your

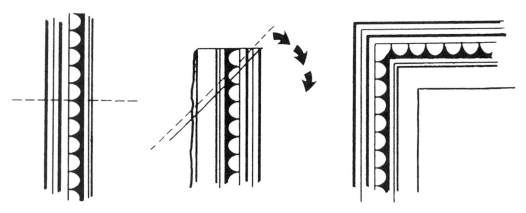

Fig. 7–8 *One way to square corners of decorative stitches is to stitch a long band of them, fold in half (top sides together), and stitch in a 45° angle from the corner. Trim to ⅛", open and press. Result: A perfect corner ready for applique onto a garment.*

Fig. 7–9 *Not all decorative stitches go around corners gracefully, as shown in the upper left and lower right corners. One way to square a corner is by drawing or basting three parallel lines, as in the upper right. The center line is worked at a 45 degree angle to the other lines.*

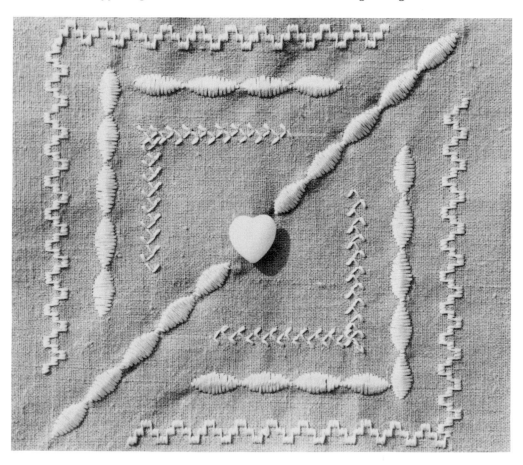

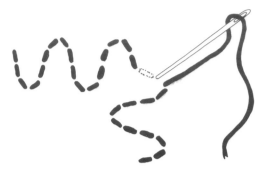

Fig. 7-10 To match the end of a line perfectly with its beginning, stop a few stitches from the join and leave a long end which is threaded through a tapestry needle. Take several hand stitches and end in the same hole where you started stitching.

fingers. Leave the needle in the fabric at the corners, pivot counterclockwise 90 degrees, and continue stitching (Fig. 7-9).

If you are stitching around a shape and two lines of stitching must meet exactly — that is, you must end the stitching exactly where you began — stop one stitch from the end. Carefully remove the fabric from the machine, pinching the last stitch and pulling to the side away from the needle. Don't jerk the fabric or the stitches may be distorted. Pull one of the top threads to the back and tie off the ends. Then thread a tapestry needle with the remaining top thread and take the last stitch by hand, entering the fabric in the same hole where you started stitching (Fig. 7-10).

Designing

To help you design automatic stitches, study other forms of continuous-line ornament: lace, quilting patterns, grillwork, wire jewelry, chainstitch in ethnic work, etc. You can also design by

Fig. 7-11 Make your "rubber" stamp by gluing string to a block of wood.

playing with string or ribbons in patterns or by making your own "rubber" stamps: glue string to a block of wood (Fig. 7-11).

And don't forget that automatic stitches can be used not as a focal point but on top of another design to unify it in a subtle way (Fig. 7-12).

Don't always think in terms of bands and borders of automatic stitches, because some of the patterns work well as isolated motifs. For example, to work a flower, baste or draw four intersecting lines as shown in Fig. 7-13. On a test cloth sew several motifs to check the tensions and to count the exact number of stitches per motif. Stop the machine exactly after the last stitch of a motif has been sewn.

On your article begin in the middle of the flower and sew one motif out, leaving the needle in the fabric at the end of the last stitch. Raise the presser-bar lever and pivot the fabric 180 degrees. Lower the presser-bar lever and sew another motif, ending exactly in the middle of the intersecting lines and ex-

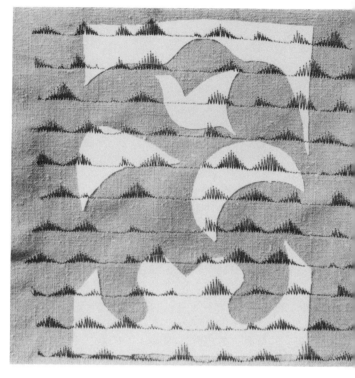

Fig. 7–12 Automatic stitches worked on top of a design can unify in a subtle way.

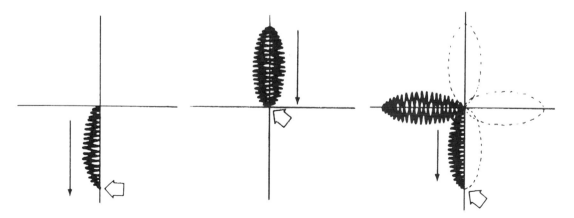

Fig. 7–13 Work an isolated motif from the center out along your marked lines, leaving the needle in the fabric at the end of one motif. Pivot the material 180° and stitch back along the marked line, ending exactly in the center. Continue in this manner on each marked line, being precise about ending in the center so the flower will not be out of kilter.

actly at the end of the motif. If the needle on the last stitch is not entering the exact center, stop the machine and reposition the fabric so the needle will enter the exact center. I am adamant about being exact because sloppiness results in distorted, unsettling flowers. Continue to sew from the middle out, along each of the eight lines radiating from the center.

After the last motif is sewn, raise the presser-bar lever and gently pull the material to the side away from the needle. Turn the fabric over and tug on the bobbin thread until the loop of the top thread appears. Pull this loop through to the back and tie off the ends.

If your machine has a serpentine stitch, a very attractive chrysanthemum-like flower can be formed by stitching back and forth from a center point (Fig. 7-14). Undoubtedly other decorative stitches based on an undulating line of stitches can be similarly

Fig. 7–14 Make a chrysanthemum flower by working the serpentine stitch around a central point.

106

formed, so experiment on your own machine. In the next chapter, you'll see similar samples worked with an attachment for the machine.

Carpets

Another spectacular use of serpentine stitch involves using a carpet fork. These are available in knitting and needlecraft stores (see Supply List) or made by bending a coat hanger into a U with square ends. Wrap the fork with any thick thread—pearl cotton, two- or three-ply wool, variegated boucle, etc. Then place a grosgrain ribbon under the fork and sew down the middle of the yarn, from the open end of the carpet fork to the closed end. Use the serpentine stitch if you have it; otherwise, a short straight stitch. Lock the last stitches by backstitching, remove everything from the machine, and pull out the carpet fork. You now have a colorful fringe to sew on a cape hood, purse strap, or baby bonnet (Fig. 7-15).

You also have the basis for a rug, believe it or not. You will need lots of yarn, backing canvas, or jute (available in rug-crafting and some needlework stores—see Supply List), and a carpet fork. Wind double strands of the yarn around the carpet fork, as explained above. On the canvas draw parallel lines 1" (2.5 cm) apart. Place the wound carpet hook on the canvas, with the left side of the fork on the middle line of the canvas. Stitch down the center of the hook with a short straight stitch or the serpentine stitch. Prevent the presser foot from catching in the yarn either by using a roller or zipper foot; by taping the front ends of your presser foot; or by putting strips of paper over the yarn and under the foot, to be torn off after stitching. When you reach the last of the yarn, leave the needle in the canvas and withdraw the fork carefully, until

within an inch of its end. Rewind the carpet fork and sew as described above until you finish the row.

For the next row, push the left edge of the wound fork firmly against the loops of the first row. After sewing this second row, cut the loops of the first row. Cut one row of loops each time you finish sewing a row.

To keep the bulk minimal between the needle and the main body of the machine, work from the center of the rug to the right side. Turn the rug upside down 180 degrees and again work from the center to the outside. Leave an

Fig. 7–16 To make a carpet, mark the backing with parallel lines 1″ apart. Lay the wound fork along the center line and stitch down the center in a serpentine or straight stitch. Work from the center out, pushing each new row firmly against the previous row. Cut the loops for a rya-like rug.

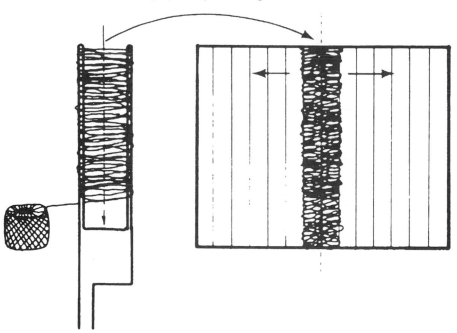

inch all around the rug for a hem. Either turn it under and bind it by hand, or stitch carpet braid all around the outside. Paint the back with latex to keep the stitches from pulling out and the rug from slipping around the floor.

This same technique can be used to make a fringe for capes, curtains, or tablecloths. Stitch close to the left edge of the fork, rather than in the center. When you remove the fork, cut the loops on the right. Sew the fringe to the article along the line already sewn on the fiber.

Judi Cull uses a finer version of this for doll hair, as well as for texture in pictures of horses and lions' manes. Carolyn Hall also uses it in Fig. 7-17.

Fill-In Shapes

In addition to emphasizing a line with automatic stitches, building patterns, and working isolated motifs, you can fill a shape with automatic stitches (Fig. 7-18). For inspiration, consult designs for the hand embroidery technique of blackwork.

Fig. 7–17 Machine-sewn yarn flossa cat by Carolyn Vosburg Hall, 15" high.

Fig. 7–18 Audrey Griese of Elk River, MN, was inspired by blackwork patterns for these automatic-stitch designs. Audrey used to write a column on machine embroidery for "Stitch and Sew" magazine.

Consider working large areas in the various patterns, bonding the back with fusible webbing, cutting out shapes, and fusing them to a backing. Cover the edges with satin stitch or a decorative stitch. To help you design the denseness of the stitches, use text cut from newspapers (Fig. 7-19).

Fagoting

Another special effect possible with automatic stitches simulates fagoting, which is a way to join two flat edges with embroidery. While experimenting, use two rectangles of fabric, both cut from a selvage so the edges are finished. On water-soluble stabilizer or on a piece of typing paper, draw three parallel lines, $1/8$" (3 mm) apart. Lay one selvage on the left line and pin the fabric to the stabilizer. Lay the other selvage along the right line and secure it to the stabilizer. With the presser foot on and ordinary sewing-machine

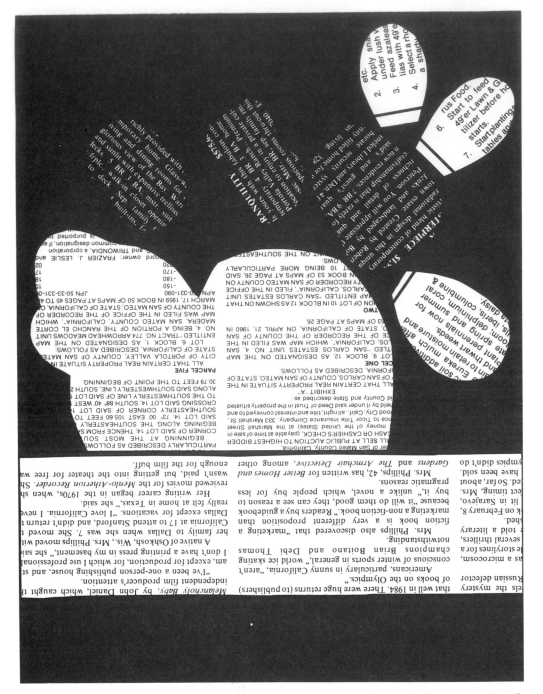

Fig. 7–19 Various size print cut from newspapers can help you design the denseness of stitch-es.

thread in top and bobbin, set up the machine for overlock stitch (if you have it—otherwise use a wide zigzag with a stitch length of 10–12 stitches/inch). See Fig. 7-20.

Stitch down the paper so that the left side of the needle swing enters the middle pencilled line on the stabilizer, and the right side enters the fabric. Turn the fabric around 180 degrees and stitch down the remaining side as before, making sure that the needle pierces the stabilizer exactly on top of the first row, and that on the other side of its swing, the needle pierces the fabric. Now either dissolve the stabilizer in cold water or carefully tear off the paper, using tweezers to remove any stubborn pieces, and separate the two rectangles of fabric. The result is a connecting line of attractive fagoting (Fig. 7-21).

Machine fagoting can be used on many garments and household articles, especially tablecloths. It is even more attractive if pearl or crochet cotton is wound into the bobbin and the fagoting is worked from the underside. You would still lay the stabilizer with the lines on it *under* the fabric next to the needle plate, even though you are working from the underside. Ordinary sewing-machine thread in a matching color is used on top. The edges to be joined are finished with a zigzag overcast or seam binding and turned under before working the fagoting. Don't use a selvage because it will shrink more than the rest of the fabric. Wouldn't this be a charming way to lengthen a child's overalls or skirt?

Incidentally, that overlock stitch makes an attractive stitch when the stitch width is set at 0. Instead of stitching back and forth in a horizontal zigzag, it stitches back and forth in a straight line, giving you a heavier topstitching. Stitched on delicate fabrics with extra-fine thread, it makes a pearly edge that resembles hand embroidery. It is also effective in heavier thread on leather and imitation suede fabrics. You can also use this stitch to strengthen seams in sturdy fabrics, like canvas in backpacks.

I know several people who augment their income by skillful, creative use of the automatic stitches. One is a dressmaker/artist who paints leather garments and then emphasizes the design with automatic stitches. Another embellishes shirts and matching bags for a clothing store. Yet another embellishes the seams of baby quilts with

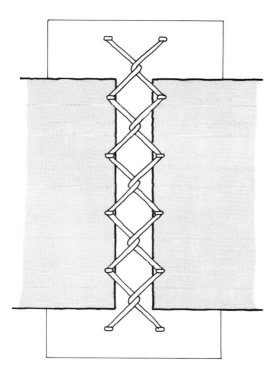

Fig. 7–20 Machine fagoting is done by laying paper under the gap between two fabric edges and zigzagging down each side, making sure the threads catch each other in the center and the fabric on the side. The paper is then torn away.

111

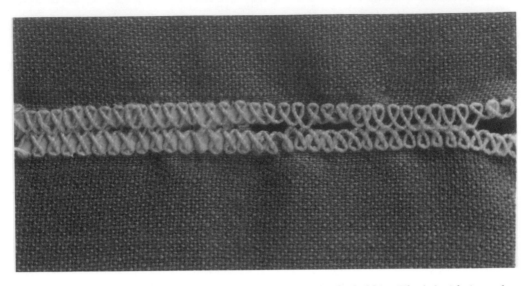

Fig. 7–21 Machine fagoting worked with crochet cotton in the bobbin. The left side is perfect, but if care is not taken to intersect the threads in the middle, gaps will occur. This was worked on paper, still visible on the left, which will be wetted and extracted with tweezers. A better choice would be to use water-soluble stabilizer.

decorative stitches. Using these stitches has definite money-making potential, which may lessen the pain of a new machine's price tag.

Variety

The major complaint about automatic stitches is their uniformity, which can lead to visual boredom. One way to break the uniformity is to work the automatic stitches with the presser foot on but in a free-motion way with the feed dogs down (Fig. 7-22). You will also need to release the pressure. (This technique does not work well on the reverse-cycle stitches, where the machine usually backs up to make part of the motif.)

Other ways to vary automatic stitches are:

1. Change the size of the motifs, either within a row or next to each other.

2. Combine pattern units (the computer machines make this fun).

3. Alternate free-form stitching with regular automatic stitches.

4. Manipulate the automatic stitches—fold, tuck, shirr, gather, cut, or rearrange.

5. Combine automatic stitches with other techniques—applique, couching, shadow work, cutwork, etc.

6. Try all kinds of threads in top and bobbin and/or use twin needles.

Each of the automatic stitches has its own potential, and not many people have yet probed the possibilities. Here is a challenge to all of us to help us think about automatic stitches in new ways. Apply these verbs to automatic stitches and see what you discover:

multiply	delay
subdue	flatten
transpose	submerge

112

Fig. 7–22 Joy Clucas, Colchester, England, works free-motion automatic stitches in flower-like shapes, surrounded by whip stitch. Joy is the author of Your Machine for Embroidery *(see Bibliography).*

weigh	destroy	concentrate	repel
fluff-up	by-pass	add	integrate
subtract	lighten	repeat	dissect
thicken	stretch	adapt	
relate	extrude		
protect	segregate		
symbolize	abstract		
divide	eliminate		
invert	separate		
unify	search		
distort	rotate		
squeeze	complement		
freeze	soften		

(Note: Verbs from *Design Yourself!*, Kurt Hanks et al, William Kaufmann, Inc., 1977.)

Until recently, we had no control over what stitches the engineers dreamed up for us. Apparently, they think we delight in Scottie dogs and duckies. At this writing, two computer

Fig. 7–23 Audrey Griese's teddy bear stitch.

machines have the capability for you to program stitches (Fig. 7-23).

We think it's time to design automatic stitches for adults. Fig. 7-24 shows our preliminary designs.

Additional Ideas

* Make a wall hanging of fabric pockets for your smaller sewing supplies. Topstitch all pockets with automatic stitches.
* Fold over 6" (15 cm) along the length of a heavy woven fabric. Fringe the edge, grouping threads by tying overhand knots. Using Mexican hand-embroidery as a design source, stitch bands of automatic stitches 2" (5 cm) above the fringe. This becomes the top front of a boat-necked tunic. Repeat for the back. Join the two at the shoulders with machine fagoting. Sew an underarm seam to fit your shape.
* Put large decorative buttonholes in a set of table napkins, fastening them to buttons on placemats. When you serve lobster, pesto, or spaghetti, show your guests that they can button their napkins to their shirts, to protect themselves from spills.
* Fill a whole length of fabric with closely stitched automatic stitches in spring colors. Overlay this with a solid-colored fabric. Satin stitch a grid

Fig. 7–24 Some designs for automatic stitches: the Falling-Asleep-at-the-Opera stitch, the Kitty-Stoned-on-Catnip stitch, and the Rat-Race stitch.

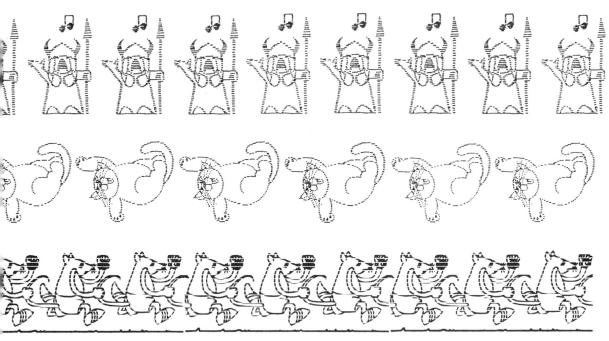

of large egg shapes all over the quilt. Cut away the egg to reveal the auto-matic-stitches Easter eggs. Machine quilt.

* Stitch the letters of "June" of your fabric calendar by securing lime-green bias binding in the letter shapes to the backing with automatic stitches. (Half the year gone and you're still not paying attention? See Chapter 2—Additional Ideas.)

Machine Accessories

Visual Glossary

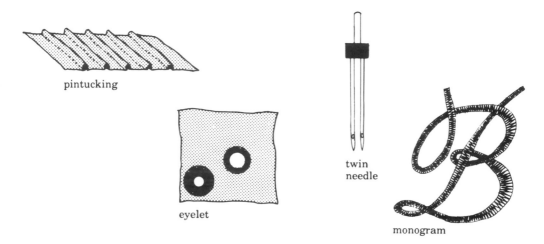

pintucking

eyelet

twin
needle

monogram

Jackie Dodson says, "Some people drink; I buy Bernina feet." It's true: once you are hooked on machine embroidery, you'll haunt your favorite store for the latest special equipment-- presser feet, needles, and needle plates. (If anyone complains about your habit, say "It's cheaper than software or camera lenses.")

Don't assume that the foot for a brand different from yours won't fit your machine. The feet are often interchangeable, depending on the length of the needle shaft and where the accessories attach (side, front, etc.). (See the chart in Chapter 6.) You can sometimes buy an adapter that allows you to use feet from a different machine — ask your dealer or a machine-embroidery teacher. You must know the shank measurement for your machine (Fig. 8-2).

I take a presser foot from my machine with me when I shop; if it fits a different brand machine, the accessories for that machine will usually fit mine. Each brand has its own line of accessories, so check the competition when you're in the market for new equipment. (I now carry a 3x5 card in my purse, listing the feet and plates I already have. I have been known to buy a foot I already own.)

I encourage you to make samples using all your special equipment. Follow the instructions given and then play with different tensions and threads. Bind your experiments into a sample

Fig. 8–1 Four name tags in three-dimensional applique by Barbara Lee Pascone of Camarillo, CA. The flower centers are worked with a tailor-tacking foot.

book (see Part Two) or paste them into your machine manual or this book.

Presser Feet

Many special presser feet have been developed for the sewing machine, with more coming out every day. To understand their subtle differences, turn your presser feet upside down and examine the grooves and wedges on the underside. Each variation is designed for a specific purpose, to help hold the fabric flat against the needle plate without interfering with the stitches already formed. For example, as discussed in Chapter 3, the applique foot has a wedge scooped out on the underside to help it move easily over the previous buildup of threads in satin stitch and automatic stitches. Likewise, the piping foot has a channel underneath to ride over the cording inside your fabric.

Presser feet fall into four general categories: those that (1) handle special fabric, (2) help manipulate fabric, (3) apply something to fabric, and (4) manipulate thread.

Machines are set up to sew medium-weight woven fabric. When you sew either lighter or heavier materials or those that are not woven—that is, when you sew special fabric—you are pushing the limits of your machine. Then it is time to change presser feet (and needles and sometimes needle plates as well), to help your machine do a good job.

Lightweight fabrics call for fine thread, a small-sized needle, and a presser foot that is flat on the bottom, so that the fabric is sandwiched tight between the presser foot and the feed

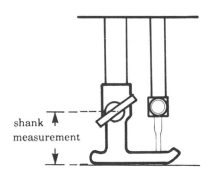

Fig. 8–2 Measure the distance from the center of the screw that holds on your presser foot to the bottom of the foot when it is in the down position. If it measures about ½" (12 mm), you have a low-shank machine; if its about 1" (25 mm), you have a high shank machine. Accessories from similar shank machines will sometimes fit your machine.

117

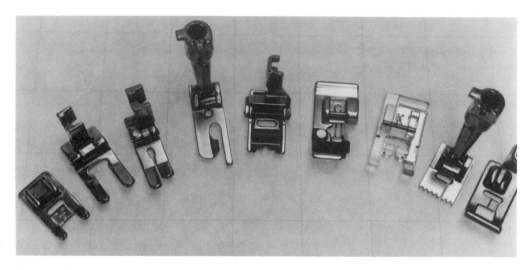

Fig. 8–3 Know your presser feet (from left): multiple cord, open-toed applique, straight stitch, rolled hem, roller, overedge, craft or embroidery, pintucking, no-snag.

dogs. If you are sewing a straight stitch and can change to a single-hole needle plate, your stitches will lie evenly on the surface. In addition, you can buy a special narrow presser foot. (The stitch formed on the old treadles was so beautiful because of its single-hole plate and narrow presser foot.)

Two feet are useful for sewing on plastics (including vinyl), imitation leather, and leather: the roller foot and the Teflon embroidery foot. The roller foot prevents the friction that makes plastic stick to the sole of an ordinary presser foot. I also use the roller foot for sewing jersey-like knits. Instead of a separate foot, Viking has a press-on glide plate for the underside of its regular presser foot, to help it move over these nonwoven fabrics.

My all-time favorite foot for keeping layers of fabric from slipping is the walking foot. You do not necessarily have to buy the walking foot made for your machine, if you know what shank size your machine has.

The quilting guide, while not really a foot, helps you to quilt accurately in the middle of large pieces of fabric. Always start from the middle of the fabric and sew outwards. Be sure the quilting guide is not pressing hard on the material, but resting lightly on the surface; otherwise it will make the fabric slide around. I also use the quilting guide anytime I cannot see the guide marks on the needle plate. For example, I recently decorated the yoke of a ready-made workshirt with automatic stitches. I used the quilting guide to keep uniform the distance of the stitches from the edge of the yoke.

Feet that help you manipulate fabric include the bias binder, ruffler, gathering, and piping feet. But the two feet used most often by machine embroiderers are the pintucking and the hemmer feet. The pintucking foot has spaced slots underneath to help guide pintucks regularly through the foot. More about this below when we talk about twin needles. The hemmer foot speeds up

118

this time-consuming process by folding under a seam allowance as you stitch. You can use either a straight stitch or a decorative stitch to secure the hem.

On thick corners I like to use the hemmer with my home-made felt wedge, which is made by folding a 3" (7.5 cm) felt square in half twice. With a straight stitch, sew along the two long parallel edges. When you approach the edge of, say, a tablecloth, where four thicknesses of cloth are waiting to harass your needle, place the short end of the felt wedge under the hemmer foot, against the edge of one hem. The foot rises over the graduated thickness of the felt without getting stuck on the added bulk of the tablecloth corners. At the corner, I sink the needle into the fabric, raise the presser-bar lever, pivot the material counterclockwise 90 degrees, place the felt wedge behind the presser foot against the edge of the tablecloth, lower the presser-bar lever, and stitch the remaining hem (Fig. 8-4).

For applying something to fabric— yarn, cord, braid, or more fabric—feet have been developed with a guide in front of the needle. Sometimes the guide is merely a hole in the cross-bar in front of the needle; sometimes the guide is under the foot in front of the needle (Fig. 8-5).

The braiding foot, with its slot in front of the needle, is similar to the hemmer foot in guiding braid, soutache, or cord evenly through the foot. Automatic stitches worked on top of these trims are good-looking. (Linda

Fig. 8–4 Felt wedge.

119

Fig. 8–5 Hole in presser foot allows cord to be applied to fabric easily.

Schulmeister of Las Cruces, NM, uses her hemmer foot for the same effect because the braiding foot for her machine is so expensive.)

Similar to the braiding foot is an embroidery foot. It has a smaller hole in the cross-bar in front of the needle than the slot on the braiding foot. A simple satin stitch worked over fine crochet gives an elegant corded edge to applique. If the design is intricate, use the foot but put the fabric in a hoop, drop the feed dogs, and release the pressure. Then you can twist and turn the work easily.

If your machine does not have such a foot with a hole in the cross-bar in front of the needle, use the multiple-cord foot instead. The multiple-cord foot also helps you apply something to fabric. I like to put four different colors of fine crochet cotton in the holes (before putting the foot on the machine) and stitch over them with the serpentine stitch or other automatic stitches (Fig. 8-6). A variation of this is to wind the elastic thread into the bobbin and then to stitch over the cords with automatic stitches. It makes a dainty gathered edge on a sleeve. If a multiple-cord foot came with your machine, turn it over. It usually has a wedge scooped out, to allow it to ride over the cords, and can be used as a substitute applique foot.

Another foot used to apply something to fabric is the button foot (Fig. 8-7). It holds the button securely to the fabric when the feed dogs are dropped. If you would like a thread shank underneath your button, so that it will sit above the buttonhole without puckering the fabric, tape a cocktail toothpick or a machine needle to the center of the button or to the foot itself. Loosen top tension slightly. The zigzag holding the button will form over the toothpick. When you remove the toothpick, you can pull the

Fig. 8–6 The multiple-cord foot holds strands of cord in place while you stitch over them with automatic stitches.

Fig. 8–7 *The ankle on this machine serves as a button foot. A machine needle has been taped to the top of the button to make a thread shank.*

button to the top of the zigzag loop. (You can also apply buttons with no foot. Tape the button to the fabric while sewing and then tear off the tape.)

The final foot used to apply something to fabric gives two kinds of applique edges. Many of the machines now have a foot with a guide or wire under it in front of the needle to hold down the fabric for accurate stitching. These feet are called topstitching, blind hemmers, overedge feet, etc. You can use them for applique in conjunction with the blind-hem stitch. The applique edge must be finished, so either use a nonfrayable fabric or finish the edge (see Chapters 2 and 3 for explanation of finishing methods—hidden applique, turned under edges, or satin stitch). For an invisible

edge, use monofilament nylon in the top and stitch around the applique. The straight stitches fall on the backing fabric and the zig catches the edge of the applique. For an edge like a hand-stitched buttonhole edging, use a thread color that contrasts with the applique. You may want to use two threads in the top. Stitch so the straight stitches fall $1/8$" (3 mm) inside the applique shape and the zig points toward the backing. (See Fig. 8-8.)

The fourth function of presser feet is to manipulate thread. I use the tailor-tacking foot for more than marking darts and basting seams. Since it leaves behind a loopy texture, I use it on items that won't be washed (pillows, wall hangings, etc.) as a suggestion of grass and seeds, or in contrast to flatter texture. Worked in circles, the tailor-tacking foot makes a fluffy flower head; this is worked easier if you lower the feed dogs and decrease the pressure, stitching from the outside of the circle to the inside (Fig. 8-9).

Bernina suggests using their tailor-tacking foot in two additional ways:

1. For a small fringe, butt water-soluble stabilizer or paper to a finished edge of fabric. Loosen top tension to 0 and sew down the middle of the two edges with a wide satin stitch. Carefully remove the bobbin thread and gently stretch the two edges apart, until they are joined only by the upper thread. Tighten top tension to normal and change to the applique foot. Anchor the left edge of the stitching with a satin stitch. Carefully remove the water-soluble stabilizer or paper, leaving a thread-loop fringe (Fig. 8-10).

2. For another form of machine fagoting, follow all the steps in (1) above, but use two finished edges of fabric and anchor both sides of the stitch with satin stitch. This provides a way to cheat an

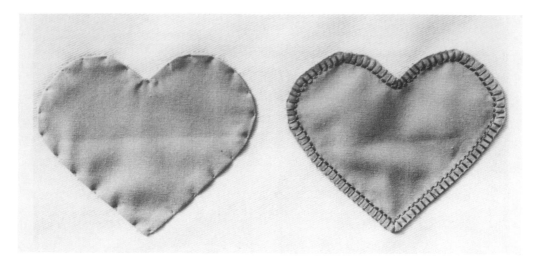

Fig. 8–8 Two kinds of applique made with an overedge foot. On the left, nylon thread is used in the top, and the straight stitches of the blind-hem stitch fall on the background fabric; the result looks like hand stitching. On the right, the blind-hem stitch is worked with the straight stitches on the applique to resemble buttonhole or blanket edging.

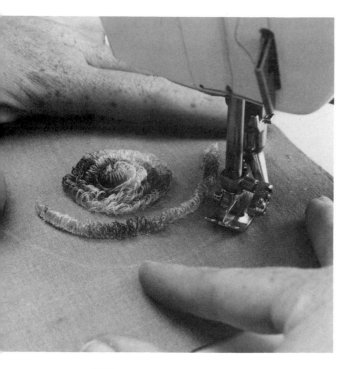

extra $\frac{1}{8}$" (3 mm) into the width of your satin stitch, and not to worry about missing an edge in the fagoting, as shown in Chapter 7, Fig. 7-21.

This discussion barely touches upon the wealth of presser feet available to you. Stay in touch with a good store and keep up on your reading to be informed of the latest. And don't be afraid to alter your presser feet—drill holes in them, tape things to them, cut off parts of them.

Needles

Three special needles give unusual effects to machine embroidery: twin needles, the wing needle, and the wedge needle (Fig. 8-11).

Fig. 8–9 The tailor-tacking foot can be used for circles or straight rows. If iron-on interfacing is afterward bonded to the back, the thread loops may be cut.

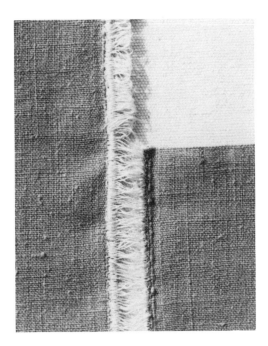

Fig. 8–10 Two more uses of the tailor-tacking foot: (top) fringe (see text for explanation); and (bottom) another form of machine fagoting.

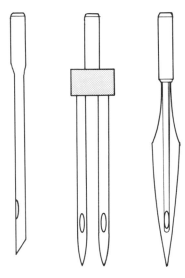

Fig. 8–11 Needles, from left: wedge, twin, and wing.

Twin needles can be used in a vast variety of ways. The most straightforward use of them is decorative top stitching of seams. The twin-needle stitch is formed on the underside the same way a single stitch is formed, except that the bobbin hook grabs two loops of top thread instead of one. Therefore if you want your twin needle topstitching to lie flat, you must loosen upper tension. It would be nice to be able to lay two parallel thick threads on the surface in one operation (that is, with twin needles); however, unlike straight stitching with a heavier thread in the bobbin, you cannot stitch from the underside with twin needles and expect the heavier thread to be laid on the surface in parallel lines of topstitching (Fig. 8-12). You could,

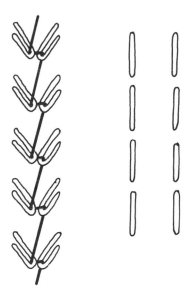

Fig. 8–12 How twin needle stitching works. (Left) underside, (right) top.

however, exploit this look by using two different colors in the twin needles and plan to make the bobbin side the eventual topside (Fig. 8-13).

Pintucking, which is a second use of twin needles, is formed when you do not loosen upper tension. The tightness of your upper tension determines how extensively your fabric is pulled. The use of the pintucking foot allows you to space rows of pintucking accurately. The grooves under the foot climb over previous rows of pintucking.

Another way to increase the bumpiness of your pintucks is to back the fabric you are pintucking with organza. Run your lines of pintucking. Then thread a tapestry needle with heavy yarn or thread—up to the size of rug yarn—and from the underside, run a line of this yarn into the channel formed by the twin needles between the organza and the fabric (Fig. 8-14). (If the garment is washable, don't use wool yarn.) And if the line to be pintucked is rounded or squared, leave a small loop outside the channel at these points, to allow for shrinkage when washing.

An alternate method for this extra-raised effect is to guide a heavy thread under the fabric as you stitch, which is then caught in the pintuck channel (Fig. 8-15). Some machines have a gadget that attaches to the needle plate,

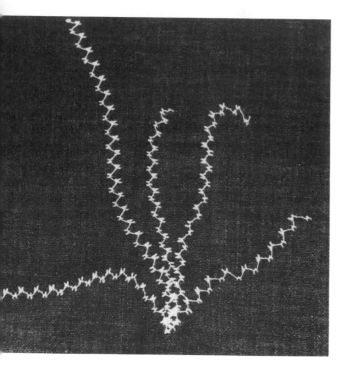

Fig. 8-13 Linda Schulmeister, Las Cruces, NM, likes the underside of twin needle zigzag. The top tension has been loosened slightly, allowing tiny loops to show on the underside.

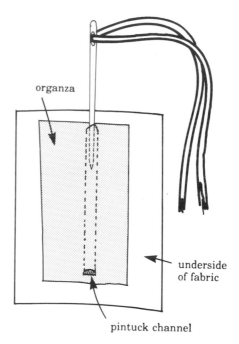

organza

underside of fabric

pintuck channel

Fig. 8-14 Make a pintuck three-dimensional by backing the fabric with organza. Then thread a tapestry needle with heavy yarn and run it from the underside into the channel formed by the twin needles between the organza and the fabric.

124

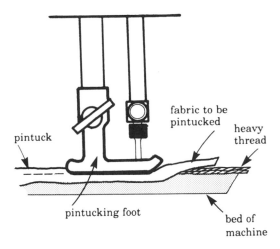

Fig. 8–15 *Another way to raise a pintuck is to stitch over a heavy thread, which is caught in the pintuck channel.*

Fig. 8–16 *Turn corners with twin needles by taking several small stitches.*

through which tucking cord for the underside can be fed. Some machines have an extra hole in the needle plate in front of the needle hole through which cord can be fed. (Judi Cull drilled a hole in her needle plate for this purpose.)

Turning squared corners with the twin needles must be done in three or four small stitches. Stop the machine with the points of the needles barely touching the fabric. Raise the presser-bar lever and half-turn the fabric (less than 45 degrees). Lower the presser bar lever and hand-turn the wheel to take one tiny stitch, leaving the points of the needles just above the fabric. Repeat these small turns until you are around the corner and then continue pintucking (Fig. 8-16).

Merry Bean has developed a stunning applique method with twin needles and gold lame tricot. See Fig. 8-17.

I like to use the twin needles to help mark fabric for hand-smocking. I run parallel lines of double stitching across a rectangle, the top and bottom of

Fig. 8–17 *Sample by Merry Bean of Arlington, VA, of her technique for outlining with a narrow gold band. She lays gold tricot lame over several layers of fabric, stitches through all layers with a double needle, and then cuts around the inside and outside of shapes, leaving the gold outline. See the color section for her screen worked in this method.*

125

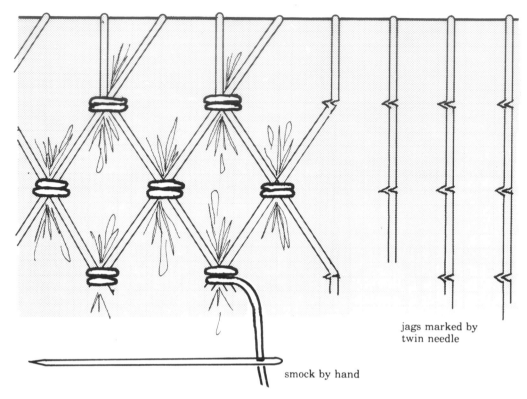

jags marked by
twin needle

smock by hand

Fig. 8–18 Use the twin needles to mark a fabric for smocking. If you have a blind hem stitch, set it for a narrow jag (otherwise the twin needles will hit the needle plate) and line up each row accurately. Smock from mark to mark.

which I have marked with machine basting. I then hand-smock the fabric (Fig. 8-18). Remember to cut out the garment piece *after* smocking. Work the smocking or pintucking area and then lay the pattern piece on top of the fabric. If there is a skirt or full area under or above the worked area (as in a sleeve), do not stretch out the fabric for cutting, because when the garment is constructed, it will not hang right. Cut the sides of a dress, for example, on the straight of the fabric, with the fullness allowed to bunch under the pattern piece (Fig. 8-19).

For another way to smock, see Theta Happ's method in Chapter 12.

Twin needles combined with automatic stitches can create very delicate effects (Fig. 8-20). In particular, the serpentine stitch lends a captivating color and pattern to otherwise ordinary materials. But watch the width of your stitch: if it's too wide, the twin needles will hit the presser foot or needle plate. This will also happen if you leave the needle decentered from a previous project. For some machines twin needles come in various widths, so you must check to be sure you can stitch the

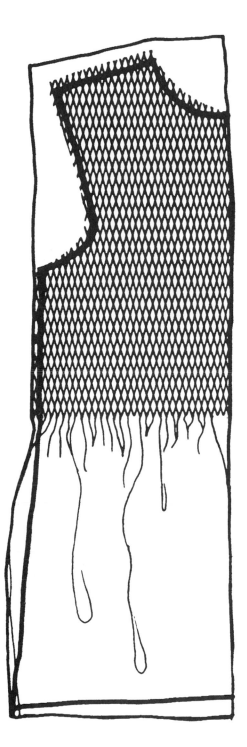

Fig. 8–19 *Smock a material before cutting out the garment piece. Then allow the material to bunch under the smocking and lay the pattern over it for cutting. Do not pull out the material flat under the smocking because the garment will not lay flat.*

entire automatic stitch without hitting the side of the presser foot or the needle plate. Handwalk the unthreaded machine through an entire stitch cycle.

Don't forget that you can free-machine embroider with twin needles, playing with different colors in the needles.

You can also buy a triple needle (Fig. 8-21).

A second unusual needle is the wing needle (also called a hemstitch needle) which makes large holes and is especially lovely on fine fabrics like organza (see Chapter 9 for more information). Try using the wing needle in combination with those automatic stitches that stitch into a central hole several times.

If a line of zigzag worked with the wing needle is sewn $^1/_4$" (6 mm) away from the bottom of a piece of organza, and then the fabric is trimmed along one side of the zigzag, a lovely picot effect is made (Fig. 8-22). More on the visual effects of the wing needle in Chapter 9.

Needle Plates

Many special needle plates are available to the adventurous machine stitcher. One of my favorites is the eyelet plate. This usually comes with an awl for piercing the fabric, to make a hole big enough to fit over the eyelet shaft on the plate. Work eyelets with the fabric on a hoop, stretching the material before making the hole with the awl. You will have to remove both the foot and the needle to fit the hoop onto the eyelet plate, and you will not be

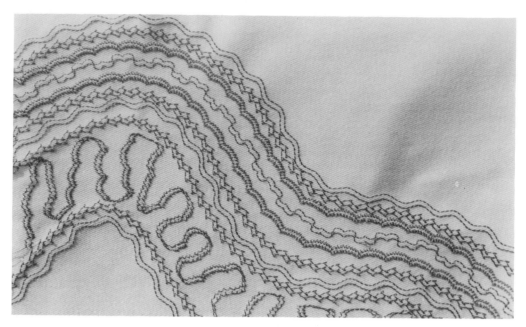

Fig. 8–20 Twin needles and automatic stitches can be worked both with the presser foot on and off.

Fig. 8–21 Mary Lou Nall of Pensacola, FL, calls this the "Accident Dress." While playing with a triple needle, she invented this yoke for a child's dress, using a three-groove pintuck and a narrow zigzag. The yoke is white batiste but the color of the threads makes it appear blue.

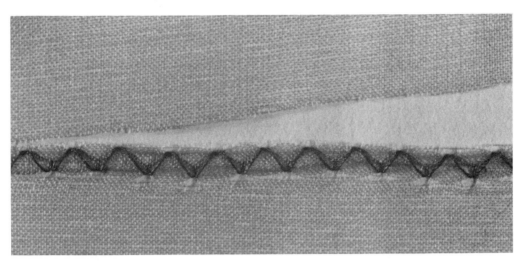

Fig. 8–22 Make this picot edge with a wing needle and an open zigzag.

able to use any foot (unless your machine has a special eyelet foot). Decenter the needle to the left and don't forget to lower the presser-bar lever. It is important to run both the machine and the hoop at a constant, medium speed so that the eyelets will be evenly formed. Stitch around at least three times for each eyelet. To end off, decenter the needle to the right, change the stitch width to 0, and take several stitches in one place to lock the threads (Fig. 8-23).

I have tried several methods to pad eyelets. One is to use crochet cotton in the bobbin and work with the underside of the fabric up, in order to make a heavier line of satin stitch. Decrease bobbin tension and tighten upper tension. Another is to make a small felt cutout, to be stitched over. Poke the awl through the felt first and then cut out a circle $^1/_8$" (3 mm) around the hole. Coax this felt doughnut over the eyelet shaft and loosen top and bobbin tensions. As you sew, hold the felt down on the side opposite where the stitches are being

Fig. 8–23 On the left is an eyelet made over felt. On the right is an eyelet in progress.

129

formed. A third way to pad an eyelet is to use a bead that has a big enough hole for the eyelet plate yet is low enough for the zigzag needle to clear. Stitch over the bead for a nice raised effect. Always experiment first on a test cloth.

Some machines have extended needle plates to sew circular designs. The fabric must be stiffened with a stabilizer, though, as it is apt to pull out of shape when stitching in circles. These plates are not cheap, but you can improvise a less expensive (but not as accurate) way to stitch circular designs.

Decide how large you want your circle and measure the distance from the center of the circle to one side (the radius). To the left of the hole in the needle plate, tape a thumbtack upside-down a radius away from the hole. Back your fabric with stabilizer and put it into a hoop. Stick the fabric over the thumbtack wherever you want the center of the circle to fall on the fabric. Now, to hold everything together, put an eraser or a cork onto the point of the thumbtack sticking through the fabric. Without stretching the fabric out of shape,

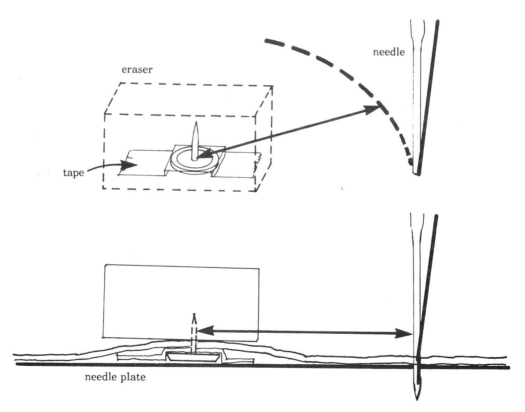

Fig. 8–24 Make your own jig for sewing circular designs by taping a thumbtack upside down on the bed of the machine a radius away from the needle. Put the material in a hoop and stick the fabric onto the thumbtack wherever you want the center of the circle to fall. Secure the fabric with an eraser impaled on the thumbtack. Keep the fabric taut between the thumbtack and the needle as you sew a circular design.

130

keep the fabric taut between the thumbtack and the needle, as you sew slowly and carefully in a perfect circle (Fig. 8-24).

A variation of this circular plate is called a flower stitcher. By varying automatic stitches and width of the zigzag, you can come up with a variety of sizes and designs (Fig. 8-25).

Some machines also have a template for perfect monogramming. It is similar to the quilting guide in that you watch an extension to the right of the machine, and by making it follow a stencil cutout of a letter, you make a perfect satin-stitched monogram. For directions on a more free-hand monogram, see Chapter 10.

The Singer computer machine makes monogramming even easier. You change to a special needle plate with a built-in hoop, position the fabric where you want the monogram, make sure you have a full bobbin, select the style

of lettering, and put a weight on the foot pedal. The machine stitches a large monogram while you have a cup of coffee.

Be sure to ask your sewing machine dealer what new special equipment has been developed for the various machines, so you can constantly expand your repertoire of machine-embroidery effects.

Additional Ideas

* Stitch an exaggerated meander pattern on a white cape with twin needles. Thread cording through the underside but pull it to the surface at some curves. Clip the cording and unravel it, for an unusual surface texture.
* Make a detachable collar of solid eyelets.
* Hemstitch a large piece of red organza with a wing needle, enough for

Fig. 8–25 Jane Warnick's flower-stitcher attachment produces designs like these.

several valentines. Insert heart shapes with satin stitch in postcard-sized pieces of interfacing on which you have already typed an address and message. Stitch the stamp on with straight stitch and mail.

* Construct a color wheel of thread, using the tailor-tacking foot.

* Use the twin needles to mark a long red rectangle for white hand- smocking. When finished, seam the panel to another blue rectangle of fabric on which you have monogrammed a white "July" for your fabric calendar. (Been on vacation? See Chapter 2 — Additional Ideas.)

CHAPTER 9

Transparent Fabrics

Transparent fabrics such as net, organza, and tulle are usually linked with bedroom curtains and wedding veils. Yet when worked with machine embroidery, the see-through quality of any transparent fabric, combined with the shadow of the bobbin thread, creates an unusual dimension.

Types of Fabrics

What are some of the transparent fabrics? Organza, organdy, net, tulle, scrim, gauze, chiffon, some muslins. Since these fabrics are not familiar to many, ask your fabric store to show you the variety of weights and textures available.

It is also useful to own a guide to fiber and fabric terms. For example, I often advise you to back a fabric with organza or organdy. But what is the difference between them? From my *Butterick Fabric Handbook*:

> At one time, organdy was a sheer, lightweight, open cotton fabric with a stiff finish; organza was the same fabric made of silk. Today, those former distinctions have almost disappeared and the names organdy and organza are used almost as synonyms. The natural fibers have been replaced by man-made fibers for their manufacture. Permanent finishes on natural fiber organdy and man-made fiber organdy have eliminated the largest objection to this fabric — its tendency to wrinkle easily and its loss of crispness. Organdy is always popular for curtains and is often used in clothing, especially for blouses and evening wear.

Other uses for machine-embroidered transparent fabrics besides wedding dresses, blouses, collars, and evening wear are pillows, lampshades, wall hangings, room dividers, and window pictures reminiscent of stained glass.

Shadow Work

The stained-glass effect, a form of reverse applique called shadow work, is achieved by stacking up layers of colored organza (or any transparent fabric you like). With a size 9/10(70) needle and extra-fine thread, sew lines of satin stitch in an interesting pattern and then cut down through the layers, close to the satin stitch, to whatever color you want to show through. Even four or five layers of the same color can be worked this way, the effect of three layers of the same color being a deeper tone than one layer.

Of course, this same reverse applique technique can be worked on any fabric. And vice versa — any of the techniques discussed earlier in the book adapt splendidly to the transparent fabrics — cutwork, heavy threads in the bobbin (metallics are especially nice), automatic stitches, free-machine embroidery, etc.

Fig. 9–1 Jackie Dodson, La Grange Park, IL, "Horses," 25" × 13½". Layers of net subtly stitched with running horses.

Fig. 9–2 Detail, Jackie Dodson "Horses."

Fig. 9–3 Shadow work is accomplished by stacking up layers of silk organza, working a design with narrow zigzag, and cutting away some layers.

A faster version of shadow work does not involve cutting down through the fabric. Called shadow applique, it is worked by inserting shapes cut from nonfrayable fabric, such as interfacing or thin felt, between two layers of transparent fabric like organza. Stitch around the shapes to hold them in place (Fig. 9-4).

Hemstitching

Zigzag or automatic stitches are appealing on transparent fabrics when worked with extra-fine thread and a

Fig. 9–4 Shadow applique is worked by inserting shapes cut from nonfrayable fabric between two layers of transparent fabric and stitching around the shape.

wing (or "hemstitching") needle (see Chapter 8). The large wing needle makes big holes in the fabric and the overall effect looks lacy and trellis-like. (Jackie Dodson says she was taught to work hemstitching on the bias because it opens up larger holes in the fabric.) Starting at the right side, stitch a line of wide zigzag with a stitch length of 10–12 stitches per inch. At the end of the row, leave the needle in the left side of the work and pivot the material 180 degrees. Sew another row of zigzag, making sure that on the left side the wing needle enters the same hole as the first row. Continue these rows until you have a piece of hemstitching wide enough for your purpose (Fig. 9-5).

You can fill small areas with hemstitching directly on the backing fabric, but another way to insert hemstitching is to lay the trellised rectangle onto a transparent backing and satin stitch any shape. Cut the hemstitching close to the outside of the satin stitch without cutting the backing fabric. Then turn the work over and cut away the backing fabric within the satin-stitch shape (Fig. 9-6). Duck-billed applique scissors make the trimming easy.

This same insertion technique can be used with net or ready-made lace (Fig. 9-7). Lay either a strip of lace or one motif from a lace panel on top of the fabric and satin stitch down or around the edge. Then carefully cut away the background fabric from the underside. This technique is used in French handsewing to insert lace on the sleeves of a blouse, either crosswise or lengthwise, and as isolated motifs inserted anywhere on garments (if the see-through area falls at a crucial point, back the lace with a flesh-colored fabric—the effect is riveting).

I have not included more French handsewing techniques because they

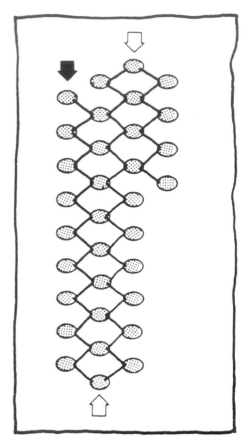

Fig. 9–5 Hemstitching can be started from either the right or left side. From the left, begin hemstitching with the wing needle at the black arrow using a wide open zigzag. At the bottom of the row leave the needle in the fabric on the right side of the zigzag and pivot the material 180°. Stitch the second row so that on the right side the needle enters the same hole as the first row. Continue in this manner.

are more related to garment construction than machine embroidery. But check the Bibliography for an excellent book on French handsewing by machine.

Manipulation of machine tensions, used in conjunction with the transpar-

Fig. 9–6 To hemstitch small shapes, work the hemstitching separately and apply to another fabric. Then cut away the fabric in back of the hemstitching.

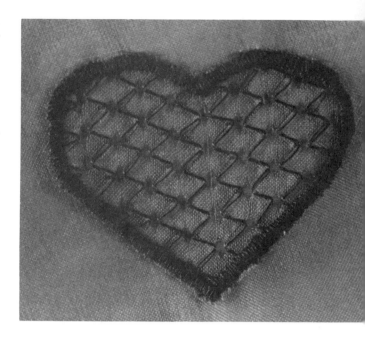

ent fabrics, adds an extra dimension to your work (Fig. 9-8). When either top or bobbin tension is loosened, the loops of thread either throw a shadow on the surface of the fabric or create a shadow under it. Organza is one of my favorite fabrics on which to work free-machine embroidery because, while it is lightweight, it is woven stiffly enough to be able to maneuver freely without a hoop. But be careful about backing organza with stabilizer (other than water-soluble stabilizer) because when you tear it away, the threads sometimes either pucker up or pull the organza out of

Fig. 9–7 Tecla inserts colored organza between transparent fabrics and outlines them with twin needles. The centers of the flowers have net inserted. Satin stitch flowers and dots fill out the design on this lingerie jumpsuit.

glazed-back Dacron batting for filler, but loose batting can be used if it is backed with a piece of organza. Cut a 4" (10 cm) tall tube from pantyhose or nylons. Cut and open out the tube to lie flat, place it over the batting, and back it with organza if you want. Using a size 9/10(70) needle and extra-fine cotton or rayon sewing machine thread, free-machine embroider a face on the nylon. If you wish, you may sculpt the face first by pinching a nose and cheeks. Try to plan your direction of stitching so that the entire face can be stitched in one operation. I usually start at the side of any eyebrow next to a temple (Fig. 9-9). When you have completed the face, cut off the extra organza on the back and put another wad of batting behind the face. Draw the nylon around the wad to the back and stitch it all together. Then work the stuffing inside the head back and forth

Fig. 9–8 By manipulating tension on transparent fabric, you can soften the lines of the design. On the left of the plant, the light-colored bobbin loops break up the dark-colored top thread. On the right, the bobbin is tightened and the line becomes dark.

shape. Either spray-starch the fabric or use water-soluble stabilizer.

Once again, let me emphasize the importance of a test cloth for experimenting. The time to discover whether or not a technique looks good or puckers badly is *before* you tackle the actual project.

Doll Faces

Here's another use for free-machine embroidery on transparent fabrics. One of the handcrafts that can be easily adapted to the machine is making stocking-face dolls. I like to use the

Fig. 9–9 A stocking-face doll can be made by free-machine embroidering features on nylon backed with batting and organza. Then pull the nylon around behind the face, stuffing with more batting and stitch closed. Add hair by hand-tacking yarn to the head.

with your fingers until you are pleased with the modeling of the face. Add hair by hand-stitching yarn over the head (Fig. 9-10) or using the fringing technique described in Chapter 7.

Darning

Some transparent fabrics, like scrim and curtain netting, are woven in loose grids. You can fill in the spaces with sidewards zigzag to simulate the hand-embroidery technique of net darning (Fig. 9-11). Or you can change the shape of the grids, pulling them together either vertically or horizontally or both, giving the impression of needleweaving.

Openwork

So far, we've treated transparent fabrics as a whole, stacking them and embroidering on them. But when we begin to manipulate the fabric itself, removing parts of it and replacing the cutouts with machine stitching, we open a whole new area of machine embroidery, one that raises exciting possibilities for play.

For example, you can create an open, transparent area in any woven fabric by removing a band of horizontal threads. Satin stitch groups of three or four threads vertically. Then work patterns horizontally across the threads (Fig. 9-12). This is called openwork or drawn thread (and also "hemstitching").

Needlelace

The most exciting technique for manipulating transparent fabrics is similar to needlelace in hand embroidery. Machine needlelace can also be adapted for any closely woven or nonfrayable fabric. Stretch your fabric in a hoop and set up the machine for free-machine embroidery: size 9/10(70) needle, stitch

Fig. 9–10 Prairie Schoolmarm.

length 0), universal tension, darning foot on, pressure released, and feed dogs covered or lowered (both optional—I use the darning foot and don't bother with the feed dogs).

For your first attempt, trace around a quarter so your cut-out will look like a true circle instead of an amoeba. Put the hoop and fabric under the needle, bring up the bobbin thread, and lock the first stitch. Stitch a straight stitch in free-machine embroidery about three times around the penciled circle. This is to strengthen the fabric, be-

139

cause next you will remove the hoop from under the needle and cut away the circle close to the stitching (but don't remove the fabric from the hoop). Now put the fabric back under the needle, bring up the bobbin thread anywhere on the circumference of the circle, and lock the first stitch. Since your stitches could pull loose if you didn't take care, stitch one-quarter of the way around the circle, right on top of your previous stitching, and stop with the needle in the fabric.

Now drive the machine at an even speed while you stitch *across* the circle. You'd think the machine would object to stitching on thin air, but if you make it go as fast as a stitch is formed, the threads merely twist around each other and are not pulled into the bobbin area.

When you reach the opposite side of the circle, take a few stitches in the same place to lock the threads to the fabric and then stitch along the circumference half-way around the circle. Now stitch across the circle to the far side again, making an X in the center. Take a few stitches in the same place to lock the threads and stitch a short way along the circumference to bisect one of the four pie shapes. Stitch across the circle, running the machine fast, and

Fig. 9–11 Marina Brown, New York, NY, removes threads from linen and then darns shapes into the cutout areas. She works with the straight stitch only.

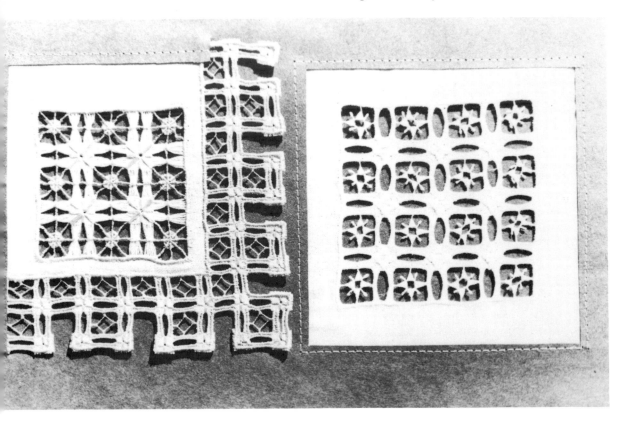

140

Fig. 9–12 Mary Ray Osmus of Benicia, CA, shows openwork in progress. On the left and top, threads have been removed. On the right, threads have been bundled, with some connected by stitching in the centers. On the bottom, the work is completed. You can use a zigzag; Mary uses the straight stitch only.

lock the threads on the opposite side. Now stitch along the circumference to the middle of another pie shape. This time run the twisted threads to the center intersection only. Then stitch in spirals from the center out, as if you were making a spider web. Quit spiralling whenever you're pleased, and stitch out to the edge in the middle of the remaining pie shape. Lock stitches at the edge, as before. If you wish, satin stitch the edge of the circle and embellish this

edge with free machine straight stitch (Fig. 9-13).

If your machine balks at stitching over space, try this. After making the initial circle and cutting it out, back your piece with water-soluble stabilizer. Follow the remainder of the directions. At the end, dissolve the water-soluble stabilizer with cold water and lacy stitches will remain.

If you want to form a shape in the center of your hole, you must also lock

141

Fig. 9–13 On the left is a circle worked in needlelace. On the right a needlelace circle is in progress. The needle is about to stitch to the center for spiraling.

your threads on the grids laid across the hole. Sew back and forth one or two stitches to lock the threads. Otherwise, your threads will slide to the center of the hole. The twists of thread can be thickened by satin stitching over them.

You can use this needlelace technique, also called air stitching, to hold down shisha mirrors, as explained in Chapter 5. You can also use the technique on heavier fabrics. The cutout does not have to be worked in a circular design. Study hand needlelace and cutwork for ideas.

Once you've mastered needlelace, you can bypass fabric completely, in two ways: (1) by anchoring your stitch-

Fig. 9–14 Moyra McNeil of West Wickham, Kent, England, worked the edging to this handkerchief in straight stitch on water-soluble stabilizer.

142

es on a cord, wire, or a ring; or (2) by using water-soluble stabilizer.

In the first method, you can twist a shape from wire or cord or use a macrame ring. Anchor your machine threads on the outside edge by stitching carefully over the edge several times. Then drive the machine across the open area to make a pattern (Fig. 9-15). If you want to cover the edge completely, you can free-machine satin stitch over it, joining intersections of the outside cord with satin stitch (Fig. 9-16).

In the second method, use water-soluble stabilizer in the background. Lay cord, twine, wire, whatever you want on the stabilizer and decorate the spaces between. When you are done, wet the piece and the stabilizer will dissolve. If you shape the stitching while the stabilizer is still a gelatinous glob, it will dry in that form.

Judi Cull has adapted the traditional hand-embroidery method of Battenberg lace to machine needlelace,

Fig. 9–15 Bambi Stalder, Penngrove, CA, tree ornaments worked in needlelace with metallic thread. The largest ring is 2" (5 cm) wide.

Fig. 9–16 Twist a shape from cord, cover it with satin stitches, and work needlelace in the intersections. Sample worked by Jackie Dodson.

Fig. 9–17 Top of flop box (see Part Two) designed and worked by Jackie Dodson on leather and corduroy. The stitching on the linen threads resembles needleweaving (see text).

using water-soluble stabilizer to hold the lace tape in place while she connects the open areas with stitching (Fig. 9-18). Battenberg lace tape is constructed on the bias and has a heavier thread incorporated into one or both edges. You can pull this heavy thread to make the tape curve without bulky gathers.

What method will you invent with water-soluble stabilizer? Study the photos in this chapter for ideas—and play.

In closing, I hope I've inspired you to experiment on all the transparent fabrics with the techniques you've learned so far—net and printed voile, for example, both work magnificently. And don't forget the watercolor-like blending you can achieve by layering transparent fabrics over solid fabrics and stitching on top (Fig. 9–19).

Additional Ideas

* Blow up the design of one lace motif from a bride-to-be's dress. Stitch a

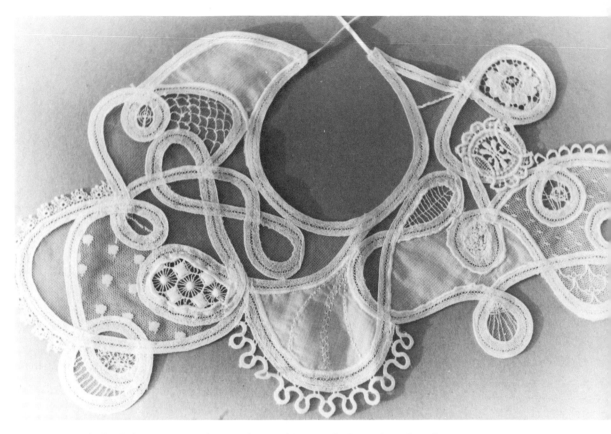

Fig. 9–18 Judi Cull, Sacramento, CA, works machine-made Battenberg lace in an asymmetric design.

Fig. 9–19 Jackie Dodson's favorite way to blend shapes is to stitch around the edges with variegated thread in similar shades as the fabric.

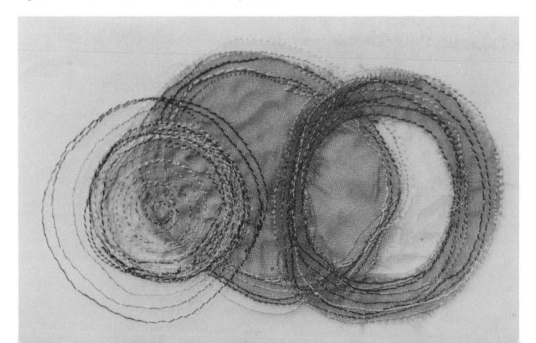

facsimile of it in net darning for the center of a wedding pillow. Inset the the stitching in silk organza. Work the couple's name and wedding date in shadow applique around the lace.

* Using a narrow zigzag, stitch snow-flake designs on water-soluble stabi-lizer. Dissolve the backing. Add a hanging wire and send one each in homemade holiday cards.

* Insert machine-made doll faces into the centers of purchased ribbon bows, to spice up present wrappings.

* Using a loosely woven fabric like scrim, needleweave large overlap-ping circles resembling seed pods for a room divider.

* Work a rectangle of yellow hem-stitching on transparent fabric and satin stitch this in the form of "Au-gust" to red transparent fabric. Cut away the excess hemstitching and work cutwork circles in the corners of the red before appliqueing to your fabric calendar. (You tend to skip the ends of chapters, don't you? See Chapter 2 — Additional Ideas.)

CHAPTER 10

Ordinary Materials
for Messages

Now that you've learned the machine-embroidery techniques and effects possible on your machine, you're ready to apply all this knowledge in a variety of ways on the different fabric scraps you hoard.

This chapter covers handling small bits of fabric, knits, special edges, and other valuable tidbits. But since so many of our projects are gifts for specific people, the chapter also covers monogramming, lettering, and other forms of personalizing.

In choosing materials for gifts that will be worn or laundered, remember to select machine-washable, colorfast threads and fabric.

Bits and Knits

Since the best-looking work is done when the fabric is stretched, you will usually use a hoop. But suppose the fabric you want to use is smaller than the hoop—how do you handle it?

You have many choices. One is to put water-soluble stabilizer into the hoop and applique the small bits to it. Later you can dissolve the stabilizer and cut the applique to the size you want.

Jackie Dodson prefers to use the Karen Bray method of applique (see the illustration in Chapter 3), tracing the shape she wants on the small bit of fabric, placing it, untrimmed, on a backing, which is in the hoop. If she has a

large enough piece of applique fabric, she will put it in the hoop, too. She straight stitches around the applique shape. Then she trims it close to the stitching and satin stitches over the edge. "This is my favorite method to prevent puckers," she says, laughing, "although I admit my applique method makes more and smaller fabric scraps" (Fig. 10-2).

Another way to apply small bits of fabric is to use a Teflon pressing sheet and fusible webbing, as explained in Chapter 3. When you bond the small piece to the larger, it will not move around (Fig. 10-3).

These techniques work well with woven fabrics, but you may want to work on stretchy fabrics, like jersey and knits, which is sometimes difficult until you learn a simple trick. Set up the machine for zigzag with the presser foot, loosening top and bottom tensions slightly. Use a ballpoint needle. Set the stitch length at 10–12 stitches per inch to make an open zigzag. Hold another piece of sewing machine thread on top of your fabric on the seam line, over which you will zigzag. Hold the extra thread slightly taut, but don't pull so hard you pull it out. If you have a presser foot with a hole in the cross-bar, put the thread through it and hold in front of the presser foot. This extra thread prevents the fabric from stretching (Fig. 10-4).

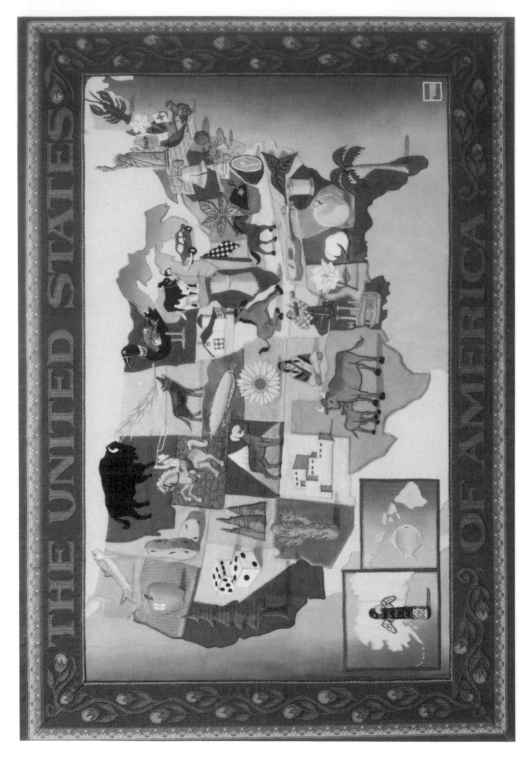

Fig. 10–1 Poster for American Express by Margaret Cusack, Brooklyn, NY. Photo courtesy of the artist.

Fig. 10–2 Apply small shapes by the Karen Bray method of machine applique (see text). Sample worked by Jackie Dodson.

Take the fabric out of the hoop, cut close to the edges, press with a damp cloth, and then remove the extra thread by pulling gently. Now set the stitch length for closely spaced zigzag, and satin stitch the edges, using your fingers to the sides of the presser foot to guide the material evenly into the machine.

There are two other ways to avoid stretching knits. First, you can back the fabric with stabilizer, so it won't stretch badly when you put it into the

hoop. Some people also put stabilizer on top of the knit fabric (obviously your design has been traced on the stabilizer first). The second trick, if possible on your machine, is to decenter the needle to the left, which makes the stitches more regular on tricot, jersey, and other knits.

Special Edges

Should you want to make a round patch from your applique, you can either trace around a round object, like a

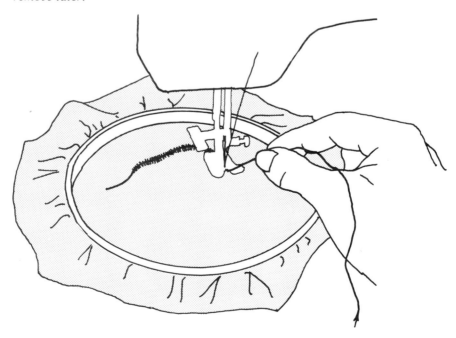

Fig. 10–3 Jini Smith, Schaumburg, IL, uses a Teflon pressing sheet and fusible web to apply small shapes to a backing. Here she plays with the initial of her first name, as she does in her books (see Bibliography).

cup or an embroidery hoop, or use the upside-down tack method shown in Chapter 8. The latter is far more precise. Incidentally, for all satin stitches, begin stitching at the side of the patch, rather than at the top or bottom, so that the eye of someone looking at your work is not drawn to those starts and finishes (Fig. 10-5). I prefer to finish the edge of a round patch with two rows of satin stitch. The first row is worked with the fabric in the hoop. Then I remove the hoop, trim close to the satin stitches, and satin stitch again, over the first stitches. This hides any stray threads from the first stitching. If you are applying a patch to something like

Fig. 10–4 To avoid stretching knits, satin stitch over an extra thread, which you remove later.

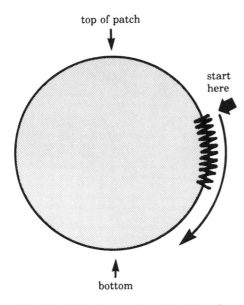

top of patch

start here

bottom

Fig. 10–5 For less noticeable joins, begin stitching at the side of a patch rather than at the top or bottom.

a jacket, use the second row of satin stitches to attach it to the jacket.

A variation of this edge is to work the first row of satin stitches in the hoop, as before. Remove the hoop and cut off excess material close to the stitches. Set your stitch length to 10–12 stitches per inch and your stitch width to a narrow zigzag. Lay a piece of 3- to 5-ply crochet cotton or any thick thread along the edge of the patch and zigzag over it, taking care that the cord stays exactly at the edge. (If you only have a thinner crochet cotton in the house, double the cord.) The embroidery foot on some machines has a small hole in the front through which you can feed this cord. I find it helpful to hold this strand slightly above the front of the embroidery foot so that the cord was guided into the right-hand groove of the embroidery foot (Fig. 10-6). You will have a hanging loop if you start a doubled strand of crochet cotton at the top of the patch,

leaving as much loop as you need to hang the patch on a tree or wherever you hang patches. Finish by threading the two cut ends into a tapestry needle and sliding them under the satin stitch on the back.

If you were using this cording on a square piece of fabric, you would zigzag to within $1/8$" (3 mm) of the corner, set the stitch length to 0, and hand-turn the wheel to make three stitches, leaving the needle in the inside edge. Raise the presser bar and turn the work. With your left finger make a loop with the cord, lower the presser foot, and make three more stitches by hand. Now set the stitch length back to 10–12 stitches per inch and zigzag for a few inches. Stop the machine, leaving the foot down, and gently pull the cord from in front of the foot until the loop you made at the corner disappears. Push the six corner stitches toward the point with a pin until they are arranged evenly. When you reach the place where you began, cut off the cord, and overlap the satin stitch about $1/2$" (1.3 cm) (Fig. 10-7).

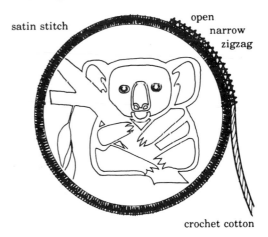

satin stitch

open narrow zigzag

crochet cotton

Fig. 10–6 For a special edge, satin stitch once around the patch and cut away excess fabric. Then sew an open narrow zigzag over crochet cotton around the edge.

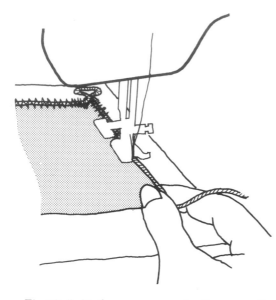

Fig.10–7 At the corners, make three small stitches on each side, leaving a loop of crochet cotton hanging out. Return to an open narrow zigzag. Stop machine with the foot down and gently pull the crochet cotton until the loop disappears.

You can dazzle the troops by working this corded edge in a scallop pattern, using an automatic scallop stitch and a close zigzag setting. Work the automatic stitch on paper first, with an unthreaded machine, watching how the needle moves through the scallop. Then thread the machine with extra-fine machine-embroidery thread top and bobbin. Hold the cording thread (fine crochet cotton is nice) first to the right slightly, then to the left, as the needle moves through the scallop. At the base of each scallop, make sure the needle pierces the fabric (Fig. 10-8).

Since the corded edge is such an attractive one, here's a third variation. Use the buttonhole foot. Its double grooves on the underside help form perfect satin stitches. Either lay crochet cotton on the edge of the patch or stitch from the underside, laying a heavier bobbin thread on the surface. Then satin stitch from the topside over the crochet cotton, using extra-fine thread in top and bobbin. I find it helpful to decenter the needle to the left, so I can control exactly where the needle enters on each side of the crochet cotton.

As before, take the fabric out of the hoop and cut close to the first line of stitching. Now decenter the needle to the right. Widen your zigzag and lay another line of crochet cotton to the right of the first one. This should fit exactly into the second groove of the buttonhole foot and the zigzag should be wide enough to cover both the second cord and the first line of stitching. Satin stitch all the way around the circle and you have a special edge (Fig. 10-9).

Fig. 10–8 Mary Nall, whose triple-needle yoke was in Chapter 8, here cords a scalloped edge on a child's dress. She has also added automatic stitches as trim.

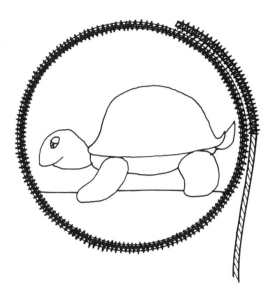

Fig. 10–9 Another special edging is made by stitching a row of satin stitch over crochet cotton, and repeating it in a second row.

Monogramming

The easiest and fastest way to show off your machine-embroidery skills is to purchase a simple item — sweatshirt, towel, napkin, placemat, bag (preferably on sale, of course) — and to add the initials of the giftee. This is called monogramming.

In choosing the style of lettering and the method of working, you have many options. Match the style of lettering to the person. For example, a casual person will not appreciate a flowery script, nor will a more formal person like avant-garde letters. Go to a good art-supply store and pick up one of the type-style books available from manufacturers of press-on letters. This will give you an idea of the variety of type styles available. You can also buy iron-on transfer letter patterns from the major pattern companies (McCall's, Simplicity, etc.).

Once you have chosen a type style, decide whether you want to embroider one, two, or three initials. If you choose one, make it large and ornate. If you choose two, make them the same size. If you choose three, either make them all the same size and in the order to be read (Robbie Losey Fanning = RLF) or make the initial of the last name larger and in the center (rFl) (Fig. 10-10). If the person has a Mc, O', or St. in her (or his) last name, it must be included in the monogram.

Be creative, however; there are no set rules for the arrangement of the letters. Play with the actual shape of the letters. Experiment with overlapping, intertwining, nesting, or combining. Make them fit a shape, such as a circle, oval, or diamond, or inside something whimsical, like a butterfly wing. Flop them, repeat them, mirror them (Fig. 10-11). As long as you can still distinguish the letters and the design is pleasing, anything goes. The easiest letters to combine are the symmetrical ones — A, H, I, M, N, O, Q, T, U, V, W, X, and Y. The others can be difficult.

RLF
RFL

Fig. 10–10 When monogramming, either use letters of the same size or center a larger letter (always the family name) between two smaller ones.

Fig. 10–11 Monogram designed by Deems Taylor for Edna St. Vincent Millay.

Sometimes it's easier to use lower-case letters.

The most straightforward kind of monogramming for machine embroidery is handwriting script worked in a satin stitch (Fig. 10-12). For practice,

Fig. 10–12 Handwriting script in a monogram graces these handtowels, worked on a Viking/White computer machine. Photo courtesy of Viking/White Sewing Machine Company.

choose a medium- to heavyweight fabric that can withstand a lot of satin stitch pulling at its threads (burlap would not be good, but denim is perfect). Back the fabric with stabilizer. Put the fabric into the hoop and write your favorite person's initials (all right, write your own name) in pencil. Use white pencil, chalk, or wax if the fabric is dark. Since the tension must be perfect for monogramming, practice on a test cloth in the hoop first. If you wish, lower or cover the feed dogs. Take off the presser foot and put on the darning foot. Set the stitch length at 0 and do not set a zigzag width yet. Extra-fine sewing-machine thread will make your monograms neater and more precise. I also stitch over a piece of knitting yarn to raise the monogram slightly. Be sure you have a full bobbin because this technique uses lots of thread.

Draw up the bobbin thread and lock the first stitch, cutting off the end threads. Now set the machine to whatever zigzag width you prefer (I like the third widest setting). The line you drew should be in the middle of the zigzag as you work. Let the machine run quickly to make a neat satin stitch, but move the frame slowly and steadfastly. Don't rotate the hoop as you stitch. Instead, imagine what Joyce Drexler of Speed Stitch calls a horizon line printed on the fabric. Make sure you don't tilt the horizon line as you stitch; keep it level (Fig. 10-13). At the end of each letter, raise the needle, set the zigzag to 0 for both width and length and take a few stitches in one place to lock the threads. Now raise the presser bar, pull some top thread through the take-up lever, and gently pull to the side until you can clip the top thread. Don't worry about the bobbin thread—most of it will be covered by satin stitch, and the remaining parts can be cut off since all stitches

154

Fig. 10–13 As you work the monogram, imagine that there is a "horizon" through it: Keep the line level.

Fig. 10–14 Combine automatic stitches with free-machine embroidery.

are locked at the beginning and end of each letter. Start the next letter by lowering the needle into the fabric, taking a few stitches in the same place to lock threads, setting the zigzag width, and stitching as for the previous letter.

You can also use a block-letter style, where you do turn the hoop, guiding the line of the cartoon under the needle as if it were a traditional seam line. For this style, you may prefer lowering the feed dogs but leaving on the presser foot, for greater control.

For either script or block, if you fill in the letter unevenly, don't hesitate to go back and fill in more.

These techniques are the most used, but be creative. Try combining the precision of work done with the presser foot on with free-machine embroidery. Work letters in automatic stitches and intertwine them with free-machining, or vice versa: intertwine freely stitched letters with the precision of automatic stitches. Use techniques like cutwork, needlelace, and shadow applique for your letters, embellishing them with machine embroidery (Fig. 10-14).

As for placement of monograms, try to determine how the final item will be used. If, for example, you are monogramming napkins, will the family fold the napkins on the diagonal? Then the monogram should also be placed on the diagonal, with the base of the letter towards the corner. If you are monogramming bridal sheets, will the sheets be turned back? Then the letters must also be read when the sheet is folded back.

One way to side-step the problem of making mistakes while working monograms on pockets, sweaters, etc., where a goof would be unfixable, is to work the monogram on a separate piece of fabric, like organdy or water-soluble stabilizer. Once you are happy with the work, place the monogram, still in the hoop, on the garment and pin it in place. Then take the hoop off the separate fabric and put it back on, this time with the garment included. This method only works when the design allows for a second line of stitching on top of or beside the first.

As for centering the monogram, be like a carpenter: measure twice, stitch once. Use a ruler or tape measure to guarantee accurate placement; don't eyeball it. If your monogram is large, make sure the base is parallel to the floor or it will be disturbing to viewers.

Don't be afraid to take pockets off of purchased garments for monogramming. It's easy to sew them back on.

Lettering

You may also want to applique or stitch whole names, words, or phrases. Be sure to match the technique you choose with the style of lettering. If, for example, you want something precise, don't use free-machine embroidery (unless your skills are top-notch). It's like coloring inside the lines in kindergarten—not likely.

If your lettering must be readable from a distance, as in banners, be sure you use a visible color scheme. In *How to Attract Attention with Your Art,* Ivan Tubau lists these color combinations as the most striking (in order of most impact): black on white, black on yellow, red on white, green on white, white on red.

All lower-case letters are hard to read from a distance. Choose either all upper case or a mixture of upper and lower.

As for how far apart your letters should be, watch advertisements and titles on movies for ideas. Fashions in spacing change; sometimes the letters are jammed together, touching at the

base, and other times they are spaced apart, often with small stars between them. Between words, the standard advice is to leave the equivalent of a capital O.

You can copy an alphabet onto graph paper from letter-style books and blow it up to any size, using a method from Chapter 1. But it's more fun to manipulate letters to fit a space or shape (Fig. 10-15). Put tracing paper over the

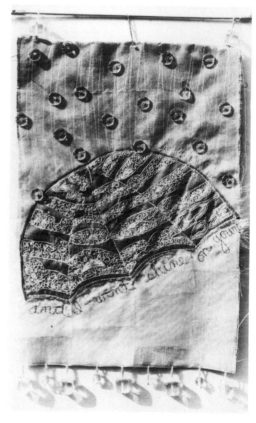

Fig. 10–15 Make letters fit a space. The free-machine scribbling in the umbrella reads "Please don't rain on my parade" (underneath: "and I won't shine on yours"). By Robbie Fanning, organza over silk, 6" × 10".

156

shape and copy it. Count how many letters you must fit into the shape. Roughly divide up the space with pencil lines. Then cut out the letters free-hand from the tracing paper. You may not like your first several attempts, but keep trying. Tracing paper is inexpensive and you won't have wasted your time goofing on the actual item. When you're done, use a spot of glue to stick the letters down and trace them again for stitching. If you work from the underside, you can stitch right through the paper—but remember to reverse the letters or they will be backwards.

To curve a message around a circle, first copy it on a straight line. Clip between letters, keeping them connected by the line; then bend the letters around the circle perimeter.

But for smaller, more intimate lettering, you can write messages with free-machine embroidery on your work (Fig. 10-16) or with the lettering function on your new computer machine (Fig. 10-17).

Other Forms of Personalizing

You can personalize gifts with more than letters and words. Most people have a favorite animal or flower (Fig. 10-18). You can also use heraldic signs and family crests. Hilde Lee has built up a business of embroidering motifs from people's china plates onto placemats (Fig. 10-19). Claire Whitmore stitched a scene from a friend's town on a skirt border (Fig. 10-20). All of these say, with the added impact of color and texture, "You're special to me."

Additional Ideas
* Use symbols of the career of your giftee on Betty's Box (Part Two)—

Fig. 10–16 Joy W. Saville, Princeton, NJ, "Karen's quilt," 80" × 110". Cotton applique on corduroy. Tiny machine-quilted messages connect the figures.

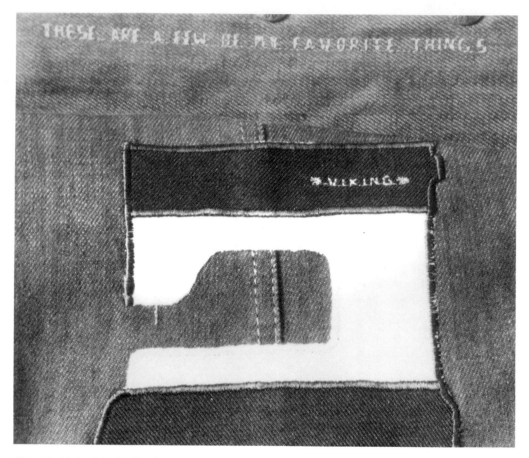

Fig. 10–17 Levi jacket by Gayle Domorsky, Flint, MI. She has appliqued favorite items all over the jacket and written with her computer machine "These are a few of my favorite things."

pharmacist, attorney, physician, stockbroker, etc.
* Make a family banner with appliqued symbols, phrases, and meaningful objects.
* Blow up the logo on a business card to the size of a purchased picture frame. Depending on the intricacy of the design, applique and free-machine embroider it.

Fig. 10–18 A personal patch designed for Kali Koala Fanning.

Fig. 10–19 Hilde Lee of Menlo Park, CA, reproduces motifs from people's china in free-machine embroidery on placemats.

Fig. 10–20 Claire Whitmore, Montgomery, AL, appliqued familiar scenes around the base of a purchased Levi skirt.

* Monogram purchased sheets and pillow cases for a new bride.
* Superimpose "September" over a solid background of zigzag shading, leaf shapes, fall colors. (Trace around real leaves if you can't draw.) Work everything *but* the letters "September." (Catch up with the rest of us by reading Chapter 2—Additional Ideas.)
* Read (and re-read) the excellent books on lettering recommended in the Bibliography.

CHAPTER 11

Unusual Fabrics

By now you realize that any fiber system is fair game for machine embroidery. Anything that is woven, knit, poured, or crushed together to make a surface through which a needle will pass can be explored for its potential in machine embroidery. Naturally, some of your attempts will be unsuitable for anything but the wastebasket, but some will be both usable and striking.

Felt

Felt is especially well-suited to machine embroidery. It works up fast and its bright colors are cheerful to sew on. All of the machine embroidery techniques covered in the book look attractive on felt because the sewing thread lies on the surface of the fabric, with no background weave competing for attention.

However, I have always been somewhat annoyed at the claims that satin stitch on felt is easy. Until I learned to use extra-fine thread and to loosen both top and bobbin tension, my attempts at satin stitch on felt looked terrible. Appliqueing felt to felt requires either fusing or machine basting. If you choose the latter, baste with either a long straight stitch or a long zigzag before working the satin stitch. Use lots of finger control to keep the felt from moving around too much. Felt is sold as washable (polyester) and unwashable (part wool). If your fabric store does not carry a 50% wool felt, check with an interior decorator. Wool felt, of course, is not washable, so plan to dryclean it.

I learned an interesting treatment for felt from artist/author Jean Ray Laury. Using the thinner felts of 75% rayon, she tears shapes with pliers, which gives a soft, fuzzy edge. This is then stitched to a background with free-machine embroidery (Fig. 11-2). I also tried this technique with loose polyester batting, free-machine embroidering the centers of puffs torn from the batting and fuzzing the edges.

Another edge treatment is to cut down the middle of a piece of felt with pinking shears, which produces a sawtooth pattern on both edges. Separate the two edges about 3" (7.5 cm) apart and applique them to a lighter or darker backing of felt. Apply a piece of rickrack trim down the center of the 3" (7.5 cm) gap and secure it with a narrow automatic stitch. The serrated edges of the trim complement those of the felt.

Plastic

Transparent plastics also adapt superbly to machine embroidery. These are available in various weights at hardware stores. The mediumweight pliable plastics are easiest to work with. Don't pin anything to plastic because the pin holes remain. For the same reason, you can't afford to make mistakes. Cello-tape designs to the plastic and sew right through the stabilizer and tape, pulling both off when

Fig. 11–1A Ultrasuede and vinyl mantle by Merry Bean, Arlington, VA.

Fig. 11–1B Detail of Merry Bean's mantle.

you're finished. The automatic stitches are magnificent worked on see-through plastic; however, if the plastic is not strong and the needle holes are allowed to pack too closely together, the plastic will rip.

Because plastic has body and is weatherproof (except for long periods in the sun, which cause it—and me—to deteriorate), it is the ideal fabric to cover and protect other fabrics. Choose it also when making decorations for an outdoor living Christmas tree.

Fig. 11–2 Fuzz felt by pulling at the edges with pliers or by ripping it instead of cutting.

Fig. 11–3 Elaine Newton, Ogden, UT, stitches flowers and stained-glass scenes by sandwiching plastic between sheer materials.

Occasionally when stitching on plastic, friction builds up between the bottom of the presser foot and the fabric, causing the plastic to stick. Use a Teflon roller foot to prevent this. I also use the roller foot for leather, imitation leather, and some knits. If you don't have a roller foot, use water-soluble stabilizer or tear-away above and below the fabric. To cut down on friction between the needle plate and the plastic, pull an old sock over the free-arm of your machine and cut a hole in it for the feed dogs and needle hole.

Vinyl can be found in the form of a colored plastic backed with cloth, which makes it easier than clear plastic to sew on. The automatic stitches, in particular, work up attractively on vinyl, with the threads lying evenly on

its smooth surface. I haven't upholstered a car in vinyl and automatic stitches yet, but . . . .

Most industrial manufacturers ship their fragile wares in an amazing variety of plastics and foam, many of which can be stitched on. I've experimented with substituting plastic for batting in machine quilting. Of course the ultimate use of the article you are making determines whether or not you use plastic. I would not put an item with plastic incorporated into it into a hot washing machine, for example. On the other hand, I once made a fabric greeting card for a friend in which I backed some crepe-backed satin with a small piece of $1/8$" (3 mm)-thick opaque flexible plastic. (I don't know what to call the plastic because I filched it from a

163

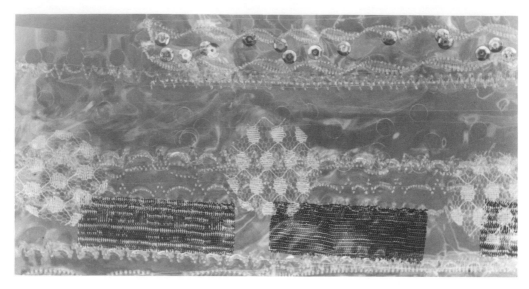

Fig. 11–4 Sample by Nancy Smeltzer, Columbia, MD, for "Champagne Party." Nancy uses a walking foot and automatic stitches on plastic with either nylon invisible or no thread, which leaves a lacy pattern of holes.

wastebasket in my husband's company.) I free-machine embroidered my friend's name through the crepe/plastic/muslin, which quilted it and brought the surface into relief. This particular plastic, pliable yet not limp, would adapt well to free-standing objects, such as small, soft boxes.

I can imagine a see-through plastic raincoat which is pintucked over colorful heavy cords—but would the coat be waterproof with all those needle holes in it?

Leather and Imitation Suede

Sewing on leather requires a special wedge needle to make a big enough hole in the fabric for the thread to pass through easily. Leather needles come in sizes. If you are free-machine embroidering, use a Size 9/10(70) and extra-fine cotton thread. A larger sized needle may tear the leather. Since you

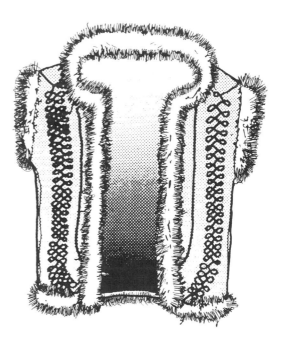

Fig. 11–5 Turn the fur on knit-backed furs to the topside for a self-trim. Then decorate the fur.

164

Fig. 11–6 Handle difficult pile fabrics like terrycloth by laying organza over the cloth, monogramming, and cutting away the organza close to the stitching.

can't put the leather in a hoop for free-machine embroidery, Linda Barker, author of *That Touch of Class/Machine Embroidery on Leather* (see Bibliography), recommends you iron two layers of freezer paper onto the back of your leather, shiny side of the paper toward the leather.

There are many kinds of leather, some of which are too thick to sew on. Your favorite sewing store will show you leather samples, or you can consult the Supply List at the end of the book. Don't overlook the chamois leather sold in grocery and auto supply stores as a possibility. Look also for the leather stripping sold in fabric stores for belting. It can be applied as trim to garments, using automatic stitches along the edges to secure the leather to the fabric. Again, as with plastics, don't pin the leather—tape or glue it. I have seen a gorgeous leather purse worked from the underside with a crochet cotton in the bobbin, laying a thick chain stitch on the surface (so far, only a few domestic machines can do this stitch).

Sewing construction on leather is different from that on ordinary fabrics. I suggest you consult a good sewing book. My favorite is *Everything About Sewing Leather and Leather-Like Fabrics* (from Vogue Patterns).

The new imitation suedes are also enhanced by any kind of machine stitching. As with other nonwoven fabrics, the sewing thread lies on the surface instead of being swallowed by a

Fig. 11–7 Marilyn Allen of The Crafty Critter, Rochester, WA, stitches the bib of a dress on plastic needlepoint canvas to resemble bargello.

165

Fig. 11–8 Use waste canvas and your zigzag to duplicate hand cross-stitch. When finished, wet the threads of the waste canvas and pull them out.

Fig. 11–9 Another way to cross-stitch is to program your computer machine. Photo courtesy of New Home.

weave. The rubber backing of these fabrics sometimes shreds rayon thread, but cotton thread works well. Free-machine embroidery without a hoop on imitation suedes is not easy because the underside of the fabric sticks to the bed of the machine, but backing with stabilizer eliminates some of the problem. Actually, I prefer automatic stitches with the roller foot to free-machine embroidery on these fabrics. Tensions must be loosened slightly to prevent rippling, and after stitching, the fabric should be pressed from the back, using a press cloth and an iron set to the manufacturer's temperature suggestion.

Loopy Fabrics

To prove how nuts I am about machine embroidery, I've even tried stitching on raw fleece and loose polyester batting. Both must be backed with organza to keep the woolly bits from being drawn into the bobbin case, but it works. I recently made a mass of fluffy clouds outlined and formed by satin stitching. I haven't yet stitched through foam or fur, but only because I don't have any in the house.

However, there is a knit-backed imitation fur that adapts beautifully to machine stitchery. Use the knit on the outside for a vest or coat, turning the fabric back on itself at all facings for a fur trim. Then use any of the machine embroidery techniques to embellish the coat front, backing the fabric with stabilizer to prevent the fur from catching in the bobbin.

Until the invention of water-soluble stabilizer, terry cloth was difficult to stitch on because the loops catch on the needle and presser foot. Yet monogrammed or appliqued towels can lend such a personal touch to your home. To cope with this, copy your design onto a rectangle of organza or nylon organdy and pin it to the right side of the towel. Put the fabric into a hoop and set up the machine for free-machine embroidery with the darning foot on, stitch length on 0, stitch width at whatever you like, extra-fine thread in the top and bobbin. For an even monogram, run the machine fast but move the hoop slowly and constantly. If you are an accomplished sewer, use a tapered satin stitch at the beginning and end of the monogram, as shown in Chapter 10. When you have finished, cut the organza as close to the satin stitch as possible. Then use your handy tweezers to remove any threads of organza that are sticking out unattractively.

Water-soluble stabilizer in this method is even easier: the stabilizer washes away when you're done stitching.

This same method of working on organza or organdy can be used in two ways to applique onto towelling. One way is to place the applique fabric on a larger piece of organza. Put the applique/organza in a hoop and pin it in position on the towel. Satin stitch around the shape. Then cut away the organza and pull out excess threads with the tweezers (Fig. 11-6).

The second method is to work a thread picture on the organza in the hoop, using any free-motion method you prefer—straight stitch, sideways zigzag, etc. Then cut out the picture, pin it to the towel, and satin stitch around the edges.

I plan to experiment with glass fabrics soon. Although they are not yet suitable for apparel, being too irritating to the skin, glass fabrics make graceful curtains, and occasionally, bedspreads. I would imagine that whip stitch worked on glass curtains would lend an intriguing shadow effect as the sun passes through.

Open Weaves

Now that we have washable needlepoint canvas, you can use free-machine satin stitch to create blocks of thread

Fig. 11–10 Beth Swider and family are stationed in Spain, where Beth is learning machine embroidery on a treadle machine from local teachers. She found this postcard there, with thread and fabric flounces added to the dancer's dress.

similar to bargello (Fig. 11-7). Also, bands of automatic stitches on ribbon can be padded and appliqued to the borders of canvas work.

Fig. 11–11 "The Left-handed Quilter" by Myrna Butler, Farmington, NM. Myrna lays fabric on cardboard cut from cereal boxes and free-machines over the surface, drawing in highlights, shadows, and details. For larger pieces, she uses grocery bags so that she can roll up the paper to get it under the head of the machine. A heavy backing prevents the thread from puckering the fabric picture. Collection of Evelyn Crittenden.

Cross-stitch embroidery uses a backing called (appropriately) cross-stitch canvas, similar to penelope canvas. This is basted to fabric, stitches are worked across the intersections, and finally the threads of the canvas are withdrawn one by one and discarded. This technique can be duplicated with zigzag by carefully matching the length and width of the stitch to the canvas so that the needle never actually pierces a canvas thread, and by matching succeeding rows of zigzag exactly, to resemble cross stitch. Using a limited color palette and choosing patterns that have solid blocks of stitches, you can come up with a passable cross stitch. I am not averse to adding isolated hand cross stitches to fill out the outskirts of the pattern (Fig. 11-8). The new computer machines make this easier; you can program them to stitch, say, six vertical crosses, then five, then four, repositioning the fabric for each row (Fig. 11-9).

Upholstery and drapery stores carry some fascinating open-weave fabrics that can be embellished in interesting ways. One is the openwork technique described in Chapter 9. Withdraw threads as if you were checking for the straight grain. Then set up the machine for free-machine zigzag and pull the exposed threads together with satin stitch. Another way is to withdraw threads as above, and work automatic stitches along the top and bottom edges of the exposed threads.

Whimsy

The last two unusual fabrics that I've decorated are used mainly for whimsy. I often free-machine embroider messages to friends on interfacing and have also used it to make tags for presents. Likewise, I've stitched small pictures on typing paper to send in letters to people I enjoy surprising.

In the late 1890s people often stitched imitations of postcards. But today, people stitch *on* postcards, a charming form of whimsy (Fig. 11-10).

Myrna Butler also stitches on paper, though you wouldn't know it because the paper is covered by fabric (Fig. 11-11).

I haven't tried stitching on flower petals or rainbows, but only because the opportunity hasn't yet arisen.

Additional Ideas

* Use simple stick figures like the symbols for the Olympics. Construct a vinyl exercise pad with six bad-back exercises zigzag-appliqued on it.
* Trace a motif from a print wrap-around skirt on nylon window screen. Fill in the colors with sidewards zigzag, cut out and applique to a matching T-shirt.
* Use two or three fall leaves from your yard as templates. Make a three-dimensional wreath of leaves made of Ultrasuede or felt scraps.
* Make a leather monogrammed book cover for your this-year-I'm-going-to-get-organized notebook, so yours won't look like everyone else's.
* Free-machine embroider an orange stocking-face pumpkin (dye the nylon) to be used as the O in "October" of your fabric calendar. Free-machine embroider the rest of the letters in black. (Feel bewitched or bewildered? Treat yourself to Chapter 2—Additional Ideas.)

CHAPTER 12

Printed Fabrics

Most of the designs we've attempted so far have been solid-colored threads on top of one-color fabrics, but machine embroidery on printed fabric opens up a whole world of possibilities. Pay attention to the photo captions in this chapter, for the artists' works point the way to that exciting world.

Machine Quilting

The easiest kind of machine embroidery on printed fabric is machine quilting a printed fabric (Fig. 12-2). Bold designs in wide widths can usually be found in custom drapery stores, but if you can only buy 45" (115 cm) or 54" (140 cm) widths, a seam can be made invisible by matching patterns exactly. If you are working on a quilt-sized piece, you generally do not have any left-over material on which to practice, so it is extremely important to practice free-machine quilting on a trial sandwich of similar fabric/stuffing/backing material. You must pin liberally (I use safety pins) and loosen both top and bottom tensions slightly, so that when you begin quilting the material does not move around and make ugly puckers. To handle recalcitrant fabrics that fight even the most skillful pinning job, put a stabilizer between the needle plate and the fabric, gently tearing away the stabilizer after quilting.

To free-machine quilt, set up your machine for free-machine embroidery, removing the presser foot and lowering the feed dogs (optional). As usual, I use the darning foot and sometimes a wooden hoop (the machine-embroidery spring hoop sometimes pops off if the quilt is thick). The hoop is both a help and a hindrance. If your pattern is large, you will have to move the hoop several times before completing an outline, which is a nuisance. But on the other hand, you waste so much time ripping out mistakes if you don't use a hoop, that the inconvenience becomes minor.

Take your time in maneuvering the hoop so that your stitches will be comparatively even. You can even challenge the legendary 12–16 stitches per inch of old-time quilters by moving the hoop slowly as you stitch and by setting the machine on slow speed (if possible on your machine).

Usually you'll have repeated patterns or motifs to quilt. When you finish one motif, raise the presser-bar lever and pull some upper thread loose above the needle. Then gently move the material away from the needle to the next starting point, changing the hoop position if necessary. Lower the needle into the fabric, lower the presser bar lever, and hold the extra thread behind the needle. Take several stitches in the same place to lock the thread and later cut off the loose threads on the front and back. They will not pull loose because you locked them. This avoids having to tie off all the threads as you go. If you doubt whether the threads will last through several washings, you

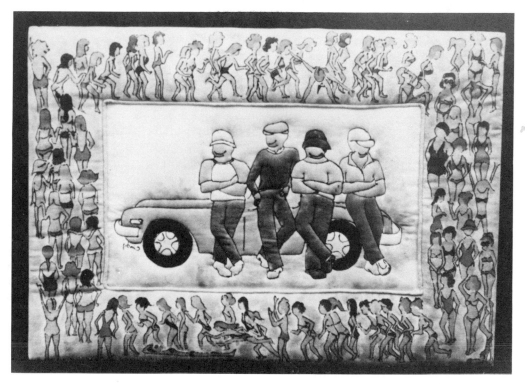

Fig. 12–1 Cindy Hickok, London, England, "Girl Watchers (When You've Seen One, You've Seen Them All)," 33" × 23". Dyed and quilted.

can pull the upper thread through to the back and tie additional knots or use a drop of fabric glue on the back.

You need not always think in terms of large projects like quilts, though. Fig. 12-3 shows a 12" (30.5 cm)-square batik handkerchief, purchased at a craft fair for under $5. It has been backed with muslin with a lightweight flannel interlining, quilted on the main outlines in a contrasting color, cut down the center, and assembled into a striking yet simple tunic top. Quilting tie-dyed fabric gives a similar effect.

Stripes, Checks, and Dots

A favorite fabric to embellish for its ready-made straight lines is pillow ticking or any striped fabric. You can stitch on the lines, between lines, zig-zag over lines, or if you're feeling energetic, you can completely cover the lines. You can also make tucks and manipulate them so that first one color, then another is exposed (Fig. 12-4). Checked or gingham fabric is also fun to embellish, as the basic shapes are already there for you to play with (Fig. 12-5).

In a variation, Carroll Labarthe uses the grid on gingham as a guide for her design, but she bastes the gingham to the underside of her fabric and works with the underside up (Fig. 12-6).

Likewise polka-dot fabrics are easily arranged into a larger pattern, al-

Fig. 12–2 Machine-quilted printed fabric.

though it can be frustrating to have a picture in your mind of a particular fabric and then to search all over town in vain for it. Again, large-pattern fabrics are often found in drapery stores and the weight of these fabrics is perfect for free-machine embroidery without a hoop.

Don't be afraid to create your own patterns if you can't find what you want. Several fabric paints are on the market, available in art and craft supply stores (or see Supply List), which can be used straight from the bottle. You want really large polka dots? Assuming you've already removed the sizing by preshrinking the fabric, merely pour some paint into a dish, dip the bottom of a flat juice glass or bottle top into the paint, and press onto the fabric. Re-ink the glass and print until satisfied. Let the paint dry and then set the colors as directed by the manufacturer. Presto!, you have your own printed fabric ready for embellishment (Fig. 12-7). A similar effect is made by using rub-

Fig. 12–3 Close-up of batik fabric quilted to emphasize the lines of the design.

Fig. 12–4 BJ Adams, Washington, DC, "Matsuri (Festival)," 61" × 26½". Striped and tucked fabric manipulated to expose different colors. Three parts can be displayed horizontally or vertically. Collection of Naperville Bank, IL. Photo courtesy of the artist.

Fig. 12–5 Mary Osmus, Benicia, CA, removes thread from gingham and works needle lace in the open spaces, using only the straight stitch on her machine.

Fig. 12–6 Carroll Labarthe, Pittsburgh, PA, detail "Jerapple jim carzanthemum." Carroll used a graphics program on an Apple computer as a take-off point for this design. She stitched gingham fabric to the back and followed its lines to make a grid on the right side, removing the grid lines after the piece was stitched.

ber stamps and indelible laundry inks (Fig. 12-8).

Be careful that your hours of machine work on printed fabric are not wasted by choosing a thread color or weight that is lost on the fabric. For example, on dress-weight linen I once started some lettering that was weak and ineffectual because the thin lines of extra-fine sewing-machine thread were swallowed by the thicker threads of the linen. I ended up using silk floss.

Color is also important. In decorating with machine embroidery, you have chosen to emphasize a particular area, so select a color that stands out—either the strongest color in your print or one that is complementary (i.e., across the color wheel from your colors). For example, I once stitched a bold red design among large green and white polka dots.

Making Fabrics

Make your own fabric by combining printed or solid fabrics into a new surface on which to stitch (Fig. 12-9). Another way to make your own fabric is to sew strips of lace and ribbons together (backed with lining fabric), interspersed with strips of machine embroidery, either with automatic cams or any of the textured stitches discussed earlier in the book.

Machine embroidery can be combined with a different kind of "printed"

174

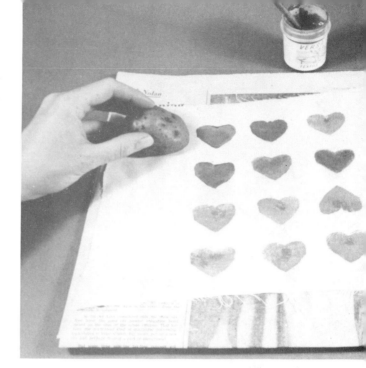

Fig. 12–7 Like your polka dots heart-shaped? Carve a heart on half a potato and print on fabric, putting newspaper underneath to soak up excess.

fabric—canvas work (also called needlepoint)—for a truly unusual look (Fig. 12-10). I have worked bands of automatic stitches on grosgrain ribbon which are sewn to the unworked canvas border with more automatic stitches. I lay flannel on the canvas for padding to bring the ribbons to the height of the canvas work. It is important to design carefully, though, and to plan from the beginning to use machine embroidery with the main design; otherwise the results can be unsatisfactory.

Embellishing Prints

It is challenging to lift part of a pattern off a fabric and to enlarge and embellish it, as pictured in Fig. 12-11. Sometimes the design of a fabric or trim can be picked up for another part of the garment. I recently made a halter dress with an attached black organza cape. On the cape in white thread, free-machine embroidered, I duplicated the swirls of the skirt fabric pattern. I've also taken the pattern off white eyelet lace used as sleeves, enlarging and satin stitching it on the bottom edge of a child's dress.

In embellishing these extensions of prints, you may want to add buttons, sequins, or beads. If you're sure the hole in the bead is large enough for the needle, you can machine sew them on by cello-taping them to the surface and carefully stitching with or without the darning foot (Fig. 12-12).

Fig. 12–8 A gentle reminder not to smoke from Barbara Lee Pascone. Rubber stamps and free-machine quilting, about 14" square.

Jackie Dodson suggests another method for beads, especially small ones. String them on monofilament thread. Then lay the beads where you want them on the surface and couch on each side of them, over the monofilament thread, to hold them in place. Also use monofilament thread in the machine if you want the couching to be almost invisible (Fig. 12-13).

Another way to embellish prints is to borrow one motif from a pattern. Cover it completely with solid stitching, zigzag or straight stitch, except for the outer $1/8$" (3 mm) of the motif. Cut out the embroidered motif and applique it to a garment, jacket, shirt, dress, purse, or pillow, by satin stitching the remaining $1/8$" (3 mm) of outline (Fig. 12-14). This is a good class project for beginning stitchers.

Another kind of printed fabric is that prepared for hand embroidery. You can easily adapt hand-embroidery designs for the machine (Fig. 12-15).

Knitting-Needle Embroidery

Sometimes the printed fabric you're covering is paper. Theta Happ, of Oklahoma City, OK, revived interest in the old Singer technique of sewing zigzag over slender steel double-pointed knitting needles, for a corduroy effect (Fig. 12-6. (See the Bibliography for her book, *Charted Needle Design*.)

Any design charted on graph paper can be used, such as cross-stitch, needlepoint, or knitting designs. You can

Fig. 12–9 Marjorie Hoeltzel, St. Louis, MO, constructs vests and coats from narrow strips of neckties machine-stitched with clear nylon thread. The neckties have been washed, dried, torn, and frayed to create additional texture.

176

Fig. 12–10 Judith B. Gross, Washington, DC, "Purple Pansy Pleasure," 34½" × 62". Inko dye stencil, hand and machine applique, needlepoint appliqued by machine, heavy threads in the bobbin.

also make any picture into a charted design by laying transparent graph paper (available in drafting or art stores), 10 squares to the inch, over your picture and coloring in the major shapes with washable colored pencils. (You can also chart any picture with a clever product called Transgraph — see the Supply List).

Set up your machine for free-machine satin stitch, with extra-fine thread in top and bobbin. Don't use a darning foot.

To stabilize the backing fabric, Theta recommends ironing freezer paper to the back of it. Lay the graph paper over the backing fabric and pin or tape the edges of the paper in position. Slide the fabric under the needle. Then place a knitting needle vertically over the left side of the picture, parallel to the lines of the graph paper. Hold the knitting needle on each side of the sewing-machine needle (Fig. 12-17).

Make sure the presser-bar lever is down. You must now determine how wide to set the satin stitch on your machine. Handwalk the machine through the first stitch, until you are sure the needle will not hit a knitting needle. You will have to experiment to find which zigzag width covers one needle without hitting the adjacent needles. (Decentering your needle helps.)

Then begin stitching slowly, filling in the picture over the needles, changing colors when you need to. Lock your stitches at the beginning and end of each color change. As you complete a portion of the picture and have covered all your needle channels, remove the

Fig. 12–11 Nancy Smeltzer, "Pastelique," 22" × 21". Machine applique and machine quilting.

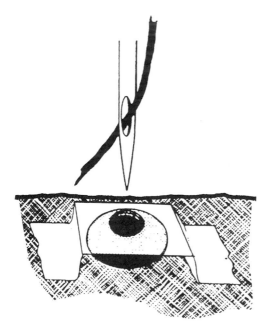

needles by gently pulling them out. (There are usually five needles per package.) Move them to the next area and begin the same process. When you are completely done, free-machine embroider around the outside of the worked picture, with or without thread. Then tear away the remaining paper.

Try the same method over curved upholsterer's needles, sanded orange or bamboo sticks, metal potato skewers, etc.

Smocking

Theta Happ cleverly extended the knitting-needle technique by pleating fabric, as for smocking, and running the knitting needles through the verti-

Fig. 12–12 To secure beads by machine, tape them and zigzag into the hole.

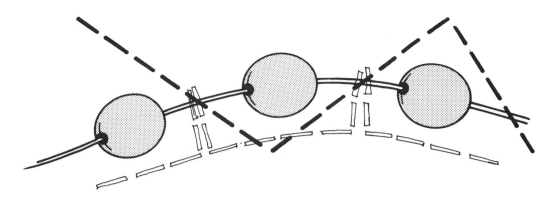

Fig. 12–13 For long rows of beads, first string beads on monofilament. Use nylon or "invisible thread" for crossing (black) or tacking (white) to hold down the row of beads.

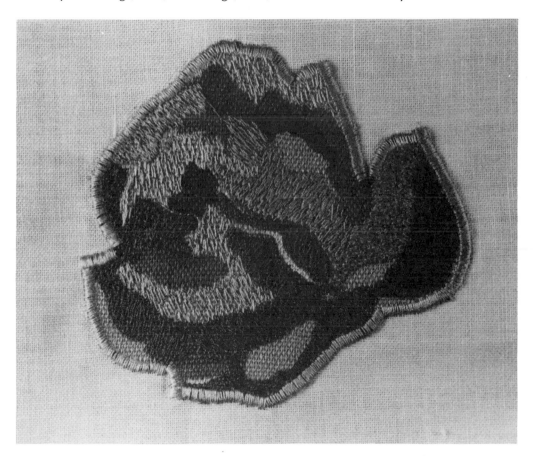

Fig. 12–14 Cover one motif from printed fabric with stitches. Then machine applique it to a backing. This is a good class project for beginners.

Fig. 12–15 Paula Kamler, Washington, MO, former educator for Pfaff Sewing Machine Company, stitched a Vaness-Ann poem meant for handwork on the machine, using automatic stitches.

cal folds on the *underside* of the fabric. Then on the topside, she free-machine embroiders with a zigzag in traditional smocking patterns. An example of her work is shown in Fig. 12-18. (Also see her book, *English Smocking on the Sewing Machine*, in the Bibliography).

Theta's method produces a smocked effect that is amazingly like hand-worked smocking, unlike the more rigid line of traditional machine smocking. Although this traditional method of machine smocking is really machine shirring, it can be used successfully on printed fabrics with regular pattern repeats, which are used as guidelines in stitching. Hand-wind elastic thread onto the bobbin, taking care not to

Fig. 12–16 Lucille Graham, Bountiful, UT, uses Theta Happ's knitting-needle technique to stitch an aardvark for Jerry Zarbaugh's Aardvark Adventures. Lucille is the author of Creative Machine Embroidery *(see Bibliography).*

180

stretch it. Load embroidery or sewing-machine thread in the top and tighten the upper tension slightly. The longer your stitch length, the more pronounced will be the gathers. Use adding machine or typing paper under the material to hold it in place, tearing the paper away later. If you plan well, you may vary the overall shape of your smocking area to further imitate the feeling of hand smocking. You can also use a decorative stitch that alternates from side to side of a middle line, and by carefully locating the line-up of stitches, create an elegant effect. Or you can use the serpentine stitch in a wide width and medium length, lining up the rows to make ogees, for a popcorn-stitch effect.

Work the smocking first and then cut out the garment. Allow the material below the smocking area to remain gathered and lay the pattern piece over the smocked material. If you were to pull the material out flat, the garment would be too small at the bottom and not hang right.

It's easy to glue machine-embellished fabric to any household object — not only recipe boxes and wastebaskets, but the telephone, the dining room chairs, your sewing machine. You will need a fabric glue like Elmer's, a razor blade, scissors, and patience mixed with whimsy. If the back of your fabric is lumpy with threads, bond iron-on interfacing or fusible web to it. Then paint your object liberally with glue and carefully smooth the fabric onto its surface, molding the fabric into hollows and over bumps. Cut slashes for anything that protrudes and trim excess neatly with the razor blade.

Fig. 12–17 Hold knitting needles on each side of the sewing-machine needle.

Additional Ideas
* Stitch a sampler of machine-embroidery techniques on the squares of plaid Thai silk. Make into a caftan.
* Use pillow ticking and decorative stitches in Dotty's Sewing Duffel (Part Two).
* Construct a telephone-book cover by sewing ribbons, lace, and strips of automatic stitching to a fabric backing.
* Free-machine quilt in blocks two colors of bandanas (or paisley fabric) backed by two solid-colored fabrics. Join and alternate colors for a reversible quilt.
* Work the word "November" in rust-colored canvas work (needlepoint),

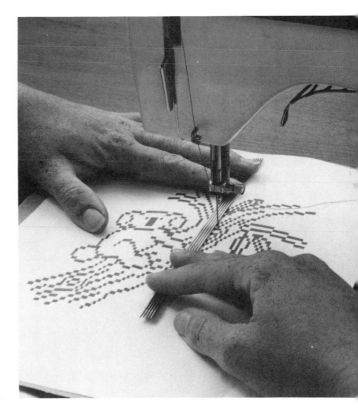

Fig. 12–18 Theta Happ, Oklahoma City, OK, worked machine smocking on this child's dress over knitting needles. The smocking is soft and elastic. Theta explains her methods in English Smocking on the Sewing Machine *(see Bibliography).*

surrounded by a cream canvas-work background. Lay a border of automatic stitching on ribbon onto the canvas and raise it to the level of the canvas work by padding with flannel. Your fabric calendar is almost done (last chance to see Chapter 2 — Additional Ideas).

CHAPTER 13

Know Your Tools

Perhaps you think it odd that I place this chapter in the middle of the book, rather than at the front. But as a teacher, I know you can overwhelm a beginner with so much minutiae about a subject that she is paralyzed.

Machine embroidery is easy: give a beginner a clean, well-oiled machine; fine thread top and bobbin; a sturdy piece of cotton fabric in a hoop. Teach her one new technique and let her take off. Let her experience the joy of making, even if her product won't win prizes at the state fair.

Later, much later, she will begin to notice the subtle differences between needles, threads, fabrics, brands of machines. She will want to upgrade her skills, to know more.

This chapter is all about those subtleties. Some of them matter more for traditional garment sewing than for machine embroidery. Others we take for granted and shouldn't. Let's start with our basic tool, the sewing machine, and the basic lockstitch.

Stitch Quality

After many hours of stitching (and a quick review of Chapter 1), you understand how a stitch is formed on the sewing machine. But the more experience you acquire with sewing, the more you realize the tiny ways you can help your machine best form that stitch. It involves the correct matching of needle, needle position, needle-plate opening, presser foot, feed dogs, thread, and fabric.

Your best straight stitch is formed by using an expensive European needle (I prefer Schmetz) in the correct size for your thread. Why expensive? Because the scarf is deep, allowing the bobbin hook to come close to the needle and grab the loop of top thread without ever missing the loop. This deep scarf requires precise machining, which is not cheap. An expensive needle also has a highly polished eye. Since the thread saws through the eye several times for each stitch, a less polished eye might have burrs on it that would catch on the thread, causing it to fray and break. Too small an eye has the same effect: it cuts into the side of the thread, causing it to snap. That's why we match the size of the needle to the thickness of the thread.

You remember that if the fabric lifts as the needle leaves the material, the loop also lifts, perhaps causing the bobbin hook to miss it. How do we prevent the fabric from lifting? By pressing it tight against the needle plate and feed dogs. But if you have a zigzag machine and are using the zigzag needle plate, you can see that there is a hole under the fabric where the fabric is not pressed tight against anything. It may look insignificant to you, but the hole is big enough for the fabric to be pulled down into the bobbin case, and it can lift slightly as the needle goes back up.

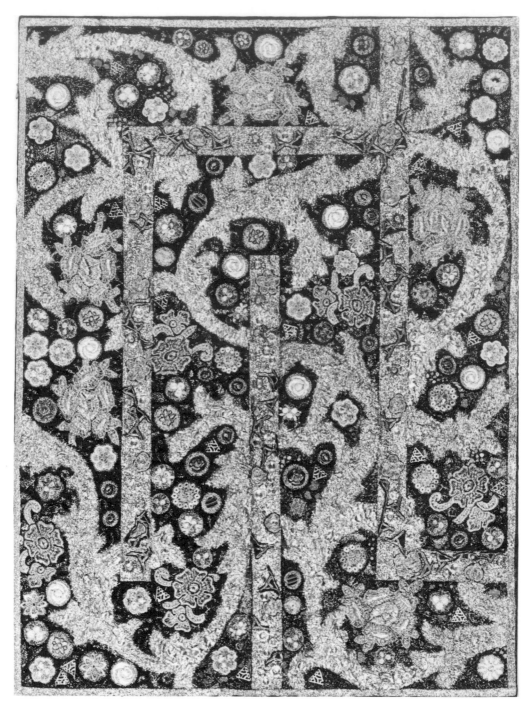

Fig. 13–1 Christine Risley, London, England, "Flower Maze," 46 × 61 cm. Christine is the author of Machine Embroidery: A Complete Guide *(see Bibliography). Photo courtesy of the artist.*

On mediumweight fabric, which resists pulling and lifting, this hardly matters. But on lightweight fabrics, like organza or tricot knit, it matters a lot. The fabric puckers along the seam line from being pulled into the bobbin case, and sometimes a stitch is skipped if the fabric lifts. How to remedy these problems?

If possible, use a single-hole needle plate and the straight-stitch presser foot, which surrounds the needle snugly and is flat on the bottom, holding the fabric securely against the feed dogs. Also use a ballpoint needle, which does not cut the fibers of the fabric but slips between them. (If the needle cuts the fiber, the fabric is skewered like a barbequed mushroom and tends to lift up when the needle rises out of the fabric.)

If you don't have a single-hole needle plate but can change your needle position, decenter the needle to the left. This supports the fabric on three sides of the opening, as well as allowing the

Fig. 13–3 Top-loading rotary bobbin system.

hook a fraction of a second more time to grab the loop. Also use a wider presser foot.

Bobbin Systems

There are two bobbin systems most often used in today's machines: the front-loading oscillator (Fig. 13-2) and the top-loading rotary (Fig. 13-3). The oscillating shuttle mechanism oscillates or see-saws back and forth to make a stitch. It never completes a full circle. The rotary, on the other hand, makes a full revolution to make a stitch.

Does this matter? After talking to hundreds of consumers and sewing-machine dealers, as well as sewing on both kinds, the answer is "no," not as far as the quality of the stitch is concerned. The only difference, and it only matters if you are lugging a machine around often (to classes, to seminars, to a distant studio, to friends' places, on an airplane), is that the oscillating ma-

Fig. 13–2 Front-loading oscillator bobbin system.

chines must be heavier to keep from bouncing around on your sewing table. If you still prefer an oscillating machine, the solution is simple: buy a suitcase trolley and cart your machine around on that. (And learn how to lift heavy objects correctly, bending from the knees, so you don't injure your back.)

Feed Dogs

When we only had straight-stitch machines, we needed merely to guide fabric forward under the presser foot. Therefore, the feed dogs were shaped in a saw-tooth pattern, like little slanted teeth. These gripped the fabric from underneath and moved it through smoothly.

But when zigzag machines were developed, especially those with a reverse cycle (which means they can stitch forward a little, then backward or sideward a little, then forward again, as with, for example, the stretch overlock stitch), we needed a different kind of feed dog, one that would hold the fabric securely as it moved it backward and forward under the needle and that would return it accurately to the same

Fig. 13–4 Saw-tooth feed dog.

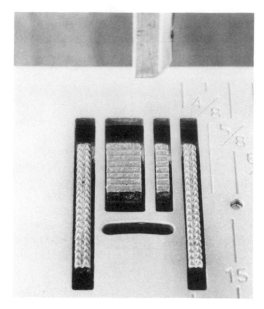

Fig. 13–5 Diamond-point feed dogs on the sides, with large saw-tooth feed dog behind.

position, so that the needle would enter the same hole as before. Thus, the diamond-point feed dogs were developed. (Some machines have a third kind of feed dog, made of rubber.)

Motors

Within the last ten years, most sewing-machine manufacturers have converted their AC electric motors to DC electronic motors. This is a more efficient use of electricity, which gives an instant torque. "Torque?" you say. "Who cares?" It means that you have greater penetration power at the needle. The needle can pierce up to eight layers of denim at a slow speed. It can also pierce all those layers of thread you make in free-machine embroidery.

Will a dealer tell you whether or not a machine you're considering buying has an AC or DC motor? No.

Presser Feet

In Chapter 8, we discussed the use of various presser feet and I won't repeat that information here. I would only encourage you to measure your shank so that you can try feet from all the brands that fit your machine. Each company has something special. The Bernina embroidery foot, for example, is painted white along the shank, which makes seeing the needle hole for threading much easier. New Home has a craft foot with small red dots on it, so you can line up decorative stitches easier. Viking has snap- on feet, which is a convenience (you can buy an adapter kit for most machines that allows you to use snap-on feet).

When you become a connoisseur of presser feet, play a game with yourself. Dump all of yours upside-down and identify them, one by one, by the shape of the underside of the foot. When you understand why they are formed as they are, you will have mastered another subtlety of the machine. Also, watch the wear-and-tear on the underside of plastic feet. After years of heavy use, the foot becomes chewed up and may need replacing.

Needles

Needle sizes refer to the diameter of the needle blade (the European size is in tenths of a millimeter). As a needle increases in size, its eye becomes bigger. Equivalent sizes in these numbering systems are:

American

9	10	11	12	14	16	18	20
65	70	75	80	90	100	110	120

European

The most important quality-control tip I can offer is to use the needle recommended for your machine. It commonly occurs in machine-embroidery classes that someone needs help because her machine is skipping stitches. When I look closely, she's using, say, an American needle in a European machine. Don't be afraid to try an expensive European needle in your machine, no matter the make. Sometimes a cheap import machine loaded with an expensive European needle performs like the most expensive, best-made machines. People think it's the machine and often it's the needle.

I've already mentioned the importance of using a well-produced needle for sewing. For machine embroidery, you must become even pickier, depending on what technique and what fabric you're using.

The needle most used in ordinary sewing is labelled 705 H (for "Hohlkehle," the German word for "long scarf"). The 705 H comes in sizes from 10(70) to 18(110). When the 705 H

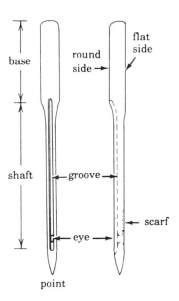

Fig. 13–6 The standard sewing-machine needle.

appeared, it was considered a break-through. It is engineered with a long scarf for zigzag, so that at no position during the formation of a stitch would the needle hit or deflect off the bobbin hook. It also has a modified ballpoint tip, called a universal point, which allows you to sew on both woven and knit fabrics. This means that home sewers do not need to change needles, which most hate to do, when they change fabric.

But the 705 H was not satisfactory for extremely stretchy material like loose knits and rubberized material, so the 705 H-SUK (refers to "synthetic") Stretch Needle was developed. It has a full ballpoint tip, which slips between the fibers instead of piercing them. 705 H-SUK Stretch Needles come in all standard sizes.

You can also buy a 705 H-S "Blue" Stretch Needle, but only in sizes 11(75) and 14(90). The blue has nothing to do with performance; it is merely a color coding. (One rumor is that it is a silicon treatment to reduce friction—not true.) The Blue Stretch Needle has the same full ballpoint tip as the 705 H-SUK, but it is a little flatter on the shank, to bring the needle closer to the hook. It was developed for flimsy knits, like Qiana, to prevent the fabric from being dragged into the bobbin case. Using a wide presser foot also helps prevent this.

The only sharp needles made today are for heavy wovens or leathers. If you were to use a ballpoint needle, you might get a slight wobble to a straight stitch, as the needle deflected off the threads instead of piercing them. Therefore, the 705 HJ (J for jeans) has an acute but round tip and is used on denim, canvas, or awning material. It comes in sizes 14(90), 16(100), and 18(110).

The leather wedge needle has a sharp cutting point. It's called 705 H-LL and comes in sizes 12(80), 14(90), 16(100), 18(110), and 20(120). Use it for nonwoven fabrics such as vinyl, synthetic suede, and leather.

For most machine-embroidery techniques, depending on the thread selected, you will use a 705 H 12(80) or 14(90) needle, the latter especially for rayon thread. This pokes a big enough hole in the fabric to allow the thread to pass freely without fraying. Some people prefer to use a 705 H-SUK.

However, if you are filling in a shape with sideways zigzag on medium- to heavyweight woven fabric, I recommend trying a topstitching needle, the 130N, which comes in 10(70), 12(80), and 14(90). It has an elongated eye with a sharper tip than the stretch or universal needles. When filling in a shape with thread, we cannot expect the tip of the needle to perform like a

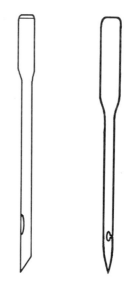

Fig. 13–7 Leather wedge needle (left) and slotted or handicap needle (right).

ballpoint tip and slip between the threads on its way through the fabric because there are too many overlapping layers. We need a needle that will easily pierce the layers of thread on in its downward trip (as does a jeans needle — 705 HJ).

This is merely an opinion, though, reached after experimenting with sideways zigzag on cotton, satin, organdy, organza, and voile. The closely woven delicate fabrics like satin and tricot hate a sharp point. They seem to demand a ballpoint tip. This leads to a finer distinction: choose your thread to match the fabric, the *size* of the needle to match the thread, and the tip of the needle to match the fabric. Incidentally, I experimented with rayon thread and was surprised to discover that each fabric demanded its own top tension setting. For example, with a tight tension nylon organdy looped on top, but it lay beautifully with a loose tension; on the other hand, cotton voile was happier with a tighter top tension. Please experiment for yourself.

Two other needles are useful to know about. One is the slotted or handicap needle which is open on one side of the eye for easy threading. This of course weakens the needle, so extra care must be taken when sewing: don't pull the material and don't sew fast. The basting needle, 130/705 RH, has two eyes, one above the other (it's sometimes called the "magic needle"). Ordinarily, for basting, you thread only the upper eye and use the blindstitch. The stitch forms only on the jag of the blindstitch, skipping all the other stitches. This gives a long basting stitch. But you can thread the eyes with two different threads. If you have trouble catching both threads in the lockstitch, decenter the needle to the left and move the needle a hair lower. All of this is to help the bobbin hook catch the two top loops of thread.

The topstitching, handicap, and basting needles are not always displayed in stores. If you don't see them in your favorite store, ask somebody — they may be in a drawer in the back. Otherwise, contact the mail-order sources listed at the end of the book.

The finish used on many modern fabrics tends to dull the tip of the needle, which is why you are advised to change to a new needle for each major project. If you pre-shrink your fabric, it removes some of this finish; however, for many machine-embroidery projects, we do not think to pre-shrink our fabric — nylon organdy, for example, or fabric we cut up to use for test cloths. Be aware that this finish may subtly affect tension settings.

One other tip about needles: I can never remember what size needle I left in the machine, especially now that I have four machines and my daughter also sews. I always have trouble reading the number printed on the needle, so I keep a linen tester by the machine, which magnifies the print. Hold the point of the needle, where the eye is, to the left to read the number, which is printed on the round part of the needle base. The lid of some needle cases has a built-in magnifier over the bases. Put your unidentified needle in a case to read the number. I also made myself sewing-machine covers for all my machines, with a dial pointing to the last needle size used (see Part Two).

Threads

If there is anything we machine-embroidery nuts take for granted, it's threads. We know what we like, but we usually have no idea of the subtle differences between types of thread. How is the thread manufactured? What are

189

its strengths and weaknesses? What do the numbers on the spool mean?

Two types of yarns are used to make thread: filament and staple. Filament yarns, which comes from silk and man-made fibers like rayon and polyester, are extremely long, thin, smooth, and lustrous; staple yarns, like cotton and linen, are shorter, thicker, fibrous, and without luster.

To produce sewing thread, slivers of the yarns are fed into rollers and drawn out in strands. These strands are spun counter-clockwise as they emerge, to increase the strength of the yarn. This is called an S-twist. When two strands are then twisted together into a two-ply machine-embroidery thread, they are twisted in a clockwise direction so they won't come untwisted. This is called a Z-twist. Sewing machines require Z-twisted sewing threads. (Just for fun, run your fingernail along the end of any machine-embroidery thread. It will untwist and you can see both the two plies and the Z-twist.)

The reasons you choose a thread for constructing a garment are not the same as for machine-embroidery. For example, 100% cotton thread has a low stretch ability. If you were to sew a seam in a knit garment with cotton thread, the stitches might pop.

Machine embroiderers, on the other hand, tend to choose threads for their fineness and texture. Cotton threads have a matte finish; polyester is slightly shinier; and rayon and silk gleam. If you want to highlight something, stitch it in rayon or silk and contrast it with surrounding areas of polyester or cotton.

We also care about how a thread behaves when it is stressed by repeated stitching. Extra-fine machine-embroidery cotton resists untwisting, so it is perfect for straight stitch, satin stitch, and reverse-cycle stitches. Polyester is strong, but it has a tendency to untwist (especially with cheaper brands). Rayon has a high sheen, but it isn't strong and it has a high thread drag. Therefore, reduce tensions and don't sew fast. But let me immediately contradict myself. Not all rayons are twisted identically; some are looser than others and may require a *tighter* tension to keep them from rolling or untwisting. (Rayon thread produced in third-world countries may be spun on second-hand equipment originally intended for a different fiber, like cotton, which explains the difference in twist.)

More important to machine embroiderers is understanding the numbering system for threads. There is no uniformity to the systems used, but generally the number describes the relationship of the length and weight, the number of plies, or the diameter of the yarn.

In the indirect method of measurement, the higher the number, the finer the yarn. Thus size 50 machine-embroidery thread is finer than size 30. In this method, the number refers to the number of 840-yard hanks per pound. Size

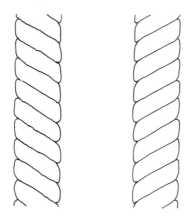

Fig. 13–8 Thread twists. (Left) S-twist; (right) Z-twist.

190

50 is 50 hanks per pound; size 30 is 30. The indirect method is used for staple yarns like cotton.

To further complicate things, some companies use English numbering, designated Ne, for cotton sewing thread and metric numbering, designated Nm, for synthetic sewing thread (referring to the number of meters of thread which weigh one gram). For both systems, the higher the number, the finer the thread. Equivalent sizes for these two systems are:

Cotton

Ne	20/3	40/3	50/3	60/3	60/2
Nm	30/3	70/3	85/3	100/3	100/2

Synthetic

The denier (pronounced duh-*neer*) method of measurement is used for silk and man-made filament yarns. It gives the weight in grams of 9,000 meters of filament. In this case, the smaller the number, the finer the yarn. This method is not used for staple yarns because their greater weight would require huge numbers on the spools.

The numbers on spools also show the number of plies: 60/2 means Size 60 with two plies.

Sometimes the number is followed by a phrase describing special processes applied to the thread, like "triple mercerized." Mercerizing is applied to cotton and cotton blends to increase their luster and to improve their strength. The threads are immersed under tension in a caustic soda solution, which causes permanent swelling of the fiber. Triple mercerized means the process has been repeated three times.

The new computer machines and the popularity of sergers, which sew faster than old machines, has put new demands on thread. The newest method of production is an air-texturing process that eliminates the old spinning techniques. This produces a strong, almost perfectly round thread with high tensile strength and hardly any defects or "nebs" (these get caught in your tension guides and needle eye and cause the thread to break). Because the thread is round, it reflects light like silk.

Thread is wound onto the spool in either vertical or cross-wound lines. A vertically wound spool empties from the top to the bottom. A cross-wound spool empties evenly until the last layer of thread, which crosses the entire spool like a giant Z-twist. The only difference between the two is that there is a slight color-cast change on vertically wound spools, making it slightly harder to match thread to fabric color. This is why you undo the thread on vertically wound spools and lay it across your fabric to match it. Merely holding the spool against the fabric is not accurate enough.

The best way to learn about the threads in your possession is to make a sample chart (Fig. 13-9). Lay down a long line of satin stitch and label each line with brand, size, and color number (optional). As Jackie Dodson says, "It's amazing to see the differences—from fuzzy to sleek, from variegated that blends beautifully to the ones that look like lengths of coral snakes, with no blending. Each rayon make is also different."

Bobbins

Buy yourself extra bobbins and a bobbin-holder case. I can never remember exactly which weight thread or brand is on a bobbin, especially if I wound it five years ago. I keep small tags in my bobbin-holder case, identifying the brand and weight (e.g., Zwicky silk, Nm 40/3).

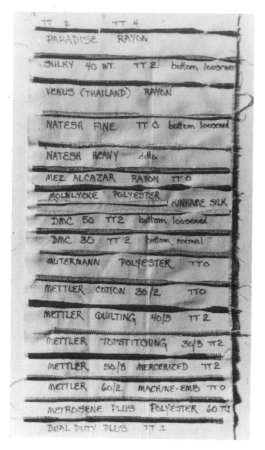

Inside the chart (handwritten):

TT 2   TT 4
PARADISE RAYON
SULKY 40 WT. TT 2 bottom loosened
VENUS (THAILAND) RAYON
NATESH FINE TT 0 bottom loosened
NATESH HEAVY ditto
MEZ ALCAZAR RAYON TT 0
MOLNLYCKE POLYESTER KINKAME SILK
DMC 50 TT 2 bottom loosened
DMC 30 TT 2 bottom normal
GUTERMANN POLYESTER TT 0
METTLER COTTON 30/2 TT 0
METTLER QUILTING 40/3 TT 2
METTLER TOPSTITCHING 30/3 TT 2
METTLER 50/3 MERCERIZED TT 2
METTLER 60/2 MACHINE-EMB TT 0
METROSENE PLUS POLYESTER 60 TT
DUAL DUTY PLUS TT 1

Fig. 13–9 Know your threads by making a sample chart.

You can also buy plastic gadgets that attach a bobbin to a spool of thread (twisted pipe cleaners or plastic-bag ties work, too).

Hoops

The purpose of the hoop is to hold the fabric taut. In the dark ages, we used hand-embroidery hoops for machine embroidery, struggling to find ways to make them ever tauter while tilting them clumsily to fit under our needle. I've had a favorite 6" wooden hoop for fifteen years, the inner ring wrapped in masking tape which has begun to deteriorate.

But, since then, hoops have been developed expressly for machine embroidery, with spring closures that make it easy to move the hoop while you're working large areas. I prefer the smaller hoops, because they keep the fabric tauter, but when working large areas, I use larger hoops so I don't have to move the hoop so often.

The problem with spring hoops is that they are not taut enough, and they tend to pop off thick fabrics. Mary Osmus solves that problem by wrapping the inner ring with 2"-wide silk adhesive tape, available from surgical supply stores. She cuts the tape in thirds the long way and wraps it at an angle.

Judi Cull wraps an extra-large paper clip around the handles of her spring hoop, so the handles cannot open all the way. This prevents them from popping off.

People who swear by screw-type wooden hoops tighten them with a screwdriver, for extra tautness. Others file a half-moon out of the inner and outer rings to aid putting the hoop under the needle.

Scissors/Shears

I have tons of both. What's the difference? Scissors are less than 6" (15 cm) long and have equal-sized finger loops. Shears are 6" or longer and often have one finger loop shaped to accept the thumb only. Most of us use the word "scissors" as a generic term for all doodads with two blades that cut. I will, too.

No scissors are eternally sharp. Everything you cut with them dulls them slightly. But synthetic fabrics are the worst, worse even than paper. If you were extremely organized, you would

Fig. 13–10 Plastic gadgets clip onto spools of thread to match bobbins wound of that thread. I keep my bobbins in a plastic screw box, with hang tags labeling the type of thread.

have one set of scissors for cutting natural fibers only, one set for synthetics, one set for paper, and one set for decoy (no matter what you tell your family, like "You die if you touch these," they will still grab the nearest pair to open Grandma's package wrapped in strapping tape).

My favorite scissors/shears are Ginghers. I have the 4" craft scissors that cut to the very point, the 6" duckbilled applique scissors, and 8" knife-edged shears. But these are so expensive ($17 for the craft scissors) that I also have lots of others, all of which I love for different reasons. For example, I have a small pair that tip up at the end, which are perfect for cutting thread ends without cutting the needle thread while doing free-machine embroidery. These came with my New Home Memory 6000.

I encourage you to treat yourself to at least one good pair each of scissors and shears. Also visit a surgical-supply store for a variety of good scissors with strange shapes. Take care of your scissors. Wipe off the lint after each use. Oil the pivot area lightly from time to time. And if necessary, hide them.

Additional Idea
* By now, you know enough to make "December" of your fabric calendar by yourself. When you finish, wrap it up and give it to someone you love.

I could not have written this chapter without the help of many generous people and companies. Thread: Carl Jorden, Swiss-Metrosene; Meta Hoge, Coats & Clark; Mary Ann Blackburn, DMC Corporation; Doug Bolles, White

Sewing Machine Co. (Zwicky thread); Joyce Drexler, Speed Stitch (Sulky thread); Jerry Zarbaugh and Debbie Casteel, Aardvark (Natesh). Machines: Don and Rich Douglas, Douglas Fabrics; Martin Redovian, Lafayette Sewing Center; Janet Stocker, Treadleart. Needles: Henry Dubens, Dubens Sales (Schmetz needles); Don and Rich Douglas. Scissors: Clair H. Gingher, Jr., Gingher, Inc.

CHAPTER **14**

Design for the Timid

Ten years ago, in *Decorative Machine Stitchery*, I offered some facile advice in a chapter called "Adapting Designs and Developing Your Own." I cannot bring myself to repeat that advice, for I don't think it is helpful to most machine embroiderers.

Two groups of people do not need to read this chapter: (1) those who are content to adapt designs for the machine from magazines, coloring books, teachers, and advertisements; and (2) those who have an in-born feeling for color and design and who are not blocked during the process of creation.

Both of these groups are fully aware of the design tricks that I covered in the earlier book: observing techniques used on ready-to-wear clothing, especially ethnic clothes; adapting hand needlework techniques like Log Cabin to the machine; using treasuries of world design as a source, such as the many Dover books; studying natural science books for color and form; playing with lettering styles; projecting a slide on the wall or fabric; cutting and arranging paper shapes; and more.

These are design tricks that anyone can use to manipulate an image (see the end of this chapter for others).

But if you are like me, groping not only toward original design, but an original statement expressed through the machine—meaning, how I perceive my world, both interior and exterior, at this stage in my life—read on. If you are like me and find your way strewn with boulders of despair, frustration, and depression, with occasional cliffs of mental blocks, read on. I'd like to share ten years of tiny discoveries about myself as creator. I write in the hopes that something I say will encourage you on your own path.

Although I write to "you," it is the teacher in me addressing the student in me.

Discovering Your Path

First and foremost, *respect your basic urge to create*. Though you may despair that you keep producing uglies, though weeks go by without picking up a drawing tool or sitting down to the machine, though you may wonder "why bother?" if creating something original can be so painful—if your inner self propels you to create, you will be happier if you do so (and conversely, you will feel a nagging dissatisfaction if you don't).

Secondly, *trust yourself and suspend judgment*. Your first task, and it may last years and change direction often, is to find out what your eye likes. Pay attention to what you actually do and see, not to what someone has told you to do and see. For example, here are my four current eyefuls: (1) I doodle endless circles when I'm on the phone; (2) I love anything that bursts out of its boundaries—an image from its frame or flowers over their border or a play where the actors move out into the audience;

195

Fig. 14–1 Verina Warren, Stanton-in-Peak, Derbyshire, England, "Bright Flowers Amidst Grasses in Splendour Grow," approx. 14" × 12". Painted and stitched with whip stitch. Photo courtesy of the artist. See also color section.

Fig. 14–2 Detail of Verina Warren's work. Photo courtesy of the artist.

(3) as a writer, I'm naturally drawn toward lettering forms; (4) and right now I keep noticing curtains in windows.

Ladies and gentlemen, if I were asked what is the most important task of our time, I would say it is to select.(Marcel Breuer)

I write all this easily and yet it has taken me years to learn to trust myself, to trust that whatever catches my eye is worth recording, and more importantly, to suspend judgment about my attempts to record what my eye likes. Too often I have muddied my vision with the I-can'ts. "I can't draw. I can't paint. I can't stitch. My eye can't see anything interesting. I can't do this."

Freeman Patterson, author of the wonderful *Photography and the Art of Seeing*, says "Preoccupation with self is the greatest barrier to seeing and the hardest one to break." When I say to myself, *"I'm* worried about making something ugly," I'm paying too much attention to me and not enough to what my eye sees. Frederick Franck, author of *The Zen of Seeing*, calls this the Me Cramp: "too much self-concern blocks direct experience of things outside yourself."

How to overcome your Me Cramp? Do. Do again. Do yet again. And suspend judgment about the end result. Savor the doing; for now, ignore the done.

This doing requires time, in terms of awareness, not in number of hours. Merely because you've put in ten cumulative hours of searching for what-your-eye-likes does not guarantee that you'll make the *click!* of awa_ness in

your own pattern—"Oh! I seem to be attracted to circles. Why didn't I see that before?" You cannot say to yourself, "I'll practice drawing for a year and then I'll be able to draw. I'll never worry about Me again."

Instead, trust yourself. Know that if you continue to slog along, observing, recording, watching yourself, you will teach yourself what you need to know next.

But looking is not enough. You must participate in looking—by making word notes, by drawing, by collage, by photographing, by collecting pictures, by whatever method you discover works for you.

At some point you may wish to learn to draw, not as a way to render an object realistically on paper, but as a way of touching shapes, of seeing the dazzling world around you (including your dreams) in new ways. I've listed my favorite drawing books in the Bibliography, but the best book for teaching yourself to draw is *Drawing on the Right Side of the Brain* by Betty Edwards. You're never too old to learn, either. My mother, Roberta Losey Patterson, taught herself at age 64.

All of this doing requires two things: frequent practice and abundant materials.

As for the first, I recently read about a physicist who trained an electron microscope on a violin. When a string was plucked, the molecular surface of the wood began to vibrate and continued to vibrate for 24 hours. But if the string was not vibrated again, the wood became inert. Apparently, musicians know this. An instrument played daily is alive from the first moment. But an instrument not played for 24 hours is dead for the first 15 minutes.

You are fighting yourself for the first X minutes if you have not looked, drawn, painted, stitched for some time. Yet the more often you work, the more you and your tools resonate.

If your schedule is packed, you will have to find ways to free time. One way is to write on the calendar exactly when you plan to work ("M–W–F, 7:30–9:30 pm, resonate"). Another is to leave your materials out where you can see them. Use the old Hemingway trick of always stopping in the middle of a piece (I often quit stitching with the needle down in the fabric) so that the momentum of working and the urge to complete make it easy to work the next day. For some, the best way to free time is to take a class (as long as it does not interfere with trusting yourself, suspending judgment, and finding out what your eye likes). Finally, always carry a note-

Fig. 14–3 Merry Bean Muse made for Robbie Fanning. She leans against Cloud 9 and carries a sewing machine and a notebook with pencil. She has another fright wig for those days when Robbie feels like a witch.

198

book and pen with you. Even the busiest person can squeeze in five minutes here and there of recording what she sees.

Frequent practice is essential to finding what your eye likes, as are abundant materials. You need as many good art materials as you can afford. I used to draw on paper torn from steno pads with blue ball point, but I'm so much more sensuously involved in drawings on good art paper made with my Size 2 Rapidograph.

I've come to realize that "Believe in yourself" means "Spend money on yourself." You deserve the best you can afford, because it will inspire you to do more. Of course you *can* work with any material you have—from drawing with a stick in the sand to sewing on a $98 machine with cheap white thread on 59 cent muslin made in Taiwan. But as in cooking, the results are not as pleasing as, say, pesto made with basil from the garden, freshly grated parmesan, pine nuts, extra-virgin cold-pressed olive oil, and freshmade noodles.

I am my own worst enemy sometimes. I will plan to work and I will have abundant materials, but they will be all over my workplace. I tend not to want to work unless my work area is friendly and approachable. Yet I continue to pile junk all over the surface until my work area disappears (a definite metaphor for my mind). I must periodically—often, daily—clear the clutter or I can't and don't work.

I also need easy access to my raw materials: fabric squares cut to standard sizes; machine threaded and ready; lots of drawing, graph, and construction paper, pens and rulers, ready to grab.

At this point, you've trusted your basic urge to create and started paying attention to what your eye likes, which I'll call your theme. In the process, if you've stayed alert to your own patterns, you've discovered something important: *you are your own best teacher.*

Alexander believes strongly that we learn by doing things, by following an example, by trial and error. This belief follows from his notion that all matter in the universe is created out of "mind stuff," that it has an organic predisposition to fall into order and that if we watch and listen carefully we can align our efforts with that order. (From CoEvolution Quarterly, fall 1984, referring to Christopher Alexander, author of "A Pattern Language.")

Everything you need to know for the next stage of your journey as creator is inside you, if you pay attention. It may be as simple as realizing that your drawings need dark and light areas. It may be realizing you are ignoring the negative space in your designs. Or it may be realizing that you are afraid of color. But step by faltering step, the more you create, the more you will reveal to yourself what you need to know next. Then what?

How you conquer what you need to know next depends on your style of learning. For you, it may be to take a class, to be guided in a systematic way by an experienced teacher. For me, it is

> **Design as process, and design as product, encompass practically any aspect of life. Design can be urban design or architectural design or product design or dressmaking, but it can also be cooking or singing or making war or making love. (Hans Holbein)**

slower and more painful—but it's my best way. Someone outside could easily hand me a list: "Here are the principles of design and here are the elements of design. Do this and that and then you will know everything." But I seem to need to experience both the chaos of not-knowing and the subsequent uncovering of one or two parts of knowing, as if in order to toddle, I need to fall down a hundred times before I can shakily stand and say, "Oh, I see: *this* is what works!"

It helps me to teach myself by keeping track of my journey in a visual and written diary. It also helps me to read books, though the ones with the information in condensed form are often too rich for me to digest yet. Someday I'll be ready for them. I keep only one or two currently inspiring books on my worktable (the rest are elsewhere). Any more would overload my mind.

But my best way of teaching myself is to make analogies between what I know well and confidently and what I know half-well and insecurely. For me, what I know well is writing. I know how to assemble disparate parts into a coherent whole. But it could as easily

be what I know about playing soccer on a team or putting together a meal or planting a garden. I can transfer what I know well in one area to what I need to know as creator. You can, too.

Some of you may remain in this state of grace forever, happily drawing, noodling, experimenting, doing. But some may want to move on to another level, one that is even more demanding: taking a theme, examining it from all sides, rearranging the parts into a new whole, stitching the results, and opening yourself to outside judgment about your piece. If you are driven to make such a piece, a statement about how you perceive the world today, read on.

First, *you must research your theme.* This point seems to be a watershed.

> **Every subject has so many attractions that I tend to work through them producing small embroidery samples. This approach gets the initial superficial ideas out of the way. Never having a preconceived idea of how the subject will be embroidered, indeed it may never get to that stage at all, I just enjoy the drawing and developing process, letting the idea progress towards the moment when only a tactile treatment of some kind will satisfy. (Jean Mould in "Embroidery" magazine, Autumn 1984)**

Some people will copy in fabric and thread exactly what they have recorded in ink. Others will plunge in, stitching the blank fabric. Unless you have tons of experience or are a natural artist, you are likely to produce either a cliched image or an ugly piece. You will disappoint yourself.

That's because you haven't worked hard enough yet. You need to go out into the world and find subject matter that expresses your theme. Where do circles appear in your sewing area, in your home, in your backyard, in your neighborhood? Where do circles natu-

rally occur in nature, in architecture, in life? What does the circle mean in ethnic cultures, in myth, in religion, in science? What other shapes are related to circles? When is a circle not a circle? How do circles show up in your dreams, in everyday language, in children's games?

You won't answer all these questions in one embroidery piece, but you may tackle one or two in a series of pieces, trying to express some aspect of how you perceive "circle" today.

In the process of research, you may run across someone else's art that per-

Fig. 14–4 Sas Colby, Oakland, CA, "Heart Book." Each fabric page relates to the heart theme. Here is the Queen of Hearts. Collection of Robbie Fanning.

fectly expresses what you want to say about circles. Should you give up? Should you copy it?

In *Banners and Flags*, Margot Carter Blair says:

> Copying another's work is wrong only when we attach our own name to it, or claim credit for the idea. Good ideas are worth repeating, and sometimes they act as a catalyst toward new directions and ideas.
>
> As a beginner or an experienced textile designer, it is worthwhile to find work we like and relate it to our own experience. If we take the time to study each element and decide why it works, we can re-create the experience of the original designer. And, in this way, we can learn a great deal about the methods of composition and the techniques used by the original artist.

Lots of people copy, lots of people don't copy. I copy. I find it teaches me things and above all it gives me consolation. (Vincent Van Gogh)

When you have researched your theme, *organize the information you've gathered* — that is, design it. This is where you can play tricks with the images you've recorded. Basically, you're playing the game of What-If: what if I cut this circle into strips and stagger them? What if I superimpose this circle on this landscape? What if I repeat the silhouette of this thread spool in a circle?

But when it comes time to design the final piece, ask yourself three questions:

1. What mood do I want the piece to have? Serenity, excitement, lushness, peacefulness, humor, drama, mystery, danger. Your selection of colors, shapes, lines, textures, light/dark, materials, and technique will depend on your answer.

2. What's the one thing I want a viewer to notice in this piece? It might be a startling combination of colors or graceful shapes or a certain texture. But in order to emphasize one thing, you need to contrast it with something else. Some of your choices are dark/light, warm/cold, high/low, big/little, formal/informal, symmetric/asymmetric, hard/soft, shiny/matte.

3. How will I integrate the interior design area with the overall shape? Some of your choices are to make the design fill almost the entire area; to use a patterned background, which acts as a transition between edge and design; to surround the main element with lines of color or texture (e.g., quilting, satin stitch, straight stitch) that connect the design to the edge; to repeat shapes or colors with slight variations; to overlay fabric or threads over the entire design; to work a complicated design in only one stitch or texture or direction; to employ an underlying grid structure, as in quilts.

If you've stitched something that disappoints you, try to ask these same questions about the piece. You may learn what you need to correct in the next version. This is admittedly difficult, to see our own work with objectivity. To train yourself, practice dissecting work you admire until you can describe it like an art critic: "The organizing principle in this piece is pattern, achieved by the repetition of shapes formed by trapunto. The basic square grid, stacked four cubes wide by eight high, is varied by two rows extended to the right of the piece by nine cubes in which the square is bisected by a diagonal line."

Easier than words, of course, is to sketch what you like, "describing" a piece visually.

It also helps to let a piece sit for awhile. Hang it or set it where you can eye it from time to time. You can also view it upside down, in a mirror, or with a reducing lens or the wrong end of binoculars. Removing the color also helps, so photocopy the piece or photograph it in black-and-white (a Polaroid camera would be handy). All will help you gain some distance from your work.

Beyond this, I cannot offer any more or it would be the blind leading the blind. As for me, I am trying to work small and uncomplicated pieces, often limiting myself to one technique or color or texture. I like what Barbara Smith taught me: K.I.S.S. Keep it simple, stupid. I need to be less niggling and more bold in my approach, which I'm learning by cutting things up, tearing shapes, manipulating my initial images. Sometimes I give myself permission to make something intentionally ugly, to make something bad, for in order to know what is bad, I must recognize what's good. My work is telling me that I need to explore color theory more systematically and to think about how the piece will be displayed before I begin working, instead of after.

My bouts of frustration and despair are less frequent, as long as I keep working. When they occur, I try to *do*, not think about doing. For I have found that doing is magic. Once I plunge in and keep going, I astonish myself with what I produce.

So my final word to you is:

Another month into the stitching and it became drastically apparent that something is wrong with the design. It is much too busy, there is no relief! So a review of what I'm doing is in order. I followed as many of the rules of good design as I know ...balancing darks with lights, large with small, tying the design together with two main colors, and balancing that against elements that combine colors no two alike in the same combinations. Plus sparkling it all over with whites and lights to let the design "breathe." (Beverly Dieringer, "Needlepoint News," July-August 1980)

Checklist of Design Tricks
* Repeat the same-size motif in rows or by rotating it 360 degrees or by flopping the motif upside-down.

* Repeat the motif in different sizes, perhaps overlapping some.
* Cut up the motif and rearrange the parts (strips, exploded fragments, etc.).
* Place the motif on a patterned background, perhaps a smaller or larger version of the motif.
* Work the negative shapes around the motif.
* Use tracing paper to superimpose images on each other (e.g., your drawing over a magazine page).
* Distort the proportions of your image—blow up, reduce, elongate, etc. (Projecting with a slide projector or opaque projector makes this easy.)
* Make the motif fit a shape (circle, square, rectangle, diamond).
* I recommend that you read all the good books on design listed in the Bibliography.

Part II

GIFTS FOR FAMILY AND FRIENDS

Note: The brand names I used for supplies are in parentheses
in materials lists.

Sewing-Machine Cover

Dust and lint are the enemies of your machine. Be kind: make covers for all your machines. I can never remember what size needle is in the machine, so I put a dial on the front of my sewing-machine covers, pointing to the last size needle used. I stitched a plastic 35 mm slide sleeve to the cover in which to store needle cases.

$^3/_4$ yd (.7 m) prequilted or heavy fabric
2 packages (3 yds or 2.7 m each) double-fold bias tape

1 plastic 35 mm slide sleeve (optional)
Nonfrayable fabric scraps (Ultrasuede and felt)
Graph paper, pen, scissors

1. Measure the height of your machine. If you leave a flat-bed extension on it most of the time, measure from the needle plate to the top of the machine. Measure the width of your machine. Make a paper rectangle the height and width of your machine plus 1" (2.5 cm) on each side. Trace the

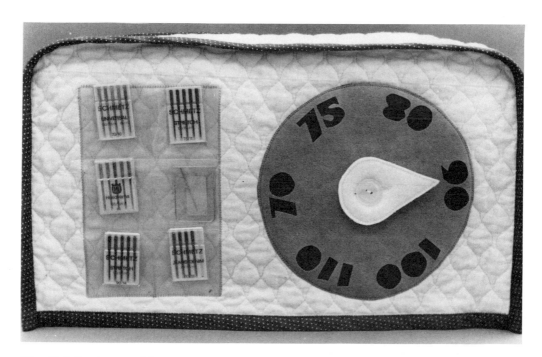

Fig. II–1 Sewing machine cover.

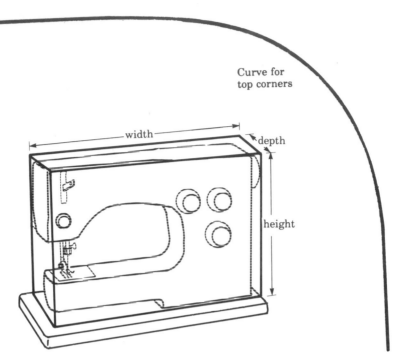

Curve for top corners

width

depth

height

Fig. II–2 Cut pattern pieces to fit your machine.

curve in Fig. II-2 on the two upper corners.

2. Using your paper pattern, cut out two rectangles of prequilted fabric. These will be the front and back of the sewing-machine cover. For the connecting piece of fabric that corresponds to the depth of your machine, cut a strip of fabric 6" (15 cm) wide and as long as two heights plus one width of your paper pattern.

3. Embellish the front part of your sewing-machine cover. (I cut numbers from a circle of Ultrasuede corresponding to the European needle sizes. I placed the Ultrasuede over red felt and zigzagged both to the prequilted fabric. Then I sewed a button into the middle of the circle by machine and buttoned a felt dial to it.)

4. Sew the 6" (15 cm) wide strip to the front and back fabric pieces in a $\frac{1}{2}$" (1.3 cm) seam allowance. Cover the seams by sewing the bias binding over them.

Jane's Tote with Pillow

The older I get, the sorer I get whenever I have to sit for any length of time. I needed a tote with a small padded pillow inside, to be carried to volleyball games, classes, lectures — wherever seats become harder with each passing moment. When my bottom starts to ache, I pull out the pillow and sit on it. This tote is made of sturdy canvas and embellished with shisha. (Tote designed and made by Jane Warnick. See Chapter 5 for her discoveries made while stitching the bag.)

- $1/2$ yd (46 cm) 44" (112 cm) wide sturdy fabric such as canvas
- 1 yd (91 cm) 44" (112 cm) wide pre-quilted fabric for pockets, lining, and pillow
- two 12" (30.5 cm) squares of comfort-type batting
- 1 spool extra-fine machine-embroidery thread (Natesh)

Fig. II–3 Jane's tote with pillow.

Heavyweight thread for bag construction (Dual Duty)
Shisha: 5 small, 3 medium, 2 large
Jean needle (16(100) 705 H-J)
Iron

1. To make the bag straps, fold the fabric, selvages together. Press the fold in place. Cut off 3" (7.6 cm) parallel to the selvages. Press in the raw edge 1" (2.5 cm) the long way. Press the selvage over the raw edge, forming a 1" (2.5 cm) wide strap. Topstitch along both edges; then stitch two more times between the lines of stitching for reinforcement.

2. Measure $2^1/_2$" (6.3 cm) from the bottom fold of the remaining fabric. Make a clip on each side of the fabric. This marks the 5" (12.7 cm) bottom of the bag. Turn in 3" (7.6 cm) along both long sides of the fabric and press. This defines the area for stitchery (Fig. II-4).

3. Decorate the bag front and/or back as you wish. Jane cut circles of construction paper and moved them around the bag until she liked the placement. Then she made shisha flowers.

4. Make two pockets for the back side of the tote from the pre-quilted fabric. One is short for keys; one is long for glasses. Cut the short pocket 8" x 5" (20 cm × 12.7 cm); cut the glasses pocket 7" × 14" (18 cm × 36 cm). Fold the short pocket in half to 4" x 5" (10 cm × 12.7 cm) and sew a $^1/_2$" (1.3 cm) seam. Move the seam to the center and press it open (Fig. II-5). Stitch across one end in a $^1/_2$" (1.3 cm) seam, trim corners, and turn rightsides out. Press. For the glasses pocket, bring the 7" (18 cm) ends together and stitch a $^1/_2$" (1.3 cm) seam. Move the seam to the center and press open. Stitch across one end in a $^1/_2$" (1.3 cm) seam, trim corners, and turn rightsides out. Press. For each pocket, turn in the remaining open side $^1/_2$" (1.3 cm) and press. Now position

the pockets on the back side of the tote: measure 3" (7.6 cm) above the clip for the bottom of the bag. The stitched ends of the pockets are parallel to the sides of the bag. Topstitch the two pockets in place.

5. For the lining, cut a piece of prequilted fabric to the same size (18" x 38" or 46 cm × 97 cm) as the bag. Fold it in half and mark the bottom with clips, $2^1/_2$" (6.4 cm) up from the fold, as you did in Step 2. If you would like pockets inside your bag, construct them as in Step 4.

6. Turn under $^1/_2$" (1.3 cm) at the top of the bag and press. Then open the pressed edges out. Rightsides together, sew the side seams of the bag in a $^3/_8$" (1 cm) seam. Press open. Repeat Step 6 for the lining.

7. To box the bottom corners, fold one side seam so that it lies along the bottom fold in the fabric (Fig. II-6). Extend a line on either side of the clips in the side seam perpendicular to the side seam. Stitch along this line. Repeat for the second seam line. Then do the same with the lining. Turn the bag rightside out. Pin the triangle against the bottom of the bag and then stitch it in place to make a sturdy bottom for the bag.

8. With the upper edge of the bag opened out, pin a handle in an arc 4" (10 cm) on either side of the center line of the bag, raw edges of handles and bag even (Fig. II-7). Be certain the selvage-edge side of the handle will point down when you carry the bag. Repeat with the second handle on the other side of the bag. Stitch handles to bag along the ironed creases. Open out handles, forcing $^1/_2$" (1.3 cm) pressed edge at top of bag to fold inside.

9. Press again the crease along the sides of the bag and the bottom. Topstitch creases $^1/_8$" (3 cm) from the edge.

10. Turn top of lining in $^1/_2$" (1.3 cm)

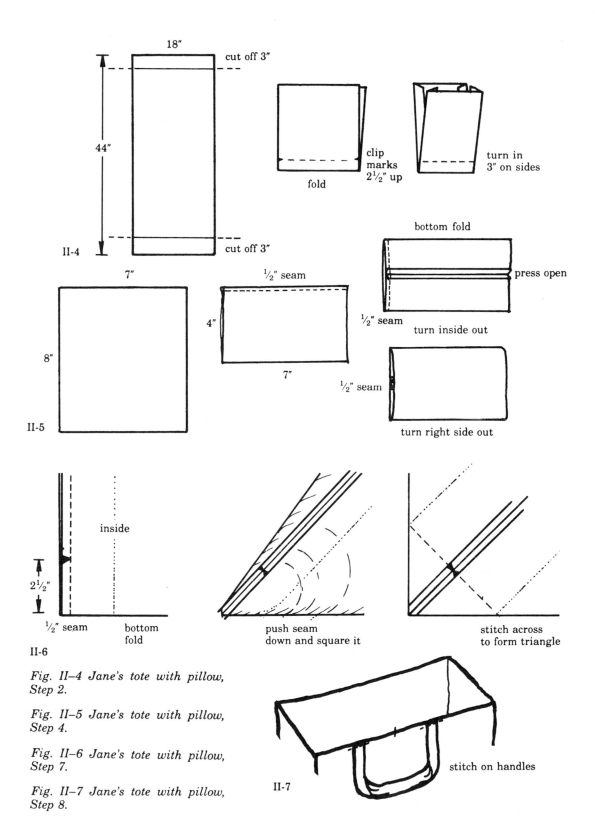

18″

cut off 3″

44″

II-4

cut off 3″

fold

clip
marks
2½″ up

turn in
3″ on sides

7″

8″

II-5

½″ seam

4″

7″

½″ seam

bottom fold

press open

½″ seam

turn inside out

½″ seam

turn right side out

inside

2½″

½″ seam

bottom
fold

II-6

push seam
down and square it

stitch across
to form triangle

Fig. II–4 Jane's tote with pillow,
Step 2.

Fig. II–5 Jane's tote with pillow,
Step 4.

Fig. II–6 Jane's tote with pillow,
Step 7.

Fig. II–7 Jane's tote with pillow,
Step 8.

II-7

stitch on handles

and sew close to edge. You still haven't turned the lining rightside out — and you shouldn't. Slip the lining inside the tote, wrong sides together, matching side seams. Stitch the tops together along the same line you previously stitched the lining.

11. To make the pillow, cut two 12" (30.5 cm) squares of pre-quilted fabric and two 12" squares of comfort-type batting. Place the fabric, rightsides together, on top of the double layer of batting and pin all layers together. In a ½" (1.3 cm) seam, stitch 3½ sides. Trim batting close to stitching. Trim corners. Turn rightside out. Tuck in the open edge ½" (1.3 cm). Stitch ¼" (6 cm) from the edge all the way around, to give the effect of piping.

PROJECT 3

Betty's Soft Box

Betty Mason developed this soft box. It is perfect for storing presser feet. I use the walking foot to stitch through thick layers of fabric and batting without the

Fig. II–8 Betty's soft box.

danger of layers creeping. (Directions reprinted with permission.)

½ yd (46 cm) each, outer fabric and lining
1 yd (91 cm) of 6–8 oz quilt batting
2 pieces of ribbon about 6" (15 cm) long
Graph paper, pen, ruler, glue, cardboard or acetate
Ordinary thread (Dual Duty)

1. Cut a 5" (12.7 cm) square of graph paper. Glue to cardboard or acetate and cut out for a template.

2. As shown in Fig. II-9, draw around the template on the right side of the outside fabric. The drawn line is your sewing line. Sew around the outside edges of the box with a short straight stitch. Embellish the right side of the fabric any way you wish (Betty put shisha mirrors and a message on the outside and the inside).

3. Turn the outside fabric over and place it rightsides against the lining fabric. Pin securely. Adding a ¼" (6

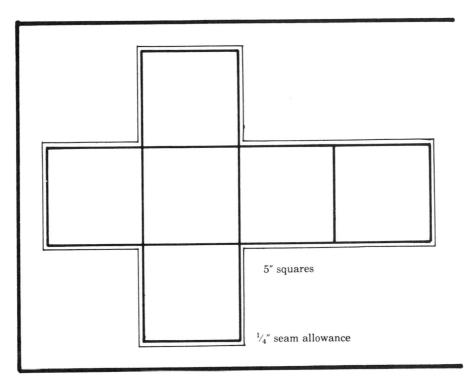

5″ squares

¼″ seam allowance

Fig. II–9 Betty's soft box, Step 2.

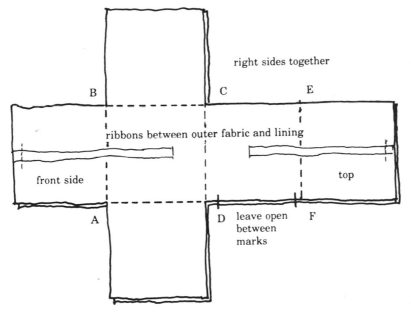

right sides together

B   C   E

ribbons between outer fabric and lining

front side   top

A   D leave open F
between
marks

Fig. II–10 Betty's soft box, Step 3.

mm) seam allowance around the stitched line of the box, cut out the two layers of fabric. Do not unpin the fabric, but insert one ribbon between the two layers of the lid end, making raw edges of ribbon and fabric even. Insert the second ribbon between the two layers of the front side (Fig. II-10).

4. Leaving the fabric pinned together, lay them on top of a double layer of batting, the wrong side of the lining against the batting. Cut the batting to the same shape as the fabric. You now have a double layer of batting pinned to the box fabric.

5. Sew around the box through all layers on the same line of stitching you already made, leaving open a portion as shown in Fig. II-10 for turning rightside out. Clip across corners. Clip into corners to release the seam, so that you can turn the box rightside out without puckers.

6. Turn rightside out. Push corners out with the eraser end of a pencil. Slip-stitch opening closed. Stitch the bottom square of the box (A to B to C to D), as well as from E to F to form a lid. Bring slides up to meet each other and whip stitch sides together.

PROJECT 4

The Flop Box

The flop box is a clever hexagon designed by Jackie Dodson and Pat Pasquini. The sides of the box are not connected. When the tie is undone, the box flops open flat to reveal a padded interior with ribbons to hold down your scissors and other sewing supplies. It can also be a jewelry box, cosmetics case, or wedding ring box.

The top of the box offers an opportunity to use some of those small stitched samples you've never made into anything. Jackie decorated the top of this one with linen threads over chamois, suede, and Ultrasuede. She added turquoise beads and porcupine quills, as well as beads made from dried carrots. Directions reprinted with permission of P.J. (very) Ltd.

Heavyweight (8-ply) poster board, available at office-supply stores: 11" × 22" (28 cm × 56 cm)

Fabrics for the outside and inside of the box: 18" (46 cm) square piece for each

1 yd (91) cm $1/4$" (6 mm) grosgrain ribbon for outside

$1\,1/4$ yd (115 cm) 1" (2.5 cm) grosgrain ribbon for inside

12" x 24" (30.5 cm × 61 cm) piece of bonded batting

Heavy craft glue (Velverette or Tacky)

6 $1/2$" (1.3 cm) plastic rings (available at sewing stores)

Hobby knife (X-acto)

Wooden popsicle stick, fingernail file

Fig. II–11 Flop box.

Sewing needle, transparent thread, scissors, dressmaker pins, 12 clip clothespins, ruler, pencil, Wash 'n Dri's

1. For the outer part of the box (called the "exterior"), you will cover two large poster board hexagons with fabric over batting. Then you will cover six poster board rectangles (called "exterior walls"), with fabric over batting. For the inner part of the box (called the "interior"), you will cover two different poster board hexagons, slightly smaller than the exterior hexagons, with lining fabric over padding. Then you will cover six small poster board rectangles (called "interior walls"), slightly smaller than the exterior walls, with lining fabric over padding. The 1" (2.5 cm) ribbon will be included in this last part.

2. Using Fig. II-12, make paper patterns for six sizes of hexagons as indicated by A-F in Fig. II-12. Carefully cut out poster board shapes using the hobby knife. When you are done, you will have 12 poster board rectangles ("walls") in two sizes and four poster board hexagons in three sizes. Cut batting to fit each poster board piece, except for the bottom exterior piece (the box would not sit flat if it were padded). Except for the top exterior fabric, which has a $7/8$" (2.2 cm) seam allowance, cut outside fabric $5/8$" (1.6 cm) larger than the exterior poster board pieces. Cut lining fabric $5/8$" (1.6 cm) larger than the interior poster board pieces.

3. Embellish the exterior top fabric of the flop box as you wish. Assemble each piece as shown in Fig. II-14.

4. Gluing Tips. Since this project requires a lot of gluing, here are some tips. Neatness is the key. Use a wooden popsicle stick for spreading glue. A fingernail file helps fold fabric over cardboard while gluing. When applying

215

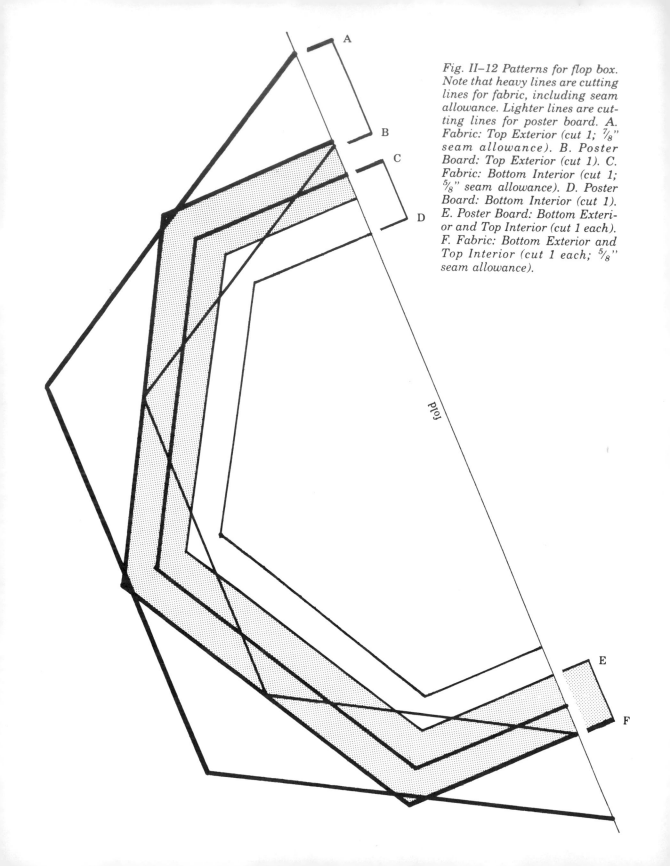

Fig. II–12 Patterns for flop box. Note that heavy lines are cutting lines for fabric, including seam allowance. Lighter lines are cutting lines for poster board. A. Fabric: Top Exterior (cut 1; ⅞" seam allowance). B. Poster Board: Top Exterior (cut 1). C. Fabric: Bottom Interior (cut 1; ⅝" seam allowance). D. Poster Board: Bottom Interior (cut 1). E. Poster Board: Bottom Exterior and Top Interior (cut 1 each). F. Fabric: Bottom Exterior and Top Interior (cut 1 each; ⅝" seam allowance).

fold

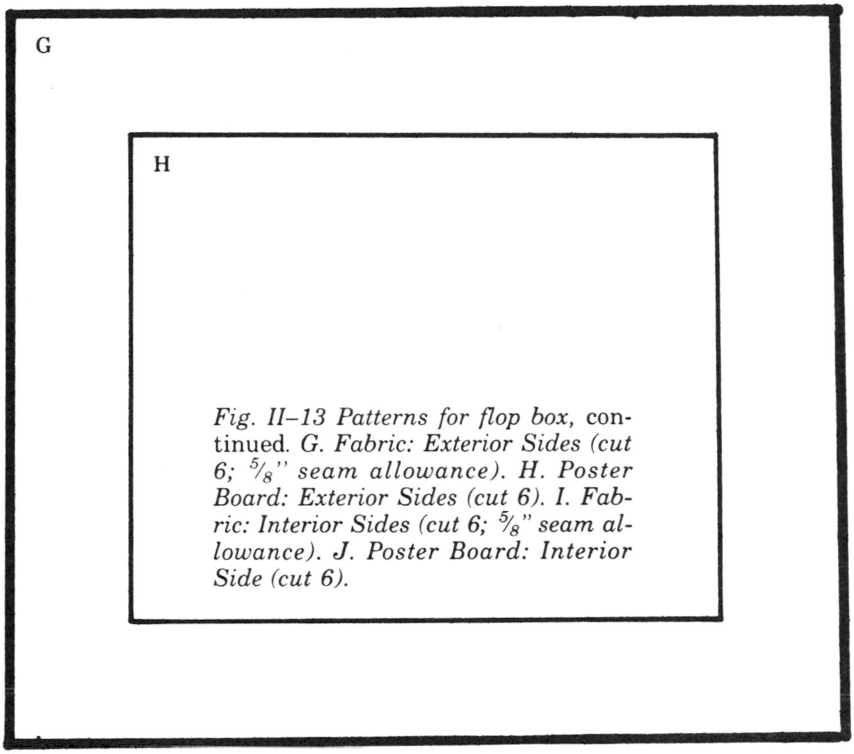

G

H

Fig. II–13 Patterns for flop box, continued. *G. Fabric: Exterior Sides (cut 6; ⅝" seam allowance). H. Poster Board: Exterior Sides (cut 6). I. Fabric: Interior Sides (cut 6; ⅝" seam allowance). J. Poster Board: Interior Side (cut 6).*

II-13

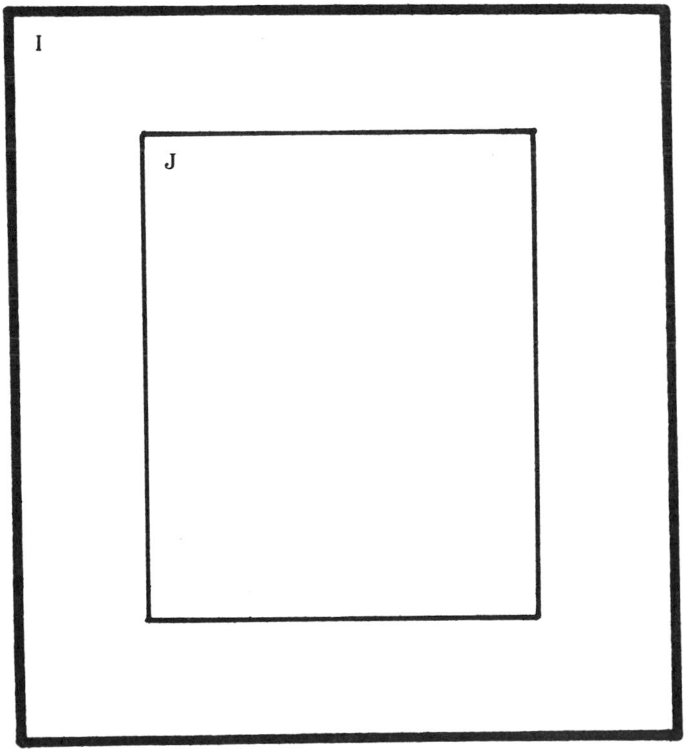

You'll have these pieces:

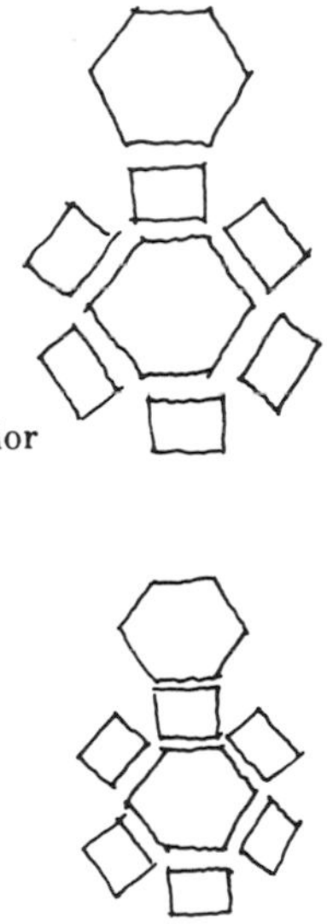

Exterior

I

J

Lining

II-14

Fig. II–14 How the flop box goes together.

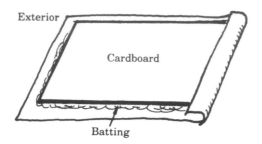

Exterior

Cardboard

Batting

Fig. II–15 Padding and covering the poster board

glue to lining fabric, all of the $^5/_8$" (1.6 cm) allowance may be covered with glue as it will be hidden. When applying glue to outside fabric, however, glue only at the very edge of the fabric turnover, as some of that turnover will be visible. Pull the fabric tight enough so that it doesn't pucker, but not so tight that it bows the poster board. Dry glued pieces under the weight of books.

Place a dab of glue on the cardboard to keep the batting from moving. Then paint the underside of the fabric in the $^5/_8$" (1.6 cm) allowance and glue it over the batting and the cardboard (Fig. II-15). Use a clip clothespin to hold the fabric until the glue sets. Work oppo-

site sides and pull snugly. You do not need to miter the edges unless you are working with heavy fabric, but tuck a neat point. Complete all pieces, but remember not to pad the exterior bottom piece (pad the interior lining piece, however).

5. Cut the 1" (2.5 cm) ribbon into six 4" (10 cm) pieces. Center each ribbon on the length of an interior lining piece and take the ends to the back of the poster board. Glue the ends past the lining fabric on the back, so they will anchor on the poster board.

6. Now prepare to glue the interior lining pieces of the walls to the exterior pieces. Reserve one lining wall piece and one exterior wall piece for later. For the remaining five walls, spread glue near the edges on the backs of the interior walls and center each interior wall on an exterior wall. Clip together with clothespins until dry.

7. Cut the 1" (2.5 cm) ribbon into two 8" (20 cm) pieces. Crisscross the ribbon across the box top lining piece as shown in Fig. II-11. Glue edges to the back of the poster board.

8. Cut the remaining 1" (2.5 cm) ribbon into two 2" (5 cm) pieces. Cut the

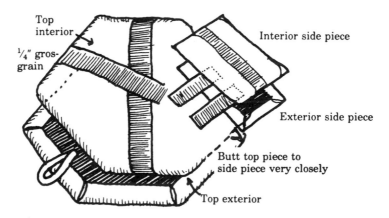

Top interior

$^1/_4$" grosgrain

Interior side piece

Exterior side piece

Butt top piece to side piece very closely

Top exterior

Fig. II–16 Assembling the flop box.

¼" (6 mm)) ribbon into two pieces, one 3" (7.6 cm) long and one 33" (84 cm) long. Loop the 3" (7.6 cm) narrow ribbon in half and position it where you want the front of the embellished hexagon. Glue the ends of the looped ribbon to the underside of the top exterior hexagon, anchoring the ends to the poster board, not to the fabric. Place the two 2" (5 cm) lengths of ribbon on the side opposite the looped ribbon. Glue in place for use as a hinge, with 1" (2.5 cm) extending out over the edge of the hexagon (Fig. II-16).

9. Now glue the top lining piece over the inside of the top exterior piece, as you did in step 6.

10. Take the last unassembled wall set. Butt the exterior side wall to the side of the top hexagon where the rib-bon hinges hang out. Glue ribbon hinges to the wrong side of the wall exterior piece. Then glue the lining piece over the wall exterior piece, securing the ribbon hinges in between. Allow to dry thoroughly.

11. Fit walls of box, including the one attached to the top piece, to the bottom piece and sew by hand with a whip stitch and invisible thread. Sew at the bottom hexagon edges only, not along the sides of the walls.

12. Sew a plastic ring to one side edge of each wall piece. Using the remaining 33" (84 cm) narrow ribbon, lace through all the rings and draw the sides up to form a flop box. Tie bow and flip the lid into position. You can now outfit your flop box and give it to a friend.

PROJECT 5

A Simple Thank You

This easy hanging incorporates the name of the person you wish to thank in the outside edge. Mine is for Don and Rich Douglas of Douglas Fabrics, Palo Alto, CA, for 20 years of sewing help. You can also arrange the flower petals in three smaller flowers of six petals each.

14" × 18" (36 cm × 46 cm) green felt
¼ yd (23 cm) each, petal fabric and petal lining or scraps (my satin lingerie scraps are from Lore Lingerie—see Supply List)

2 scraps for flower centers, big enough for a machine-embroidery hoop (one should be the same color as the petals and will be hidden; the other will be a contrasting color and have "thank you" written on it)
Machine-embroidery hoop
Teflon pressing sheet and fusible webbing
2 plastic rings (available in sewing stores)
1" × 13" (2.5 cm × 33 cm) strip of iron-on interfacing
Extra-fine machine-embroidery thread (Zwicky)

Fig. II–17 A simple thank you.

Graph paper, water-soluble pencil, heat-transfer pencil, iron, pencil, scissors, pinking shears

1. Warm the graph paper with the iron. Copy the petal shape (Fig. II-18) onto the graph paper with the heat transfer pencil. On the back side of the lining, transfer the petal shape 18 times, leaving $\frac{1}{2}$" (1.3 cm) between petals.

2. Place the lining rightsides together with the petal fabric. Pin in the middle of each petal. Using a short stitch, sew around the curved edge of the petal, leaving the base unsewn. Use the pinking shears to cut out the petals with a $\frac{1}{4}$" (6 mm) seam allowance. The pinking shears automatically clip the curves. Turn petals rightside out and press.

3. Make two small tucks pointing toward the center of the base of each petal. These tucks will make the base measure about $\frac{3}{4}$" (1.9 cm). Sew $\frac{1}{4}$" (6 mm) from the base of each petal to secure the tucks. Sew six petals at a time, without breaking the threads between them.

4. Draw a $2\frac{1}{2}$" (6.4 cm) diameter circle on the contrasting colored flower-center fabric. Write "thank you" in handwriting script with the water-soluble pen $\frac{1}{2}$" (1.3 cm) from the edge of the circle. Put the fabric in the hoop and free-machine embroider "thank you," connecting the words with a design of leaves (I used an automatic stitch).

5. On the other flower-center fabric, draw a $4\frac{1}{2}$" (11.4 cm) diameter circle. Mark the center of the circle with the

220

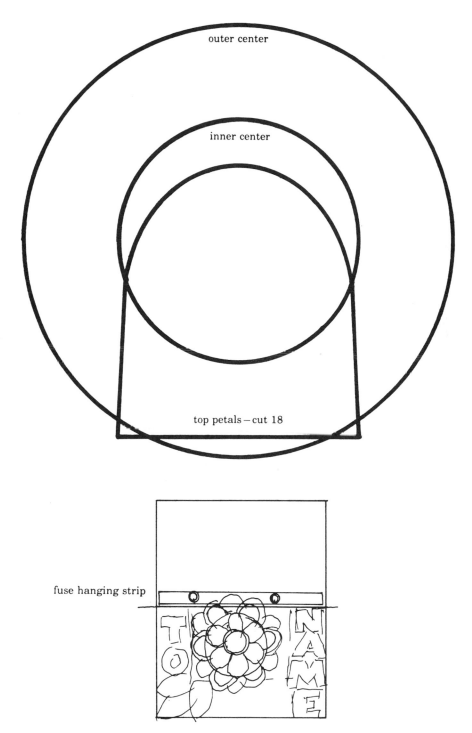

outer center

inner center

top petals — cut 18

fuse hanging strip

T O

N A M E

Fig. II–18 Simple thank you flower pattern.

water-soluble pen. Using the Teflon pressing sheet, fuse the backs of both flower centers. Cut them out on the drawn lines.

6. Fold the green felt in half so it measures 14" × 9" (36 cm × 23 cm). Press fold. Open out the green felt and place it underside up. Center the strip of iron-on interfacing along one side of the fold and fuse it, to strengthen the edge.

7. With the green felt opened flat and the fused edge of the fold away from you, mark a flower center $2^1/_2$" (6.4 cm) down from the fold and centered between the side edges. Arrange 12 flower petals (two groups of six petals) in a circle around the marked flower center. The bases of each petal should be touching. Pin the petals in place and stitch them to the green felt with a zigzag. Lay the larger circle of fabric you prepared in step 5 over the petals and fuse, using the Teflon sheet to protect the petals. Then stitch it in place with a zigzag. Place the remaining six petals in a circle around the center. Pin and then zigzag in place. Fuse the remaining circle over the petals and then stitch the edge in a satin stitch. Free-machine embroider stamens in the cen-ters of each of the petals on top, as well as on the spaces between these petals.

8. By machine, sew the two plastic rings $^1/_4$" (6 mm) from the fold, on the rightside of the interfaced strip and 4" (10 cm) from each side. Fold the felt in half, wrong sides together, and pin edges. Some of the petals will extend above the fold.

9. Cut 2" (5 cm) strips of graph paper. In block letters, plan the message you want to write along the outside edges. Mine says "To Don & Rich" with my name and the date written on the petals at the lower left corner. When you are satisfied with your letters, pin them in place 1" (2.5 cm) in from the edges. Cut three leaves from graph paper and pin them 1" (2.5 cm) in from the lower left edge of the felt. Straight stitch through the paper, tearing it off when you are finished. I free-machine embroidered the centers of the O, D, and R. I also free-machine embroidered my name and date in the centers of the leaves. With sharp scissors, trim the outside edges of the felt close to the stitching. If you wish, cut out the centers of letters. Surprise your friends with your simple thank you.

PROJECT 6

The One-Hour Gift

Our friends were coming for dinner near the holidays and suddenly I realized they would be bringing us a gift. I needed something to give in return, something that could be made in an hour. I had already made challah bread for them, so I decided to make a special bread warmer for it. The lettering function of my new computer machine made the bread warmer a bit more special

Fig. II–19 One-hour gift. Collection of Maggie Bounds and Steve Sokolow, Santa Cruz, CA.

Fig. II–20 Close-up of lettering: "Maggie and Steve."

(you could free-machine embroider a similar message).

> 23" × 20" (58 cm × 50.8 cm) piece each, fabric and lining (I used flannel for the lining)
> Extra-fine machine-embroidery thread (DMC Size 30)
> Ribbon
> Water-soluble pen, ruler

1. Cut the fabric and lining. Place right sides together and sew around three and one-half sides with a $^1/_2$" (1.3 cm) seam allowance. Clip corners and turn rightsides out. Press. Press open area inside. Topstitch around entire bread warmer.

2. Fold the warmer in half across the 19" (48 cm) length. Press lightly and open. Draw two lines on each side of the center line, each 3" (7.6 cm) away from each other. This makes five lines.

3. Program your machine to write the names of the recipients over and over. Loosen top and bobbin tensions slightly and practice on a test cloth. Stitch the names on the two outer lines. Program your machine to write a message from you, with the date, for the center line. Decorate the remaining two lines with an automatic stitch.

4. Wrap the bread in the warmer, secured with the ribbon, and answer the doorbell.

PROJECT 7

Get-Well Envelope

We have all been touched by the kindness of neighbors and friends at times when we are ill or in distress. The smallest thoughtful gesture means so much to someone who is ill or in a hospital — an unexpected visit or phone call, a gaggle of bright balloons, a stack of good magazines, a note. This get-well envelope will mean more to your loved ones because you took the time to make it.

The envelope is cheerful and simple to make. You can tuck small goodies inside (a card, chocolate, a little present). Since the bag and lining are one piece of fabric, its construction is easy. You can make several at once, through step 8 below, adding the final personalizing stitching when you are ready to send the envelope. (Designed and made by Jackie Dodson.)

> Sturdy fabric about 13" (33 cm) square (Trigger)
> Iron-on interfacing about 15" (38 cm) square
> Fusible webbing and Teflon pressing sheet
> Transparent thread
> Fine gold thread
> Extra-fine machine-embroidery thread
> Fabrics to be embellished (gold lame, yellow and peach organdy, peach transparent curtain material, red chiffon, red mesh bag, gold veiling)

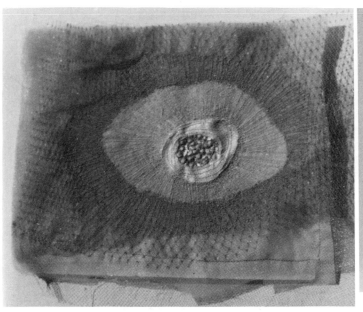

Fig. II–21 Get-well envelope.

Cording for edge (optional)
Ruler, disappearing pen, tracing paper, scissors

1. First embellish the window that
shows on the envelope. To work a design similar to Jackie's, cut a piece of
iron-on interfacing about 7" (17.8 cm)
square, glue side up (it will be ironed to
the envelope fabric later). Layer gold
lame followed by yellow organdy on top
of the interfacing. Cut a free-form circle
out of the organdy about 1" (2.5 cm) in
diameter. Now layer peach organdy,
peachy transparent curtain material,
red chiffon, and red mesh bag fabric,
cutting slightly larger circles for each
layer. Overlay gold veiling on all and
pin in place. Free-machine embroider
the yellow organdy in straight-stitch
circles around the center gold lame.
Then straight stitch in radiating lines
outward, running the machine fast and

Fig. II–22 Positioning the parts for the get-well envelope.

225

moving the material slowly. (Jackie did not use a hoop, using a darning foot instead.) Add satin-stitch blobs in the center on the gold lame (Jackie used variegated thread in yellows and oranges).

2. Put the presser foot back on, with transparent thread on top. Decide how much of your design you want to show. (Jackie's is $3^3/_4$" × $4^1/_8$" (9.5 cm × 10.8 cm), but you can make it any size.) Stitch around the design with transparent thread. This will be your guide for the edges of the fabric frame. Trim all layers 1" (2.5 cm) wider than the line you just stitched. Then trim away all layers but the interfacing $^1/_2$" (1.3 cm) wider than the stitched line. Place tracing paper over this square. Use a ruler to trace the outside of the square and the stitched line. Cut along the stitched line on the paper, removing the center rectangle. Call this your "paper frame."

3. Lay the interfacing-with-design on the lower left corner of the underside of the envelope fabric. Cut the envelope fabric two times as wide and twice as high as the square of interfacing plus 1" (2.5 cm) all around for seam allowances. Cut a second piece of iron-on interfacing the same size as the first. Remove the interfacing-with-design square. Cut a piece of fusible webbing the same size as the interfacing-with-design. Using the Teflon pressing sheet, fuse the webbing to the lower left back of the fabric where the design will be placed. Fuse the other rectangle of iron-on interfacing to the lower right underside of the envelope fabric.

4. Lay the paper frame on the fusible webbing. Trace the edges of the cut-out rectangle. Then stitch them with transparent thread. This makes folding easier, later on. Draw diagonals from corner to corner within the stitched

square. Cut on the diagonal lines. Trim the triangle shapes to within $^1/_2$" (1.3 cm) of the stitched lines. Fold the envelope fabric to the inside on the stitched lines. Using the Teflon sheet, press. If you wish, remove the stitching lines.

5. Turn the fabric over. Place the interfacing-with-design under the cutout, using the transparent thread lines on the design as a guide for placement. Press the design in place, using a Teflon sheet underneath and a terry towel on top. You only need press the fabric frame, not the center design.

6. Use a narrow zigzag or blind-hem stitch with transparent thread to secure the design to the fabric frame.

7. Write "getwellgetwell" in free-machine embroidery or with your automatic computer machine $^1/_4$" (6 mm) outside the design on the fabric frame. Write "getwell" in scattered places on the square of fabric to the left of the design (this is the back of the bag).

8. Press the bag in half so the top edge is marked. Open the bag flat and turn it over. Fuse a 1" (2.5 cm) wide strip of iron-on interfacing along the pressed line where the bag is not interfaced. This will be the top edge of the lining. In free-machine embroidery, using either gold thread or something more subtle (a surprise is always pleasant to discover), write the person's name over and over. This stabilizes the upper edge of the lining.

9. To construct the bag, fold the fabric in half, rightsides together, so the sides meet. Sew the side and bottom edges in a $^1/_2$" (1.3 cm) seam allowance. Trim corners and seam. Turn rightsides out. Fold in the remaining open side $^1/_2$" (1.3 cm) and topstitch. Now tuck the lining inside the bag. Hand-tack the cording to the sides and bottom, so you can hang the envelope, if you want.

226

Traveler's Sewing Kit

This kit has two inside pockets to hold folding scissors and a thimble, as well as a felt flap inside to hold needles, pins, and other necessities. If you want the whole kit washable, use polyester felt for the felt flap. If the kit is a gift, tuck in some pre-gummed labels with your name and address on them, to make it easy to receive a postcard from the traveler.

Felt rectangle, $1^3/_8$" x 4" (3.5 cm × 10 cm)
2 pieces sturdy fabric for outside at least $6^1/_2$" × 5" (16.5 cm × 12.7 cm) (Ultrasuede is elegant)
Interfacing (optional)
2 rectangles lightweight fabric for pockets, $6^1/_2$ × $2^3/_4$" (16.5 cm × 7 cm) each
Bias binding or strips of Ultrasuede

Fig. II–23 Traveler's sewing kit.

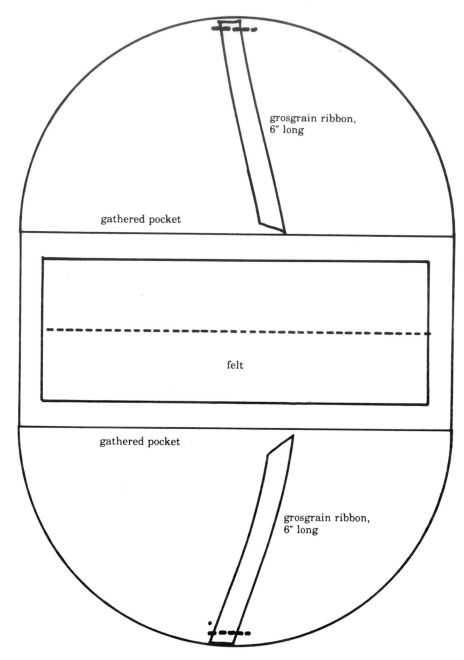

grosgrain ribbon,
6″ long

gathered pocket

felt

gathered pocket

grosgrain ribbon,
6″ long

Fig. II–24 Assembling the sewing kit.

2 pieces $\frac{1}{8}$" (3 mm) elastic, 4⅝" (12 cm) long

Grosgrain ribbon

Travel supplies: folding scissors, dark and light thread rewound onto cardboard, buttons, safety pins, hook and eye, needles, pins, thimble, Band-aids

1. Crease felt long way. Sew buttons to one side of crease nearer outside edge. Sew hook and eye to other side.

2. Center felt on right side of one fabric foundation as shown. Sew along crease.

3. To make pockets, turn under one long edge of each pocket $\frac{1}{4}$" (6 mm) and press. Turn another $\frac{1}{4}$" (3 mm) and press. Stitch close to fold. Thread elastic through opening and gather pocket. Sew elastic in place. Smooth gathers and pin center bottom of pocket to foundation fabric. Pin rest of pocket in place. Turn foundation over and trim off extra pocket even with foundation. Baste pocket in place along edge. Repeat for second pocket.

4. Embellish outside fabric. If it's a gift, a monogram is always appreciated. Interface if desired. Wrong sides together, baste foundation fabric to outside fabric around edge with a zigzag.

5. For ties, cut two pieces of narrow grosgrain ribbon, each 6" (15 cm) long. Sew to ends of case as shown.

6. Sew bias binding around entire edge of case.

7. Pin safety pins, needles, and pin to felt. Tuck thimble and thread into one pocket and scissors into other. Bon voyage!

PROJECT 9

Nina's Quilt Module

Nina Stull works full-time in a custom monogramming business. She still likes to make machine-quilted quilts in her free time, so she has simplified the process, using this clever quilt module. She often repeats one or two designs in the center, and achieves variety by using lots of colors in the connecting bands. (Directions used with permission.)

For each quilt block you will need:

Backing fabric, 10" (25.4 cm) square

Center quilt fabric, 5" (12.7 cm) square

Batting, 10" (25.4 cm) square

Fabric strip to surround center quilted fabric, about 28" (72 cm) long and 3" (7.6 cm) wide

9" (22.8 cm) square graph paper glued to sandpaper or acetate

Walking foot

1. Lay the backing fabric wrong side up on a flat surface. Lay the batting on it. Then center the 5" (12.7 cm) square quilt fabric on the batting and pin. Machine quilt the center image.

2. Lay the long fabric strip along the top edge of the center quilted fabric, rightsides together. Using the walking

Fig. II–25 Nina's quilt module.

foot to prevent the layers from creeping, sew a $\frac{1}{2}$" (1.3 cm) seam and trim the strip even with the right edge of the center fabric (Fig. II-26). Flip strip out and pin in place. Repeat for the bottom edge of the center quilted fabric. Flip strip out and pin. Now sew a strip along the right and left edges of the center quilted fabric. Flip and pin. Pin all around the outside edges.

3. Center the 9" (22.8 cm) square template over the quilt module and mark the edges. Trim all edges. Nina says the puffiness of the quilt hides any inaccuracy. You're done with the basic quilt module. Make as many as you need for your quilt.

4. To connect modules, cut long strips of 2" (5 cm) wide fabric (this gives a 1" connecting band—if you want it larger, adjust now). Cut two 9" (22.5 cm) long strips and place right sides against the front and back of the right side of a quilt module. Place a strip of 2" (5 cm) wide batting on top. Sew a $\frac{1}{2}$" (1.3 cm) seam. Trim the batting close to the stitching. Sew a second quilt module to the top connecting band, right sides together. Trim the batting close to the stitching. On the underside, handstitch

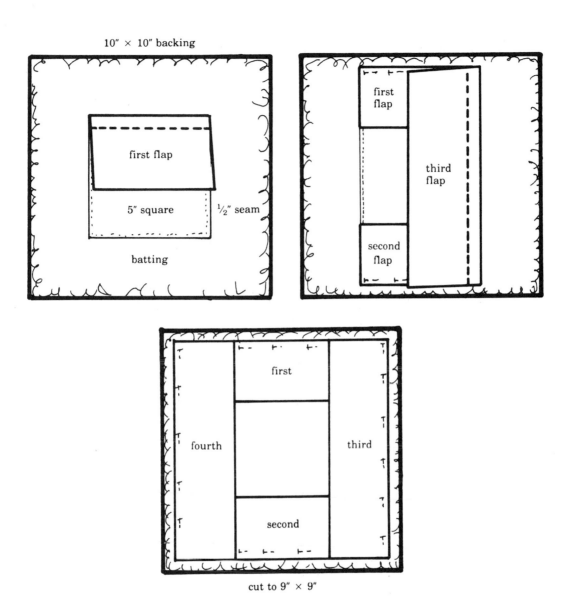

Fig. II–26 Making the quilt module.

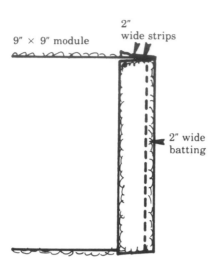

9" × 9" module

2" wide strips

2" wide batting

Fig. II–27 Connecting the modules.

the connecting fabric to the second quilt module. Machine-quilt on the connecting bands $\frac{1}{4}$" to $\frac{1}{2}$" (6 mm to 13 mm) from the seam line (try a narrow zigzag for a soft line). (Fig. II-27.)

5. Continue connecting quilt modules across the quilt this way. Then use the same technique to connect the rows. Bind the edges with a double layer of bias binding.

PROJECT 10

Portable Book Cover

Roberta Losey Patterson noticed someone carrying this portable book cover on a nature hike. It has inside flaps to hold the pages of your book open. It also has an outside pocket for a short pencil and a small notebook. Best of all, the long straps make it easy to carry around, so that you may sneak in some reading whenever you find yourself with spare minutes. It's designed for books up to $5\frac{1}{2}$" × $8\frac{1}{2}$" (14 cm × 21.6 cm). Scale up the design and make a second one for larger books.

> Sturdy dark-colored fabric (denim, canvas, upholstery fabric) or interfaced lighter fabric, 10" × 20" (25.4 cm × 50.8 cm)

10" × 20" (25.4 cm × 50.8 cm) lining (cotton print is attractive)
2 yds $1\frac{1}{2}$" (3.8 cm) wide strap material (belting is fine)
7" x $5\frac{1}{2}$" (17.8 cm × 14 cm) sturdy fabric for pocket
7" x $5\frac{1}{2}$" (17.8 cm × 14 cm) lining for pocket
Iron-on tape (optional)
Pin or masking tape
Extra-fine machine-embroidery thread (Sulky)
Iron, press cloth, Teflon pressing sheet, fusible webbing

1. Decide how to embellish the pocket. The left 1" (2.5 cm) of the pocket will be a pencil pocket. Center your design

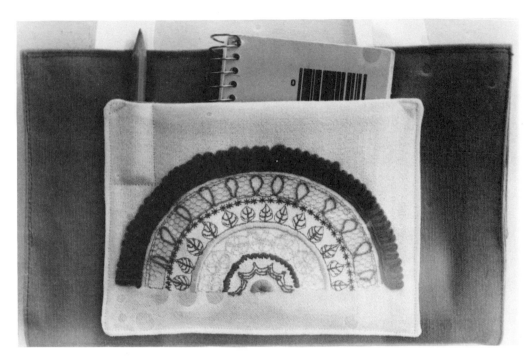

Fig. II 28 Portable book cover.

between the stitching for the pencil pocket and the right side of the pocket. If the bottom of the design is not obvious, mark the bottom on the underside of the pocket with a pin or small piece of masking tape (Fig. II-29).

2. Place the lining on the pocket, right sides together, and stitch all four sides in a $\frac{1}{2}$" (1.3 cm) seam allowance. Carefully make a 3" (7.6 cm) slit in the lining only, parallel to the long edge of the pocket and 1" (2.5 cm) from the bottom edge (which was marked by your pin or tape).

3. Turn the pocket right side out through the slash. Press it face down into a towel so the embroidery won't be flattened. Close the slash with herringbone stitch or iron-on tape.

4. Position the pocket on the right side of the book cover, as shown in Fig.

II-30. Stitch around three sides near the edge of the pocket. Reinforce the stitching at the top edges. Stitch a line parallel to the left side of the pocket and 1" (2.5 cm) in, to make a pencil pocket.

5. Lay the sturdy book cover right side up on a flat surface. Cut two straps from the belting, each 3 ft (.9 m) long.

6. Make a U shape of each strap. Lay each on top of the book cover, each cut strap 2" (5 cm) from the long edge of the book cover. Stitch across the ends inside the $\frac{1}{2}$" (1.3 cm) seam allowance.

7. Lay the lining right sides together with the book cover. Stitch around all sides in a $\frac{1}{2}$" (1.3 cm) seam. Carefully slash the lining $2\frac{1}{2}$" (6.4 cm) in and parallel to the short side of the book cover. Turn the book cover rightsides out. Close the slash with iron-on tape or

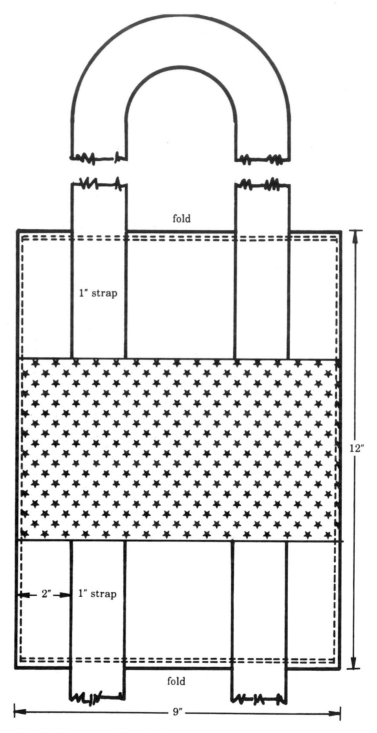

Fig. II–29 Assembling the book cover.

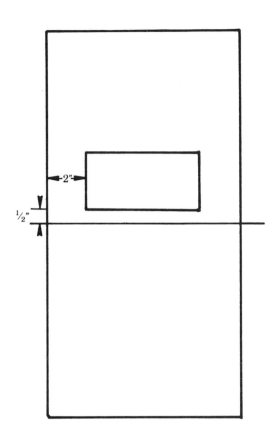

Fig. II–30 Positioning the pocket.

←2"→

½"

stitching and press the cover, using a damp press cloth to avoid iron marks on the heavy fabric. Don't iron your embroidery.

8. Turn in each short end of the book cover $3^1/_2$" (8.9 cm). The straps should lie flat, as shown in Fig. II-29, protruding in a U beyond the book cover. Stitch around the entire book cover close to the edge. Stitch the two ends a second time for added strength.

PROJECT 11

Machine-Embroidery Sample Book

Here's a way to display your stitched samples and still be able to regroup them or to remove them to show classes (Fig. II-31). If you like to work with a bigger hoop, say 8" (20.3 cm), you should make a larger book. These pages fit 6" (15.2 cm) samples. You may want to make two books, one for your first

Fig. II–31 Machine-embroidery sample book.

test-cloth attempts, and one with the same techniques in a small finished design.

> Rectangles of non-frayable fabric such as felt, 7" × 14" (17.8 cm × 35.6 cm)
> 2 notebook clasps
> Stitched samples trimmed to 6" (15.2 cm) or smaller

1. Cut several rectangles of felt, so you always have more ready than you need. Fold the rectangle in half to make two 7" (17.8 cm) squares. Stitch $\frac{1}{2}$" (1.3 cm) in, parallel to the fold. This makes a book spine. Make two straight-stitch buttonholes 2" (5 cm) above the bottom and below the top edges within the $\frac{1}{2}$" (1.3 cm) book spine (Figure II-32).

2. Trim the samples to 6" (15.2 cm) or smaller. Zigzag the edges. Center a sample on each fabric page. Sew those on the left side of the fabric page at the

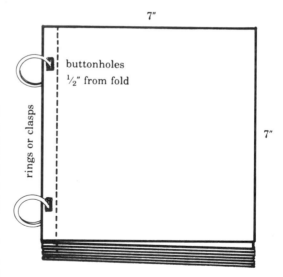

7"

buttonholes
$\frac{1}{2}$" from fold

rings or clasps

7"

Fig. II–32 Assembling the sample book.

236

bottom edge with a zigzag or straight stitch. Sew those on the right side of the fabric page at the top. This allows you to fold the sample out and study the underside. If you wish, you can type or write the machine settings you used on a piece of interfacing or paper and fuse or sew it to the page underneath the sample. Be sure to lift any sample on the other side of the page before stitching the paper in place.

3. Lay the pages on top of each other and connect through the buttonholes with the notebook clasps.

PROJECT 12

Dotty's Sewing Duffel

I first saw this clever duffel in southern California at the "Treadleart" studio, where Dotty Niewig, its inventor, worked (she now lives in Australia). It has plenty of pockets for thread, scissors, pens, hoops, and all the other supplies you carry to class with you.

I appliqued the outside with enlarged versions of my three favorite presser feet—applique, buttonhole, and regular. While the directions are long, making the bag does not take a long time. I finished mine in less than a week of leisurely evening sewing. (Directions reprinted with permission from Dotty Niewig.)

2 yd (1.6 m) of 48" (127 cm) wide heavyweight fabric (duck, denim, or heavy twill)

1 12" (30 cm) wide vinyl floor tile, trimmed with paper-cutting shears to an $11\frac{1}{2}$" (29 cm) circle

1 piece of plastic needlepoint canvas, 10 squares per inch, $38\frac{1}{2}$" $\times$ $5\frac{3}{4}$" (98 $\times$ 15 cm) (can be pieced together from smaller

pieces if you can only buy precut pieces like tablemats)

2 lengths of $\frac{3}{8}$" (1 cm) nylon or cotton cord, each cut 54" (1.4 m) long

1 piece of $\frac{3}{4}$" (1.9 cm) wide elastic, 39" (1 m) long

Graph paper, pen, ruler, marking pen, iron

Denim needle (16(100) 705 H-J)

Heavyweight thread (I used Metrosene Plus)

1. *The big picture:* The order of working is to start by making paper patterns if you want to make more than one bag; otherwise measure and mark directly on the fabric. Then cut out fabric pieces, mark the pockets, sew the hems in the pockets, and construct the bag.

2. *Make paper patterns* for the following pieces:

One each:

$38\frac{1}{2}$" x 13" (97 cm x 33 cm) inside ring (A; see Fig. II-34)

6" x $57\frac{1}{2}$" (15 cm x 146 cm) spool pockets (B; see Fig. II-34)

Fig. II–33 Dotty's sewing duffel.

6½" x 45½" (17 cm x 116 cm) inside
pockets (C; see Fig. II-34)
48" x 22" (127 cm x 56 cm) outer bag (E)
  Two each:
12½" (32 cm) fabric circle for bottom
(D)
⅜" (1 cm) nylon or cotton cord, 54" (1.4
m) long
  3. *Cut out fabric.*
  4. *Hem edges of pieces B and C (Fig.
II-35).* Hem one edge each of pattern
pieces B and C. The hem will be folded
to the outside of the fabric, making a
smooth inside for the top of the pockets
you'll soon stitch. Make the hem by
folding down ½" (1.3 cm) to the outside
of the fabric; press. Fold ½" (1.3 cm)
down again and stitch close to the hem
edge and the top edge.
  5. *Mark pieces A, B, and C as follows:
Inside Ring A* — Fold in half lengthwise
and press. Open flat. Mark off ¼" (6
mm) on each end for side seams. On one
half of fold, draw a line perpendicular
to the fold every 2" (5 cm) (19 times).
On the other half of the fold, mark lines
as shown in Fig. II-34A. *Spool Pockets
B* — Mark off ¼" (6 mm) on each short

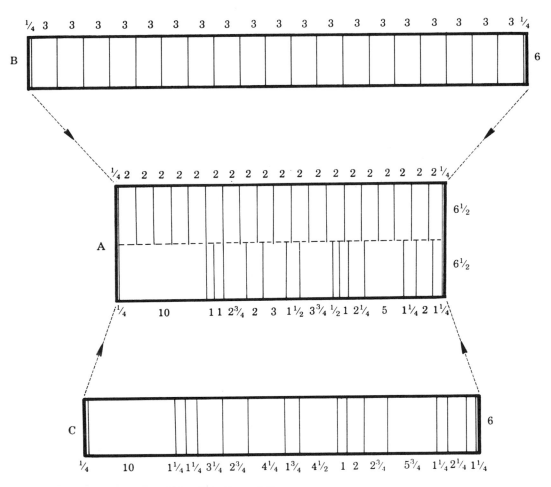

Fig. II–34 Dimensions of pieces A, B, and C.

end for side seams. Then draw a line across the rectangle every 3" (7.6 cm) (19 times) as shown in Fig. II-34B. *Inside Pockets C* – Mark off ¼" (6 mm) at each end for seam allowances. Then draw pocket lines as shown in Fig. II-34C.

6. *Attach spool pockets (B) to one side of inside ring (A) (Fig. II-36).* Lay B on top of the side of A marked off every 2" (5 cm), with the hem of B near the fold of A. Align the markings on B with the markings on A, keeping the bottoms of the two fabrics even. Sew on each line, backtacking the stitches securely at top and bottom. To make B fit A, make ¼" (6 mm) pleats on each side of the stitched line. Sew across the bottom to secure the pleats. Then sew again 2" from the bottom. This will make 3" (7.6 cm) deep spool pockets.

Lay the elastic along the last line sewn, with the top of the elastic on the sewn line. Sew the elastic parallel to the pleats in the center of each pleat, backtacking the stitches securely at top

239

and bottom. Now you can fit thread spools both inside the pockets and outside, held by the elastic. Zigzag the bottom edge to finish it.

7. *Attach inside pockets (C) to other side of inside ring (A) (Fig. II-37).* Lay C over the other half of A, matching the marked lines, as you did in Step 6, with the hem of C near the fold of A. Sew the lines, backtacking at top and bottom. Some of these pockets should be pleated, as in Step 6. They are all different widths, so judge for yourself. Sew across the pleats at the bottom to hold them. Zigzag the bottom edge to finish it.

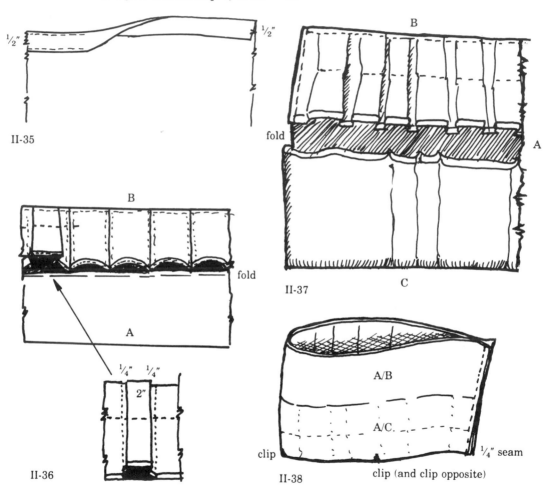

II-35

II-36

II-37

II-38

Fig. II–35 Hem edges of pieces B and C (Step 4).

Fig. II–36 Attach spool pockets B to one side of inside ring A (Step 6).

Fig. II–37 Attach inside pockets C to other side of inside ring A (Step 7).

Fig. II–38 Stitch seam of inside ring A and mark the ring into quarters with small clips (Step 8).

240

8. *Stitch inside ring (A) to make a circle.* Place the right sides (with the pockets) of A together and sew across the short end in a $^1/_4$" (6 mm) seam. Lay the piece flat, with the seam at one end. Directly opposite the seam, clip into the edge on the A/C side. Now open up the circle and put the clip up to the seam line; this makes two new "folds." Clip into the A/C edge at the resulting two folds. You've now marked the piece into quarters (Fig. II-38).

9. *Construct the bottom of the bag D (Fig. II-39).* Fold one of the fabric circles into four quarters and mark each with a clip into the edge. Repeat with the other fabric circle. Place the two circles wrong sides together, quarter marks matching, and sew half way around with a $^3/_8$" (1 cm) seam. Insert the floor tile into the fabric. Sew the remainder of the circle, using a zipper foot to get as close to the floor tile as possible

10. *Sew A to D (Fig. II-40).* Match the quarter marks on A/C to those you made on D (the bottom) and pin. Using the zipper foot, sew a $^3/_8$" (1 cm) seam.

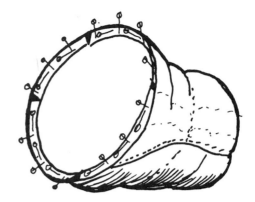

Fig. II–40 Sew inside ring A to bottom D (Step 10).

Now the inner pockets are connected to the bottom of the bag.

11. *Embellish the outside bag.* Before you construct the outside of the bag (E), embellish in any way you want. You will make a tuck $9^1/_2$" (24 cm) below the top unfinished edge of the bag to help it fold down for use. Make sure your decoration is compatible with this tuck.

12. *Construct outside bag (Fig. II-41).* (1) With wrong sides of E together on

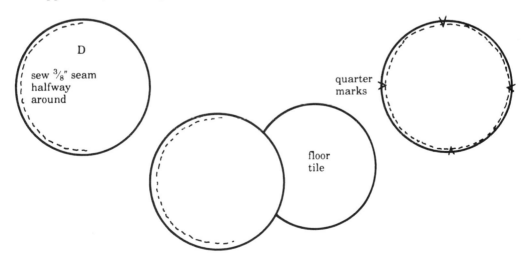

Fig. II–39 Construct the bottom of the bag D (Step 9).

241

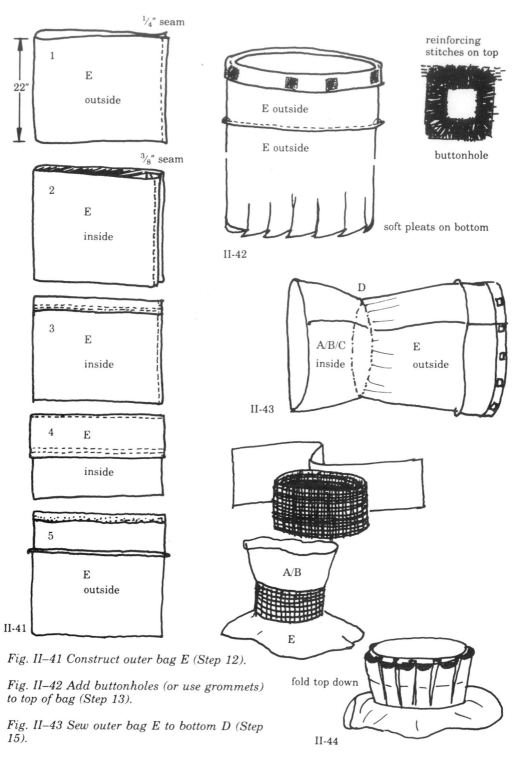

¼" seam

1

E

outside

22"

⅜" seam

2

E

inside

3

E

inside

4   E

inside

5

E

outside

II-41

reinforcing
stitches on top

E outside

E outside

E outside

buttonhole

soft pleats on bottom

II-42

D

A/B/C

inside

E

outside

II-43

A/B

E

fold top down

II-44

Fig. II–41 Construct outer bag E (Step 12).

Fig. II–42 Add buttonholes (or use grommets)
to top of bag (Step 13).

Fig. II–43 Sew outer bag E to bottom D (Step
15).

Fig. II–44 Reinforce inside ring A with needlepoint canvas and stitch in place (Step 16).

the short end, sew a $^1/_4$" (6 mm) seam. Press seam open, then to one side. (2) Turn right sides out and sew another $_3/_8$" (1 cm) seam. You have just encased the raw edge in a French seam. (3) To hem the top of the bag, fold the top of the bag to the inside $^1/_2$" (1.3 cm) and press. Fold an additional $1^1/_2$" (3.8 cm) and press. Topstitch close to the folded edge and the top edge. (4) To make the tuck, fold the bag to the outside (right sides together) $7^1/_2$" (19 cm) and press. Sew $^1/_4$" (3 mm) away from the fold all around the bag. This helps your bag fold down easier for use.

13. *Make 10 buttonholes* (or use grommets) around the top of the bag, through which the cord will be drawn. Alternate the distance between buttonholes, spacing them first 6" (15 cm) apart and then $3^1/_4$" (8.3 cm) apart (Fig. II-42).

14. *Fit the outer bag to the bottom circle.* Fold the outer bag into quarters and clip the bottom edge. In each quarter make four $^1/_2$" (1.3 cm) pleats about 3" (7.6 cm) apart, for a total of 12 pleats (see Fig. II-42). Try not to obscure the quarter marks. Zigzag edge to finish it.

15. *Sew the outer bag E to the bottom D (Fig. II-43).* To sew the outer bag to the bottom, turn E inside out. Place it over the bottom D, with right sides of E to the side of D that isn't attached to A and matching quarter marks. You may need to adjust the pleat on A to fit D. Using a zipper foot, sew a $^3/_8$" (1 cm) seam.

16. *Stitch the inside ring in place, strengthening it with a ring of plastic needlepoint canvas (Fig. II-44).* If necessary, piece the plastic needlepoint canvas to make one long strip with the dimensions given in the materials list. Overlap the ends of the plastic $^1/_2$" (1.3 cm) to make a ring. Stitch. Place the plastic circle over the inside piece A/B/ C. Fold A/B over the plastic circle and pin in place at the bottom. Be careful that the material doesn't twist. If A/B doesn't fit, make small pleats until it does. You now have five edges meeting at the bottom. Sew one last time around the floor tile, using the zipper foot and a $^3/_8$" (1 cm) seam. Zigzag through all edges of the material to finish it.

17. Stitch $^3/_8$" (1 cm) down from the folded edge of A, through the fabric and plastic inside. Fold outside of bag up over inside pockets.

18. Thread the cord through the buttonholes, using one cord for half the buttonholes and the other cord for the other half. Draw together to close bag.

PROJECT 13

Two Alphabets for Machine Embroidery

Here are two alphabets suitable for machine embroidery. The script style is good for monogramming (see Chapter 10), and the block style looks good as applique or filled in with stitches. See Bibliography for a list of books on lettering.

ABCDEFGHI
JKLMNOPQR
STUVWXYZ

Fig. II–45 Commercial Script alphabet for monogramming (from Letraset Instant Lettering).

ABCDEFG
HIJKLMNO
PQRSTUV
WXYZ

Fig. II–46 Helvetica Bold alphabet for monogramming (from Letraset Instant Lettering).

APPENDICES

How to Buy a Sewing Machine

Sewing machines have changed drastically in the last ten years. You may be wondering if it is worth buying a new machine, when your old one has served you so well. Are the computer machines really worth owning?

The answer depends on what you use a sewing machine for. Do you do lots of free-machine embroidery? Do you sew garments for your family? Do you want one machine to do everything, from sewing upholstery to embroidering daisies on tricot? If the answer is yes to all these questions, it is worth investigating the new machines.

Here is a checklist of questions to ask yourself, as you investigate. Be methodical as you research your purchase. Take the same bag of fabrics and threads to each dealer (don't expect the store to provide them). Practice the same maneuver on each machine, so you have a basis for fair comparison. Keep track of each machine and each dealer.

I take lightweight denim, a machine-embroidery hoop, and extra-fine rayon machine-embroidery thread with me. As I free-machine embroider my name, I learn how easy it is to to drop or cover the feed dogs, loosen top tension, and remove the presser foot on each machine. I can assess how large the working area is and how easy it is to return the machine to normal sewing. Neither denim nor rayon are easy materials to

work with, and each machine responds differently.

Once you decide on a machine and you are debating where to buy it, I encourage you to opt for a dealer's knowledge over a low price. In the long run, you will be much happier buying your machine from a store that has classes, that has the supplies you need, that keeps up on the latest techniques and accessories, and that can service your machine ten years from now.

I also encourage you to buy the very best you can afford. Even though Tony and I are unusually old-fashioned about debt—if we don't have the cash, we don't buy—I *would* borrow from a credit union or bank to buy a top-of-the-line sewing machine. In the long run, it would be worth it. In 1970 we bought an expensive Elna Super for $315. That was a lot of money for us, new parents and new homeowners. Sixteen years later the Elna is still going strong and the pleasure of sewing on it has cost me about $20/year. That is a good deal.

If your budget is fixed and you're not willing to get a loan, consider buying a used top-of-the-line machine from a good dealer.

While you are looking around at machines, ask other consumers about their machines and their favorite dealers. Remember, though, that you can do almost all the techniques in this book on any machine, no matter what somebody tells you. Home sewers are passionate about their choices; one will swear by one brand, another will swear at it. As long as you stick to the major brands, you really can't go wrong.

Here's what to ask yourself. For each machine, keep a written list of the answers.

Vital Statistics
Brand, Model Number, and Year
Oscillator or Rotary?
Weight
Color
Dealer
Price
Length of Guarantee

Efficiency
1. Is the machine easy to thread? Is the thread spindle vertical or horizontal?
2. Can you decenter the needle?
3. How easy is it to wind a bobbin?
4. Does the light illuminate the work area well?
5. Can you extend the working area with a clip-on surface, extra bed, case for the machine, built-in table, etc.?
6. Is a free-arm important to you? If you will be making children's clothes, will a cuff, pant leg, or neck opening fit around the free-arm?
7. What will it be like to work on this machine at night? Can you see the dials? Does the color of the machine affect you?
8. How much room is there under the presser foot?
9. Is the foot pedal well-designed or will it give you shin splints to use?
10. Can the machine be switched to slow speed? If not, is it important to you?
11. How do you carry the machine (built-in handle, carrying case, etc.)?
12. How extensive and well-written is the manual?

Stitches
1. Does it perform the meat-and-potatoes stitches (straight stitch, zigzag, buttonhole, possibly blind hem) easily and well on all weights of fabric? Does it skip stitches or balk at any of these?
2. Will you need reverse-cycle stitches (e.g., stretch overlock for knits)? If so, does the machine have them?
3. How wide is the satin stitch? Can you easily taper them?
4. Will you need to consult the manual every time you make a buttonhole because you can't remember how to do it?
5. How many stitches are built in? How many are silly or redundant? Can you update stitches with cams, stitch programmers, cartridges, etc?
6. Does the machine show you the beginning and end of an automatic pattern?
7. Is there a pressure regulator? If not, do you care?

Machine Embroidery
1. Does the machine convert to free-machine embroidery easily? How do you drop or cover the feed dogs? Is it easy to put in the bobbin? Can you manipulate top and bobbin tensions easily? Does it have a darning foot or spring and if so, do you like embroidering with it?
2. Is the needle plate even in height with the rest of the machine? Does your machine-embroidery hoop catch on any ridges? Is the working area big enough for the hoop? If not, can you extend the working area with a flat-bed extension or other device?
3. How does the machine respond to different weights of thread in top and bobbin?
4. Is it easy to change stitch width and length? Can you, for example, taper a satin stitch easily?

5. What decorative stitches are built-in? Are they easy to use? Can you make up your own stitches? If so, do they disappear when the machine is turned off?

6. Does the needle always stop in the up position? If so, will that annoy you?

Accessories

1. Is the machine low-shank, high-shank, slant needle, or other?

2. What other brands of presser feet fit this machine?

3. Do the feet snap on, screw on, clip on, etc.?

4. What feet come with the machine? Can you buy walking, applique, and buttonhole feet for it? What other tools and accessories are included with the machine?

5. What kind of feed dogs does it have (sawtooth, diamond point, rubber, other)?

6. What kind of needles are recommended? Can you use a good European needle in the machine?

7. If it's an oscillator and you want to manipulate bobbin tension extensively, how much is an extra bobbin case?

Education

1. Does the dealer offer instruction? How will the dealer keep you up-to-date on new techniques and accessories (classes, newsletter, mailings, phone calls, etc.)?

2. Does the brand have educational matter available (manuals, magazines, books, etc.)?

3. How do you clean and oil the machine? Is it clearly shown in the manual? How often should you oil it?

4. How will your machine be serviced? Does the dealer do it or send it out? If it's sent out, how long does it take? (Be sure to confirm this with a consumer who's used the shop—or automatically add a month to any estimate.) Where is it sent?

5. What does the guarantee cover? For how long? What doesn't it cover?

6. What makes this brand unique?

Note: The answer to "Is it worth owning a computer machine?" is: if you sew a lot, including clothing, home decorating, and machine embroidery—yes!

APPENDIX B

A Short History of Machine Embroidery

After reading this book and playing with the techniques you've learned, you already know machine embroidery is fun, even exhilarating. But you may be taking for granted two discoveries that make your attempts easy: electricity (introduced in 1921) and the swing-needle machine (available after World War II). Without these, making a zigzag, for example, was laborious.

Still, exquisite machine embroidery was worked on treadle machines in the late 1880s. The hoop was pulled from side to side to make precise zigzags or satin stitches in a maneuver called the jump stitch. Like the long-and-short stitch of hand embroidery, longer zig-zags were used to produce detailed shaded pictures. Fig. A-1 shows a picture of two cats, worked this way in 1890 on a treadle by Ella Crampton, the grandmother of Elinor Schmidt in Indianapolis, IN.

Ella Crampton was the head of the Singer office in Indianapolis and presumably received training in art embroidery from the company educators, who pioneered the free-machine embroidery techniques in their New York workrooms. In 1889 someone sent one of these pieces to a friend in England. Although fancy embroidery had been worked there for twenty years, it was always worked with the presser foot and feed dogs. The English friend excitedly showed the work to Singer/London and the company began teaching the techniques in their workrooms. Soon the techniques spread all over the world.

Constance Howard (English author, artist, and professor) says "In the Singer workrooms during the 1890s some remarkable embroidered pictures were produced, often copied from postcards with subjects from well-known paintings, portraits, landscapes and seascapes. These were stitched on domestic machines with fixed needles, the fabric being moved to give zigzag, satin and other stitches. Great patience and technical skill were necessary when embroidering these pictures, some of which were produced by highly skilled embroiderers working in their own homes."

Fig. A–1 Two cats worked in 1890 on a treadle machine by Ella Crampton, grandmother of Elinor Schmidt of Indianapolis, IN.

250

When treadles were hooked to electric motors, machine embroidery took off. Suddenly, with the new freedom of movement, people began creating much more than repetitive designs on dress or household items. And Singer helped the movement along by publishing an extraordinary book in 1911, called *Singer Instructions for Art Embroidery and Lace Work* (Fig. A-2). This 224-page jewel contained five courses of graduated study, covering 125 lessons. The first course covered basic free-machine embroidery and then expanded with cording, eyelet embroidery, applique on net, various laces, and shaded embroidery. Each lesson was accompanied by a large photo of the work in progress, with exact instructions on how to duplicate it, from thread, needle, fabric, tension, and even how many stitches per half-inch.

By the end of the book, every conceivable hand-embroidery technique had been duplicated in machine work, including beadwork, false corduroy, raffia straw work, rugmaking, and—hard to believe—embroidery on wood veneer! (See the end of this discussion for the complete table of contents from this astonishing volume.)

The Singer book was developed in the United States, but also distributed in England. In 1916 a woman named Dorothy Benson joined Singer/London. She became a skilled technician and teacher of machine embroidery and was eventually promoted to head of the workrooms in 1958. Constance Howard says, "She could imitate anything on the machine—fine canvas embroidery, lace, freely worked designs. And this was when the stitching was often examined with a magnifying glass for ac-

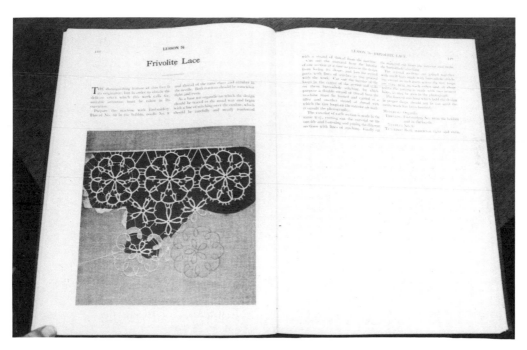

Fig. A–2 One page of my beloved Singer book, first published in 1911.

251

curacy." In 1952 Sylvan Press published Dorothy Benson's book, *Your Machine Embroidery*, the first popular book in England on the subject. Earlier she had written a book for Singer/London called *Machine Embroider: The Artistic Possibilities of the Domestic Sewing Machine* (1946).

Before long, artists/teachers saw Dorothy Benson's work and became intrigued with the potential of the machine. Two such prominent people were Rebecca Crompton, head of women's crafts, dress, and embroidery at Croydon School of Art; and Elizabeth Grace Thomson, head of fashion and crafts at Bromley School of Art. Both artists used the machine in bolder, freer ways than had been done before. In particular, Rebecca Crompton, who was initially instructed by Dorothy Benson in 1936, often combined hand and machine embroidery. She shocked the traditionalists by deliberately using raw edges as an integral part of her designs. Naturally, as an artist, she was more interested in design and color than technique. Her innovations raised the standards of machine embroidery in ways that still affect us.

Meanwhile machine embroidery in America went underground. I have no doubt it was being practiced as diligently as in England, but I have uncovered little written material. The edition of the Singer book I've studied is the ninth, published in 1941. According to Jessie Dalzell of Singer/United States Sewing Education Department, that was the last printing. After World War II, Singer published a color booklet on "fashion stitches," given free with a sewing-machine purchase. It showed some of the previous techniques, but it included an important addition: work that had been accomplished with a swing-needle (or zigzag) sewing machine.

If free-machine embroidery with a straight stitch was fun, with a zigzag it was pure glee. Now home sewers could finish edges, make satin stitches, easily fill in large shapes with thread, sew on buttons, and play with their machines more freely than ever.

One such person was Lucille Merrell Graham of Bountiful, UT. After the war, her husband dragged her into a sewing store "to see this wonderful new machine. I said 'If it's not a Singer, I'm not interested.' It was an Anchor and he bought it for me anyway as a Christmas present. Later, in the 1950s, I was working as a demonstrator for Necchi/Elna. A home economist from Denver showed us a little free-machine embroidery. I was thrilled and wanted to learn more. I heard that a competitor was giving lessons, so I slipped into her class. She gave me two or three lessons and said 'Now you're on your own.' I worked on my own, but sometimes I got frustrated. For example, there was no machine-embroidery thread available at that time and the thread kept breaking."

Before long, Lucille found herself teaching a machine-embroidery class in the new community adult school. "I didn't know how or what to teach, so I bluffed. But oh!, I worked hard from week to week to keep ahead of the students." Out of this came three self-published books on machine embroidery that started many Americans on their way (see Bibliography). Lucille also opened a teaching center and a mail-order supply business called Sew-Art International, now owned by her brother (see Supply List).

Another person who has rekindled the interest in machine embroidery is Janet Stocker of Lomita, CA, editor/publisher of "Treadleart," a magazine for machine-embroidery enthusiasts (see Supply List). Janet's mother, Virginia Verdier, was a sewing-machine demonstrator in the 1950s, so Janet grew up loving the machine. She sewed for her family and wanted to figure out how machine-embroidered patches for clothing were made. Luckily, she found one of Lucille Graham's books and another love affair with machine embroidery blossomed. In 1978 Janet began publishing a newsletter for other enthusiasts. Then she began selling some supplies and holding Treadleart parties — she and a friend would take supplies and their machines to someone's home and show people how to machine embroider. From that Janet's business grew to a full-supply store with classes, a mail-

Fig. A–4 Janet Stocker. Photo courtesy of Janet.

order company, and a bimonthly magazine.

Several other Americans have been central to spreading the word about machine embroidery. Verna Holt of Las Vegas, NV, studied with Lucille Graham and later published her own machine-embroidery books. Joyce Drexler of Speed Stitch in Port Charlotte, FL, is the only person so far to offer machine-embroidery kits, which teach a beginner how to get started. Both Verna and Joyce hold annual in-depth seminars on machine embroidery. Jerry and Scott Zarbaugh and their daughter, Debbie Casteel, of Livermore, CA, owners of Aardvark Adventures, import

Fig. A–3 Lucille Graham. Photo courtesy of Lucille.

253

Fig. A–5 Verna Holt. Photo courtesy of Verna.

Natesh rayon threads and publish "The Aardvark Territorial Enterprise," a zany newspaper about hand- and machine-embroidery techniques. (See Bibliography and Supply List for all addresses.)

Our history has been one of expanding circles: one excited person shows another who moves to a new area, taking the techniques with her. Machine embroidery is now taught in art schools, universities, evening adult education classes, and stores, as well as in living rooms between friends. Best of all, the history of machine embroidery is still unfolding.

For those of you who have wondered what all the fuss is, here's the table of contents from the 1911 *Singer Instructions for Art Embroidery and Lace Work*. (I was first shown the old Singer book by Caryl Rae Hancock. Like everyone who has seen it, I was astounded at the fineness and scope of the work. The last edition of the book was 1941 and it is very difficult to find a copy of it. Then when I wrote about it in my "Needle & Thread" column, Bessie Lizawetsky of Akron, OH, offered to sell me hers, for which I am still grateful.)

Foreword
General Rules

FIRST COURSE OF STUDY
1. First Stitches
2. Cording
3. English or Eyelet Embroidery

Fig. A–6 Joyce Drexler. Photo courtesy of Joyce.

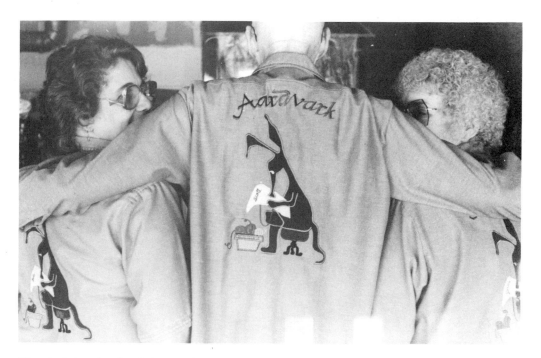

Fig. A–7 Aardvarks (left to right: Debbie Castell, Scott Zarbaugh, Jerry Zarbaugh). Shirts worked by Margo Watson of Sacramento, CA.

4. First Openwork Stitches
5. Richelieu Embroidery (Cut Work)
6 and 7. Hemstitching
8. Scalloping and Raised Embroidery Satin Stitch
9. Letters and Monograms
10 and 11. Fancy Stitches on White Goods
12. Applique on Net
13. English Lace (Braid Applique)
14. Brussels Lace
15. Filet Lace
16. Milan Lace
17. Bone Lace – First Applique
18. Embroidery on Net
19 and 20. Needle Point Lace and Venetian Richelieu Lace
21. Smyrna Embroidery
22 and 23. Venetian Lace – First Stitches
24 and 25. Shaded Embroidery

SECOND COURSE OF STUDY
26. Teneriffe Wheels
27 and 28. Mexican Drawn Work
29. Hedebo Embroidery

30. Velvet Applique
31. Battenberg Embroidery
32. Applique of Cretonne
33. Bond Lace
34. Valenciennes Lace
35. Cluny Lace
36. Fancy Lace
37 and 38. English Point Lace
39 and 40. Artistic Embroidery on White Goods
41 and 42. Renaissance Lace
43 and 44. Fancy Embroidery Points on White Goods
45. Bone Lace – Insertions
46. Fancy Lace Edging
47. Bead Work
48. Rococo Embroidery
49. Venetian Embroidery
50. Imitation Velvet

THIRD COURSE OF STUDY
51. Crochet Lace
52 and 53. Duchess Lace
54. Bruges Lace

Fig. A–8 Deb and Esther Wagner, authors of Wagner's Sewing Machine Artistry (see Bibliography), have worked many of the old Singer samples. This duck is appliqued onto thin veneer. Photo courtesy of the artists.

88.	Embroidery with Mercerized Embroidery Cotton	106.	White Lace Cushion
89.	Embroidery with Metallic Cord	107.	Altar Cloth
90.	Imitation Tapestry	108.	Table Runner
91.	Embroidery on Leather	109.	Kimono
92.	Bengal Lace	110.	Towel
93.	Crochet Points	111.	Tea Cozy
94.	Medallions	112.	Tray Cloth
95.	Mirecourt Bone Lace Edging	113.	Fancy Box
96.	Fancy Work of Raffia Straw	114.	Window Panel
97.	Imitation Embossed Velvet	115.	Runner for Dresser
98.	Sculpture Reproduction	116.	Lamp Shade
99.	Embroidery on Wood	117.	Handkerchief Case
100.	Smyrna Rug	118.	Picture
		119.	Curtains
		120.	Parasol

FIFTH COURSE OF STUDY

101.	Combination	121.	Sofa Cushion (Embroidered in Colors)
102.	Bed Spread	122.	Slippers and Bag
103.	Bed Sheet	123.	Baby Dress and Cap
104.	Table Cover	124.	Imitation Pen and Ink Drawing
105.	Boudoir Doll Lamp	125.	Amphora

APPENDIX

Organize Your Work Area

I envy those of you who have your own room to mess up. For the rest of us who must carve out a work space in a corner of the bedroom, living room, dining room, or kitchen, here are some tips.

Try to claim a small place that you can leave set up. It is discouraging enough to interrupt your enthusiasms, without having to clear your workspace so that everyone can eat dinner. A flea-market cardtable is enough. When you have extremely limited space, the key is to keep your materials simple. Every time you can't see your machine because it's covered with piles of scraps you might use someday, it's time to be ruthless. Give the scraps to Goodwill and get back to work.

Pay attention to your quirks. You don't need a lot of space, but that space must feel right. For example, I hate to sew facing a blank wall. I either need a window across from me or I need to face an open area. I also don't mind spreading material all over the bed and floor, but I feel cramped if the area around my machine is crowded with materials, threads, and tools.

The answer for me was to buy two old office desks, the kind with lots of drawers and a swing-up stand for a typewriter. The drawers hold all those miscellaneous items that threaten to overtake my work area and the swing-up stands inside receive piles of projects-in-progress. (I thought I'd use the stands to store my machines, but I discovered I like my machines out where I can see them.) Another advantage of these office desks is that you can lock the drawers, handy if you have toddlers who might eat pins. I use one of the desk tops for sewing and the other for art.

If your work area is small, like mine, you will have to go up, not out. Buy, build, beg, or borrow shelves. Then keep your eye out for anything that will hold thread and fabric and can be stacked. Some solutions used by friends and by me are: Gail Domorsky uses a Plano fishing-tackle box to store threads. This is a bin with fold-out drawers and a handle on the lid. She can then easily carry her box to classes she teaches. A three-drawer Plano box costs about $30 in 1986. Jackie Dodson uses pie safes for threads. I use plastic stacking office trays for threads (not such a great idea, because the thread gets dusty and dried-out, but I use what I have and I have lots of trays — one of these days I'll get around to making a plastic cover for them). I also have stacking clear plastic shoe boxes for threads and I recently bought five clear lingerie boxes for about $21. I like being able to see the colors I have and I need to be able to carry boxes from room to room, since I am a sewing gypsy. Check hardware and fishing stores for nifty storage compartments at reasonable prices.

I keep fabrics in cardboard boxes that once held reams of paper (check at your local photocopy center). They are sturdy and can be stacked up. One box is solely for interfacings and stabilizers. Since I can never remember which fabric is what, once I've opened the package, I store them in labeled Ziplock bags with fusing instructions inside.

After carefully organizing fabric scraps for years, until every spare corner was overrun, I decided to limit what I keep to the amount of storage space I have. Now, when I overrun, I clean house and give away fabrics I haven't touched for years. I call this Playing the Game of Condominium — if I had to move to a condominium and compress all my belongings, what could I give away? For me, it is liberating to contract rather than to expand (to some of my correspondents, this attitude is scandalous).

I keep small sewing tools in several places. One is an organizer from the hardware store, with small drawers meant for nails and screws. I also keep three small stacking bins near whatever machine I'm working on, which contain thread snips, bobbins, tweezers, ripper, etc. But what I like best is the inside of a roll-top desk that I bought at a garage sale. It has lots of little drawers, into which I pile the odds and ends we all collect. The trouble is that I can never remember what I put where, so I end up opening all the drawers to find what I want. Labeling the drawers might help.

I keep special pencils, pens, and pokers in coffee cups and glass beakers and often load up a kitchen tray with supplies, so I can carry them from room to room (I have sewing machines all over the house). Larger rulers are kept in a basket on the floor.

As for design inspiration, I keep track of ideas by making manilla files for categories of interest — circles, windows, lettering, quilts, flowers, ani-

258

mals, color, techniques, etc. Each original design is assigned its own manilla folder, into which goes my journal, sketches, first attempts, research notes, related articles, clippings from magazines, etc., plus a history of where it has been shown or who received it.

In addition to the folders, I have many (used) three-ring binders, organized into various categories, including garment sewing, into which I put more complicated items—class notes, articles, tips from readers and friends, manufacturers' instructions, etc. In these binders, I have plenty of blank paper, see-through plastic envelopes, and the kind of photo-album pages where you lift a piece of acetate and place a photo on a sticky background. The blank paper and extra holders allow me to file as I accumulate. Otherwise, the paper tends to mount up.

I also have lots of sketch books, my favorites being spiral-bound 1/4" graph paper books from Aardvark Adventures (alas, the books are no longer available). These are loosely organized into quilts, clothing, museums, and travel sketches.

What I don't have is wall space in my sewing area for display. I improvise by stringing a clothesline over my work area and hanging up stitched samples, notes to myself, pictures for inspiration. I also use a small magnetic board with magnets, propped against my shelves, on which I can display small items—a technique or design I'm pondering, a funny saying, etc. I've hammered pushpins into the edges of the shelves over my work area, from which I hang oversized plastic clips. On these I hang up pattern instructions, cartoons, notes, etc., to study as I work at the machine. Tony has promised to make me a felt-covered bulletin board,

to be inset into the back of the door next to my sewing area. I'd like to be able to display sketches and stitch samples when I'm playing What-If.

Jane Warnick has a much better way to keep track of her stitched samples than I do (Fig. A-9). She has two notebooks full of samples. (Until I get around to making sample books, I tend to throw my samples in a drawer.) Judi Cull has a clever way to display her teaching samples: on herself. She's made a simple dress with a set of detachable collars, on which she has worked samples of the techniques she is teaching. She changes collars as she teaches each new concept.

All this describes my primary sewing area—but with four machines, a daughter who loves to sew, a husband I like to be near, and a small house, I have other areas. I bought a handy portable table made by Sirco that lifts into a support around the free arm of the machine. Either Kali or I are always using it, often in front of the TV during football season (if you can't lick them, join them). I also have a portable cardboard cutting table, an ingenious device by Daynell (see Supply List), that I can set up and take down in seconds. I prefer to work in an L-shaped area, with another surface to my left—but our house is too small for such a permanent work area. The cardboard table allows me to make an L, but easily to clear it away when I'm done.

I also leave a machine set up on the back porch off the kitchen. I often leave the needle down in a project, so that when I get up in the morning, I can work for 10 or 15 minutes while making coffee. If I see it, I do it; if I don't see it, I don't work. (This is why I don't like to store my machine with the case on; somehow it's uninviting to me—yet I

FLOWER
STITCH/TECHNIQUE

THREAD: Top NATESH LIGHT STITCH: Straight   Zigzag

Bobbin ___"____"_____   Cam_____

GROUND FABRIC: TREMODE _____   Length_____ Width_____

NEEDLE: ___80_____   WORKED FROM Right / Wrong SIDE

TENSION: Top _2_ (THREAD TREE)

Bobbin: Loose   Tight   (Normal) (Bypass) WHIP
                                   SATIN

FOOT: Presser Foot   Darning Foot (Free in Frame) Other_____

NOTES:_____
_____
_____
_____
_____

Fig. A–9 One page from Jane Warnick's sample books. She prints the forms on manilla stock, cuts out a window for the sample, and tapes it with artists's white tape from the back. This one shows the magazine photo that inspired the sample.

don't mind a handmade sewing-machine cover.)

If you've been counting, you realize I've only mentioned three of my four machines. The last is set up with heavy upholstery thread, because I am slowly recovering my couches. I won't say how many years this has been going on, but not sharing this machine with anyone or any other project has speeded the project.

In closing, let me remind you that organizing is not static: you don't organize once for life. It's an organic process that changes as your life changes. Sometimes you don't realize that you need to rethink your organization until it registers that the piles of unsorted stuff sitting around and driving you crazy have been there for months. Then eureka!, you think of a new, better way to rearrange your work area.

Besides, creative people are mostly messy. I'm always a little suspicious of the super-organized.

In case these suggestions are helpful, here are some favorite tools and such:

Snag repair for knits, used to pull thread ends to the back
Needle-nosed tweezers
Linen tester (bought in photography store) to magnify needle sizes
Stamp moistener to erase water-soluble pen marks
Toothbrush for brushing pile, Ultrasuede, fake fur
Basting brush for cleaning bobbin area of machine

Fig. A–10 Some favorite tools: linen tester, precut 6" squares of fabric, compressed-air cannister, stamp moistener, heavy-duty Olfa cutter, Sony Walkman to listen to Books on Tape as I sew, needle-nosed tweezers, curved-at-the-tip scissors, brush for cleaning bobbin, toothbrush.

Compressed-air cannister used by photographers to clean equipment, used everywhere on machine, including bobbin area

Elna Press

Small table-top ironing board that sits next to machine

Heavy-duty plug on top of desk with six outlets

Heavy-duty Olfa cutter and full-length cutting mat, X-acto knife

Portable light table and opaque projector

Swivel chair on coasters so I can easily get in and out from my sewing desk

C-thru ruler, Nancy Crow Quickline, long drafting T-square, flexible ruler, cork-backed metal ruler

Lots of graph paper in all sizes, including wall-size pads with 1" squares (these are not accurate, however—check yours)

Colored construction paper, ColorAid paper, felt-tipped pens, colored pencils, Rapidograph technical pens

Stack of pre-cut 6" square fabrics, ready for stitching

Sony Walkman tape recorder and tapes of good books rented from Books on Tape (see Supply List) or from the library—I love to listen as I sew

Large goose-neck lamp from art store

APPENDIX

On Collecting Machine Embroidery

I collect two kinds of machine embroidery: ethnic pieces and contemporary machine-embroidered art. My budget and wall space are limited, so I tend to buy a few small pieces each year. I currently own art by Merry Bean, Sas Colby, Katharine Colwell, Maria-Theresa Fernandes, Elizabeth Gurrier, Cindy Hickok, Peggy Moulton, Joan Schulze, Wilcke Smith, and Verina Warren.

This tells you whose work I own—but it does not tell why I collect.

Quite simply, I love to be moved, to be touched deeply, to be tweaked, to be uplifted, to be astounded, to be enriched—and to laugh. My art collection does all of that for me. Best of all, the artists' passions speak to me daily, because I work in my home and am surrounded by the pieces.

Yet I don't come from a background where art was collected. My ancestors are of Depression stock, with no extra pennies for "frills." Paying what seemed like a lot of money for my first piece was hard for me.

But I've since discovered that art is magic. I love the work. I love the relationship with "my" artists. I love sharing my collection with visitors.

How do I choose a piece? I don't—I choose an artist. Despite my love for the sewing machine, I'm not interested

262

Fig. A–11 Maria-Theresa Fernandes, Washington, DC, "Landscape USA No. 1," 5' × 1'. Paint, thread, paper, wire mesh. Collection of Robbie Fanning.

solely in technique; change that word to "soul-ly" and I'll buy. I look for evidence of the soul of an artist, the fire of creative genius. The artists I seek are the kind of people who would create something worthwhile if they lived in a cave with no audience. They are not merely creating something for sale to collectors like me. They are compelled to create and have been given an indescribable spark that lights every piece.

How do I find the artists? Most often, I see work I like in books or magazines. I track down the artist's address; then I ask her or him to send slides, descriptions, and prices, so that I often buy without having seen the piece, only the slide (which underlines the importance of artists taking good color slides).

My interest in the artist does not stop with one piece. I want to know how the artist is faring and growing. Therefore, I appreciate the professionalism of those artists who put me on their publicity list and notify me about their exhibitions, awards, conference teaching jobs, feature stories in newspapers and magazines, etc. I also appreciate receiving periodic slides and prices of new work.

My acquisition budget is small, but year by year, my home fills with magic.

APPENDIX **E**

Teaching Machine-Embroidery Classes

If you and your sewing machine love each other, you can make up to $100/day teaching machine-embroidery classes.

I'm not joking about the love affair, either. The first prerequisite for this opportunity to bring in several hundred extra dollars a month is a genuine affection for the sewing machine as a fast, effective, and creative tool—as useful on the homestead, for example, as the chain saw. If you understand your machine literally inside-out—its quirks, its possibilities, and its limits—then you are ready to teach others how to use their machines, too . . . and to make money at the same time.

In this age of hurry, many people have forsaken the time-consuming arts such as hand embroidery that once satisfied our age-old desire to bring beauty to usefulness. Yet the desire to create is still there. This is the appeal of machine embroidery: it's fast, it's easy, it's attractive, and it satisfies that universal creative urge. Remember those four points when you teach your first class.

The scope of what and how to teach machine embroidery is vast—everything from how to make machine-appliqued bookmarks to how to design a 16-foot machine-embroidered hanging commissioned by a hospital. Your first decision is what age do you want to teach, what are your own interests, and what are the interests of your community.

Some teachers specialize in working with teenagers, such as 4-H, church groups, and junior and senior high school sewing classes. The kids want simple projects that they can use immediately, and your classes should concentrate on one technique a lesson. Making a patch for their jeans or jackets using simple free-machine embroidery would be a typical two- to three-hour class.

Adults, most of whom are women, also like to walk out of your class with finished projects, although with the added years of sewing experience, they can handle more complex projects, something that may require two or more lessons to complete. Typical projects might be Christmas ornaments or small machine-made gifts like needle cases.

Some adults are primarily interested in the sewing machine as an art tool, and these people want one- or two-day intensive instruction in machine concepts, basic design, and color. They will want to make a notebook of small finished samples. Although these are the best-paying classes, naturally these groups are not numerous in a small community, so if this is your interest, prepare to travel widely to teach.

Once you've pinpointed which age group appeals to you and determined that there are enough people nearby to teach, you must decide where to hold the class. The least expensive and most profitable place for you is in your home. You do not need an extremely large place, either. I've often taught up to 25 people, two to a cardtable, in an average-sized living room. (Incidentally, sewing machines do not pull much power so you don't have to worry about overloading, but don't plug in an iron in the same room or you'll blow the circuits.) Teaching in your home, you do not have to pay a percentage to a store or set class hours to fit into someone else's room-availability schedule.

If you do decide to teach at home, an additional source of income is to sell thread, hoops, scissors, pamphlets, magazines, and books to your students. For this you'll need a resale license to buy at wholesale rates. However there is a fine line between nickel-and-diming your students to death on supplies and teaching with integrity. I used to resent classes I took with an additional $5 supply charge for materials I had at home—until I taught a class with people from outlying areas who had no access to the simplest thread. I now give students a choice: I give out a supply list and I also say "supplies available for purchase in class."

The disadvantages of teaching in your home are that you usually feel compelled to clean it before the class comes, which can be nerve-wracking and time-consuming when you're also preparing for the class and living your normal disorderly life. You have to clean up afterwards, too, and machine embroidery can be messy. You'll have to provide extension cords and outlets for all the machines, probably coffee or tea for participants, and missing supplies. Invariably, no matter how thorough your supply list, someone forgets a hoop or scissors. And invariably, no matter how eagle-eyed you are, someone walks off with your best scissors. All of these are the hidden expenses of teaching at home.

The alternative is teaching outside your home. A likely place is a fabric- or sewing-machine store. You must then decide whether each participant brings her own machine or whether you'll teach on the store's machines. Naturally, there are pros and cons to both ways. A woman knows her own machine best and ideally wants to learn how to use it for machine embroidery. But there are many cheap, out-of-tune machines, and unless you are very experienced with many makes, you and the student may become bogged down by a malfunctioning machine. Working on store machines is to the store owner's advantage. He or she not only knows the capabilities of the machines, but often makes a sale to a student with an inferior machine at home. Technically, if the student decides to buy a new machine because of your class, you should get a salesperson's commission. Talk this over with the store owner *before* you begin teaching.

I prefer students to bring their own machines to a store, but I've sewn on all models and can now fix or figure out practically every problem. I do say at the beginning of class, "I will spend up to five minutes with cranky machines but no longer than that." As a precaution, I always have my machine along or several extra store machines available for the use of the student who is suddenly without a functioning machine.

Other places to teach are in church halls (not necessarily for church groups—you can usually rent the hall inexpensively), in high school home ec rooms through adult education classes, in junior colleges, and at specialized conferences, conventions, and fairs.

How much to charge, like all classes, is how much the traffic will bear. I took a survey of ten machine-embroidery teachers around the country and the average was $5 to $7 per 2-3 hour lesson per person. Often these were in a series of three to five weekly lessons. The more complicated the lessons and the more authority you bring with you, the more money you make. For example, several teachers, myself included, teach one-day workshops all over the country for $100/day plus travel expenses. If you teach in a shop, you generally give about 20-25% to the owner for class space.

Be sure to set a minimum-maximum limit on students. It's not worth my time to prepare for a class of less than eight, but some teachers will go as low as three. As for maximum, the size of your teaching space determines this. However, I limit class size to 25; above this, no one receives enough individual attention.

How will you find students once you've decided to teach? This is where teaching in a store has decided advantages. The owner usually posts signs in the window, tells walk-in customers, notifies the store mailing list, and includes the information in newspaper advertising. I never totally rely on someone else to promote my classes. I always make up a one-page flyer, using press-on letters (available at art and stationery stores) to create the original, and photocopy onto colored stock. I post these flyers on kiosks, bulletin boards, etc. I also send notices of the class to interested groups for their newsletters and to local newspapers. After you've taught once, word-of-mouth will work to your favor for a continuing stream of students. (If it doesn't, you probably shouldn't be teaching in the first place.)

Two additional effective ways to find students are to display your own machine-embroidered work or the work of your students in a store, library, art center, etc. and to give free demonstrations of machine embroidery at stores,

festivals, shopping malls, or fairs. Have a class sign-up sheet with you to take advantage of being the center of attention.

It is not difficult to attract repeat students if you offer beginning, intermediate, and advanced lessons, and if you change the projects made in your classes often. In particular, busy women will take your classes again and again if they know that you've saved them time by testing the design first and that they can go home with an attractive finished project. Also, there is a tremendous growing interest in machine quilting, which can attract repeat students. Offer three levels of machine embroidery first, and then three levels of machine quilting.

How will you generate ideas for projects and for classes? As one teacher said, "I can't create, but I can copy." She's right: you do not have to be a top-notch designer to teach machine embroidery. As long as you cover all the basic machine concepts, you can borrow designs to use those concepts on. In case you haven't noticed, machine embroidery is popular and all the ladies' magazines have projects you can adapt for your classes. Also consult the list of machine-embroidery books and magazines at the end of this book. Many contain good class projects. Another favorite source of simple designs has always been children's coloring books.

The concepts you should cover in machine-embroidery classes are (in the words of one demonstrator) "how not to be afraid of the machine," straight stitch, zigzag and satin stitching, free-machine embroidery, outlining, monogramming, machine applique, fill-in stitches, tapering, and special effects like fringing, cording, heavy threads in the bobbin, cutwork, yarn stitchery, etc. If you are not familiar with these terms, study this book and others in the bibliography and work masses of samples until you are thoroughly comfortable with the techniques.

In class you will combine lecture and demonstration on a machine with samples of the technique being talked about, ideas for how to use it, slides, books, ditto sheets, and sketches on a blackboard. Generally, in any subject, a good teacher tells the student what she *will* learn, teaches it by example and by having the student do it, and then tells the student what she *has* learned.

If you do not feel confident in working up your own class plan, there are places and books to help you. Talk to your local fabric store owner; he or she may train you to teach in the store. If you are using a particular model sewing machine, find out when the company demonstrator is coming through. You can learn a lot by watching and by asking her how she was trained. Sometimes the company has regional training centers. Several pioneers in the machine-embroidery field have teacher-training studios and people travel from all over the country to learn (see Supply List—Training in Machine Embroidery).

To improve as a teacher, keep track of each class you teach. Have a lesson plan to follow; then critique the session afterwards by writing notes to yourself on what worked well, what confused some students, what bombed, and how you can improve the class the next time.

I asked the surveyed machine-embroidery teachers what advice they would give to people who want to start teaching machine embroidery. "Know your subject and enjoy it!" says dj Bennett of Lake Forest, Illinois. "Be thoroughly versed on things that can go wrong with the sewing machine. Have lots of samples and ideas. Work from basics and then to complex. Give them something they can use ASAP. Have compassion and patience," comes from Nancy Duncan, former demonstrator for the Riccar Sewing Machine Company. Nina Stull of Fremont, California, agrees with her. "Have a full line of samples and know a variety of techniques." Verna Holt of Las Vegas advises "Don't try a huge big project. Start with something simple and small. Complete it; then grow as you practice." "Be flexible," says Sue Osgood of Los Altos, California. "You will have all kinds of machines. Teach what the group is interested in. And don't have hurt feelings when not everyone loves every part."

And finally Barbara Sharpe of Placerville, CA says "Learn what other educators are teaching in your area and don't duplicate their teaching patterns. Develop your own style. Find an unusual use for machine embroidery and expand it. One of my unusual uses was to personalize the outdoor clothing and equipment I make for my family. I also teach a class in outdoor clothing and equipment which was doubly useful as teaching samples."

The greatest joy in teaching machine embroidery is to see someone come in the door timid about her creative abilities and then to see her leave overflowing with confidence, plans, ideas, and inspiration. If you can communicate your own enthusiasm about the machine to others, then you won't have any trouble making some extra money teaching machine-embroidery classes.

NEEDLE AND THREAD CHART

Fit the thread to the type of work or material and fit the needle to the thread

needle	*thread*	*fabrics*
8/9 (65)	extra-fine	very sheer (denier, etc.)
10/11 (70)	extra-fine cotton and polyester	lightweight and transparent fabrics (net, chiffon, organza, etc.)
12 (80)	silk twist (A), ordinary cotton, rayon	lightweight cottons
14 (90)	ordinary cotton, cotton-covered polyester, silk twist (D)	wool, flannel, medium-weight cottons, jerseys
16 (100)	heavy-duty cotton	heavy coating material
18 (110)	heavy	heavy denims, etc.

HANDY ALL-AT-ONE-GLANCE MACHINE EMBROIDERY CHART

	chapter	stitch width	stitch length	tensions top	tensions bobbin	foot	feed dog	hoop	backing	needle	thread
applique	3	v*	v	loosen	normal	applique	up	no	stabilizer	12 (80)	extra-fine
automatic	7	v	v	v	v	embroidery	up	no	stabilizer	v	v
beading	3	v	fine	tighten	loosen	embroidery	up	no	no	10/11(70)	extra-fine
cable	6	0	0	v	bypass	darning	lower	no	no	16/18(100/110)	heavy on top
circular embroidery	8	v	v	universal		embroidery	in place	yes	stabilizer	10/11(70)	extra-fine
couching-by-piercing	5	0	0	universal		darning	lower	no	stabilizer	v	invisible
couching, topside	4	0	0	normal	loosen	darning	lower	no	no	v	v
couching, underside	6	0–4	10–12	loosen	bypass	regular	in place	no	no	vv	heavy under
crosshatching	2	0	10–12	universal		regular	up	no	no	v	v
crosshatching, zigzag	3	v	10–12	universal		regular	up	no	no	v	v
cross stitch	10	v	v	universal		regular	up	no	no	v	v
cut work	3	medium	fine	loosen	loosen	embroidery	up	yes	no	v	v
detached whip stitch	5	0	0	tighten	bypass	darning	lower	yes	interfacing	v	v
edges, special	10	v	v	universal		embroidery	in place	yes	stabilizer	v	v
encroaching zigzag	5	v	0	loosen	normal	darning	lower	yes	stabilizer	10/11(70)	extra-fine
eyelets	8	v	0	universal		none	e. plate	yes	no	v	v
fagoting	7	wide	10–12	loosen	normal	embroidery	in place	no	paper	v	v
free machine embroidery	4	0	0	loosen	normal	darning	lower	yes	stabilizer	wing	extra-fine
hemstitching	9		10–12	universal		regular	in place	no	no	10/11(70)	extra-fine
monograms	10	v	0	loosen	normal	darning	lower	yes	stabilizer	10/11(70)	extra-fine
needlelace	9	0	0	universal		darning	lower	yes	no	10/11(70)	extra-fine
openwork	9	v	0	universal		darning	lower	no	no	v	v
quilting, presser foot	2	0	10–12	loosen	loosen	walking	up	no	no	v	v
quilting, free	12	0	0	loosen	normal	darning	lower	no	stabilizer	v	v
picot	8	0	10–12	universal		regular	in place	no	no	wing	extra-fine
pintucking	8	0	10–12	tighten	normal	pintuck	in place	no	no	v	v
reverse applique	9	v	fine	loosen	normal	embroidery	in place	no	no	v	v
rugmaking	7	v	10–12	universal		regular	in place	no	no	v	v
satin stitch	3	v	fine	loosen	regular	embroidery	in place	no	no	10/11(70)	extra-fine
satin stitch spots	5	v	0	loosen	normal	darning	lower	no	no	v	v
smocking	8	v	10–12	universal		regular	in place	no	no	twin	v
stocking face dolls	9	0	0	universal		darning	lower	no	organza	10/11(70)	extra-fine
straight stitch	2	0	any	universal		regular	up	no	no	v	v
topstitching	2	0	8–10	universal		regular	up	no	no	v	v
trapunto	2	0	10–12	universal		regular	up	no	organza	v	v
vari-width zigzag	3	v	fine	universal		embroidery	up	no	stabilizer	v	v
whip stitch	4	0	0	tighten	bypass	darning	lower	yes	no	v	v
zigzag, open	3	v	10–12	universal		regular	up	no	stabilizer	v	v
zigzag shading	5	v	0	loosen	tighten	darning	lower	yes	stabilizer	10/11(70)	extra-fine

*varies

Supply List

Sewing Machines

Archer-Finesse
Melex USA, Inc.
    1200 Front St.
    Raleigh, NC 27609

Bernina/East
    534 W. Chestnut
    Hinsdale, IL 60521

Bernina/West
    70 Orchard Dr.
    North Salt Lake, UT 84054

Brother Sewing Machine Co.
    8th Corporation Pl.
    Piscataway, NJ 08854

Elna, Inc.
    7642 Washington Ave. S
    Minneapolis, MN 55344

Kenmore
    Sears Tower
    Chicago, IL 60607

Necchi Logica/Allyn International
1075 Santa Fe Drive
Denver, CO 80204

Nelco
    164 W. 25th St.
    New York, NY 10001

New Home Sewing Machine Company
171 Commerce Dr.
Carlstadt, NJ 07072

JC Penney Co., Inc.
    1301 Avenue of the Americas
    New York, NY 10019

Pfaff American Sales Corp.
    610 Winters Ave.
    Paramus, NJ 07653

Riccar America Co.
    14281 Franklin Ave.
    Tustin, CA 92680

Simplicity/Tacony Corp.
    4421 Ridgewood Ave.
    St. Louis, MO 63116

Singer Company
    135 Raritan Center Pkwy.
    Edison, NJ 08837

Viking White Sewing Machine Co.
    11750 Berea Rd.
    Cleveland, OH 44111

Ward's (Montgomery Ward)
    PO Box 8339
    Chicago, IL 60680

White — see Viking White

Threads

Note: Ask your local retailer or send a pre-addressed stamped envelope to the companies below to find out where to buy their threads.

Extra-fine
DMC 100% cotton, Sizes 30 and 50
    The DMC Corporation
    107 Trumbull St.
    Elizabeth, NJ 07206

Dual-Duty Plus Extra-fine, cotton-wrapped polyester
    J&P Coats/Coats & Clark
    PO Box 6044
    Norwalk, CT 06852

Iris 100% rayon
    Art Sales
    4801 W. Jefferson
    Los Angeles, CA 90016

Iris 100% silk — *see* Zwicky

Mettler Metrosene Fine Machine Embroidery cotton, Size 60/2
    Swiss-Metrosene, Inc.
    7780 Quincy St
    Willowbrook, IL 60521

Natesh 100% rayon, lightweight
    Aardvark Adventures
    PO Box 2449
    Livermore, CA 94550

Paradise 100% rayon
D&E Distributing
199 N. El Camino Real #F-242
Encinitas, CA 92024

Sulky 100% rayon, Sizes 30 and 40
Speed Stitch, Inc.
PO Box 3472
Port Charlotte, FL 33949

Zwicky 100% cotton, Size 30/2
White Sewing Machine Co.
11750 Berea Rd
Cleveland, OH 44111

Ordinary
Dual Duty Plus, cotton-wrapped polyester — *see
Dual Duty Plus Extra-fine*
Also Natesh heavyweight, Zwicky in cotton and
polyester, Mettler Metrosene in 30/2, 40/3,
50/3, and 30/3, and polyester Metrosene Plus

Metallic
YLI Corporation
45 West 300 North
Provo, UT 84601

Machine-Embroidery Supplies

(hoops, threads, patterns, books, etc.)

Aardvark Adventures
PO Box 2449
Livermore, CA 94550
Also publishes "Aardvark Territori-
al Enterprise"

Clotilde Inc.
237 SW 28th St.
Ft. Lauderdale, FL 33315
$1 catalog

Craft Gallery Ltd.
PO Box 8319
Salem, MA 01971

Crafty Critter
PO Box 16124
Duluth, MN 55816

D&E Distributing
199 N. El Camino Real #F-242
Encinitas, CA 92024

Verna Holt's Machine Stitchery
3221 Joanne Way #B
Las Vegas, NV 89108

Nancy's Notions
PO Box 683
Beaver Dam, WI 53916
Catalog $.60 in stamps

Patty Lou Creations
Rt 2, Box 90-A
Elgin, OR 97827

Sew-Art International
PO Box 550
Bountiful, UT 84010

Speed Stitch, Inc.
PO Box 3472
Port Charlotte, FL 33952
Catalog $2

SewCraft
Box 6146
South Bend, IN 46660
Also publishes newsletter, catalog
$.50

Treadleart
25834 Narbonne Ave.
Lomita, CA 90717
Catalog $1, also publishes
"Treadleart"

Troy Thread & Textile Corp.
2300 W. Diversey Ave.
Chicago, IL 60647

Sewing Machine Supplies

The Button Shop
PO Box 1065
Oak Park, IL 60304
Presser feet

Sewing Emporium
1087 Third Ave
Chula Vista, CA 92010

Miscellaneous

Application's
871 Fourth Ave
Sacramento, CA 95818
Release Paper for applique

Berman Leathercraft
145 South St.
Boston, MA 02111
Leather

Books on Tape
PO Box 7900
Newport Beach, CA 92660
1-800-626-3333
Oh frabjous joy! Listening to good
books while stitching!

Boycan's Craft and Art Supplies
PO Box 897
Sharon, PA 16146
Plastic needlepoint canvas

Cabin Fever Calicoes
PO Box 54
Center Sandwich, NH 03227
Wonderful fabric colors, books on color, $2.75 catalog

Ceci
PO Box 1602
Lemon Grove, CA 92045
Thread holders and clever gadgets — $1 catalog

Clearbrook Woolen Shop
PO Box 8
Clearbrook, VA 22624
Ultrasuede scraps

CR's Crafts
Box 8, East Main
Leland, IA 50453
Fake fur, doll and teddy bear parts, $2 catalog

Judi Cull
PO Box 60902
Sacramento, CA 95860
Packet of worksheets for machine embroidery, $4.50

Daisy Chain
PO Box 1258
Parkersburg, WV 26102
All kinds of thread for hand embroidery, $2 catalog

Daynell
Box 5793
Portland, OR 97228
Portable cardboard cutting table

The Fabric Carr
170 State St.
Los Altos, CA 94022
Sewing gadgets

Folkwear
Box 3798
San Rafael, CA 94912
Timeless fashion patterns, catalog $1

Gick Publishing
9 Studebaker Dr.
Irvine, CA 92718
Great Shapes (cardboard shapes) — ask your local retailer

The Green Pepper Inc.
941 Olive St.
Eugene, OR 97401
Outdoor fabrics like Goretex, catalog $1

Heritage Crafts
10966 Sutter Way
Nevada City, CA 95959
Patch-Catcher is a clever magnetic pin-up board

Home-Sew
Bethlehem, PA 18018
Lace for French handsewing, catalog $.25

Libby's Creations
PO Box 16800 Ste. 180
Mesa, AZ 85202
Spool-It Horizontal Spool Holder

LJ Originals, Inc.
516 Sumac Pl.
DeSoto, TX 75115
TransGraph

Lore Lingerie
3745 Overland Ave.
Los Angeles, CA 90034
1 lb. of silk remnants, $9.45

Osage County Quilt Factory
400 Walnut
Overbrook, KS 66524
Washable fabric spray glue

The Pellon Company
119 West 40th St.
New York, NY 10018
Wonder Under machine applique supplies

The Perfect Notion
115 Maple St.
Toms River, NJ 08753
Sewing supplies

Salem Industries, Inc.
PO Box 43027
Atlanta, GA 30336
Olfa cutters

Solar-Kist Corp.
PO Box 273
La Grange, IL 60525
Easy Way Applique Teflon pressing sheets

Stacy Industries, Inc.
38 Passaic St.
Wood-Ridge, NJ 07075
TransFuse Teflon pressing sheet

Summa Design
Box 24404
Dayton, OH 45424
Charted designs for knitting-needle machine sewing

Tandy Leather Co.
   PO Box 791
   Ft. Worth, TX 76101
      Leather

Tecla's
   120 E. Birch
   Brea, CA 92621
      Pad of technique sheets, $2

Books
(used and new)

Books in Transit
   2830 Case Way
   Turlock, CA 95380

Jo Bryant Books
   630 Graceland SE
   Albuquerque, NM 87108

The Crewel Elephant
   124 East 13th St.
   Silverton, CO 81433

Bette Feinstein
   96 Roundwood Rd
   Newton, MA 02164

Museum Books, Inc.
   6 West 37th St.
   New York, NY 10018

Quilting Books Unlimited
   156 S. Gladstone
   Aurora, IL 60506

Jane Starosciak, Bookseller
   117 Wilmot Mews
   San Francisco, CA 94115

Wooden Porch Books
   Rt 1 Box 262
   Middlebourne, WV 26149

Magazines
(write for current rates)

Aardvark Territorial Enterprise
   PO Box 2449
   Livermore, CA 94550
      Zany inexpensive newspaper filled
      with information about hand and ma-
      chine embroidery

disPatch
   1042 E. Baseline
   Tempe, AZ 85283
      Newpaper about quilting and ma-
      chine arts

Fiberarts
   50 College St.
   Asheville, NC 28801
      Gallery of the best fiber artists, in-
      cluding those who work in machine em-
      broidery

Needle & Thread
   3750 S. University Dr.,Ste. 201
   Ft. Worth, TX 76109
      Creative uses of the sewing ma-
      chine; Robbie writes a column

SewCraft
   Box 6146
   South Bend, IN 46660
      Free newspaper with machine-em-
      broidery projects

Sew News
   PO Box 1790
   Peoria, IL 61656
      Stylish monthly tabloid mostly
      about garment sewing

Stylepages
   PO Box 358
   Cary, IL 60013
      Ideas for creative clothing

Textile Booklist
   PO Box 4392
   Arcata, CA 95521
      Book reviews

Threads
   Box 355
   Newtown, CT 06470
      Glossy colorful magazine on all fi-
      ber crafts; Robbie is a Contributing Edi-
      tor

Treadleart
   25834 Narbonne Ave, Ste I
   Lomita, CA 90717
      Bimonthly all about machine em-
      broidery

Training in Machine Embroidery

California Association of Machine Embroiderers
(annual) — see address under Groups listing

Verna Holt's Machine Stitchery
   3221 Jeanne Way #B
   Las Vegas, NV 89108

National Machine Embroidery Instructors Association
      (annual) — see address under Groups listing

National Standards Council of American Embroiderers
    Carnegie Office Park
    600 Bell Ave.
    Carnegie, PA 15106
      Correspondence course in machine embroidery written by dj Bennett

S.M.A.R.T.
    (annual — location changes)
    Speed Stitch Inc.
    PO Box 3472
    Port Charlotte, FL 33952

Theta's School of Sewing
    2508 NW 39th St.
    Oklahoma City, OK 73112

Videos

Machine Embroidery (97 minutes) and
Machine Quilting (87 minutes)
    Learn by Video
      PO Box 27352
      Salt Lake City, UT 84120

Machine Applique and Embroidery (1 hour) and
Machine Quilting (1 hour)
    Nancy's Notions
      PO Box 683
      Beaver Dam, WI 53916

Groups

California Association of Machine Embroiderers
    PO Box 523
    Westminster, CA 92683
      $30/year, includes newsletter

Embroiderers' Association of Canada, Inc.
    25 St. Leonards Ave.
    Toronto, Ont. M4N 1K1
    Canada
      Quarterly magazine

The Embroiderers' Guild
    PO Box 42B East
    Molesey, Surrey, KT8 9BB
    England
      Quarterly magazine — very inspiring

Embroiderers' Guild of America
    200 4th Ave.
    Louisville, KY 40202
      Quarterly magazine, "Needle Arts"

National Machine Embroidery Instructors Association
    c/o Sew-Art International
    PO Box 550
    Bountiful, UT 84010
      Publishes quarterly "Stitchery Garden" and has annual conference of certified instructors

National Standards Council of American Embroiderers
    PO Box 8578
    Northfield, IL 60093
      Quarterly magazine, "The Flying Needle"

Bibliography

Over the years, many friends have shared their favorite design and color books with me. Of these many friends, I'd especially like to thank Jane Warnick, Margaret Vaile, Bea Miller, Wilcke Smith, Marjorie Coffey, Lois and Walter McBride, and Marilyn Green. Note: Make friends with your public librarian; he or she can help you find all these books.

Good Books on Drawing

Edwards, Betty, *Drawing on the Right Side of the Brain,* JP Tarcher, 1979.

Nicolaides, Kimon, *The Natural Way to Draw,* Houghton Mifflin, 1975.

O'Neill, Dan, et al, *The Big Yellow Drawing Book,* Hugh O'Neill & Assoc., 1974.

Rottger, Ernst, and Dieter Klanta, *Creative Drawing/Point and Line,* Van Nostrand Reinhold, 1983.

Thiel, Philip, *Freehand Drawing,* Univ. of Washington Press, 1981.

Good Books on Design

Blair, Margot, and Cathleen Ryan, *Banners and Flags,* Harcourt Brace Jovanovich, 1977.

Bothwell, Dorr, *Notan/The Dark-Light Principle in Design,* Van Nostrand Reinhold.

d'Arbeloff, Natalie, *Designing with Natural Forms,* Watson-Guptill, 1973.

de Sausmarez, Maurice, *Basic Design: The Dynamics of Visual Form,* Van Nostrand Reinhold, 1964, rev. 1983.

Dendel, Esther, *Designing from Nature,* Taplinger, 1978.

Evans, Helen Marie, *Man the Designer,* Macmillan, 1973.

Garrett, Lillian, *Visual Design/A Problem-Solving Approach,* Reinhold, 1967.

Gatto, Joseph A., et al, *Exploring Visual Design,* Davis, 1978.

Graves, Maitland, *The Art of Color and Design,* McGraw-Hill, 1951.

Hanks, Kurt, et al, *Design Yourself!,* William Kaufmann, 1977.

Howard, Constance, *Inspiration for Embroidery,* BT Batsford/Charles T. Branford, 1966.

Joyce, Carol, *Designing for Printed Textiles,* Prentice-Hall, 1982.

Landa, Robin, *An Introduction to Design,* Prentice-Hall, 1983.

Maier, Manfred, *Basic Principles of Design* (4 volumes), Van Nostrand Reinhold, 1977.

Meilach, Dona Z., et al, *How to Create Your Own Designs,* Doubleday, 1975.

Prohaska, Ray, *A Basic Course in Design,* North Light Publishers, 1980.

Stoops, Jack, and Jerry Samuelson, *Design Dialogue,* Davis, 1983.

Thiel, Philip, *Visual Awareness and Design,* Univ. of Washington Press, 1981.

Wadsworth, John W., *Designs from Plant Forms,* Universe Books, 1910, 1977.

Wong, Wucius, *Principles of Two-Dimensional Design,* Van Nostrand Reinhold, 1972.

Good Books on Color

Albers, Josef, *Interaction of Color,* Yale Univ. Press, 1963.

Birren, Faber, *The Textile Colorist,* Van Nostrand Reinhold, 1980.

Ellinger, Richard G., *Color Structure and Design,* Van Nostrand Reinhold, 1963, 1980.

Grumbacher Color Compass, M. Grumbacher, Inc., 1972.

Hickethier, Alfred, *Color Mixing by Numbers,* Van Nostrand Reinhold, 1963.

Horton, Roberta, *An Amish Adventure: A Workbook for Color in Quilts,* C&T Publishing, 1983.

Howard, Constance, *Embroidery and Colour,* Van Nostrand Heinhold, 1976.

Itten, Johannes, *The Elements of Color,* Van Nostrand Reinhold, 1970.

Justema, William and Doris, *Weaving and Needlecraft Color Course,* Van Nostrand Reinhold, 1971.

Libby, William Charles, *Color and the Structural Sense,* Prentice-Hall, 1974.

McKelvey, Susan R., *Color for Quilters,* Yours Truly, 1984.

Reiss, John J., *Colors,* Bradbury, 1969 (children's book).

Sargent, Walter, *The Enjoyment and Use of Color,* Dover, 1923.

Good Books on Pattern

Appleton, LeRoy H., *American Indian Design and Decoration,* Dover, 1950, 1971.

Baumgartner, Victor, *Graphic Games,* Prentice-Hall, 1983.

Edwards, Edward B., *Pattern and Design with Dynamic Symmetry,* Dover.

Humbert, Claude, *Islamic Ornamental Design,* Hastings House, 1980.

Proctor, Richard M., *The Principles of Pattern,* Van Nostrand Reinhold, 1969.

Proctor, Richard M., and Jennifer F. Lew, *Surface Design for Fabric,* Univ. of Washington Press, 1984.

Stevens, Peter S., *Handbook of Regular Patterns,* MIT Press, 1980.

Wade, David, *Geometric Patterns and Borders,* Van Nostrand Reinhold, 1982.

Books for Visual Inspiration

Bager, Bertel, *Nature as Designer,* Van Nostrand Reinhold, 1976.

Diethelm, Walter, *Visual Transformation,* Hastings House, 1982.

Fassett, Kaffe, *Glorious Knits,* Clarkson N. Potter, Inc., 1985.

Gerster, Georg, *Grand Design: The Earth from Above,* Paddington Press, 1976.

Sandved, Kjell Block, *Butterfly Magic,* Viking, 1975.

Strache, Wolf, *Forms and Patterns in Nature,* Pantheon Books, 1973.

Books That Speak to Me

Edward, Betty, *Drawing on the Artist Within,* Simon and Schuster, 1986.

Field, Joanna, *On Not Being Able to Paint,* JP Tarcher, 1957, 1983.

Franck, Frederick, *The Zen of Seeing,* Vintage Books, 1973.

Jung, C. G., *Man and His Symbols,* Doubleday, 1969.

Patterson, Freeman, *Photography and the Art of Seeing,* Van Nostrand Reinhold, 1979.

Good Books on Machine Stitchery

Bakke, Karen, *The Sewing Machine as a Creative Tool,* Prentice-Hall, 1976.

Barker, Linda, *That Touch of Class/Machine Embroidery on Leather,* (c/o Treadleart, 25834 Narbonne Ave., Lomita, CA 90717).

Bennett, dj, *Machine Embroidery with Style,* Madrona Publishers, 1980.

Better Homes & Gardens, *Creative Machine Stitchery,* Meredith, 1985.

Boyd, Margaret A., *The Sew & Save Source Book,* Betterway Publications, 1984.

Bray, Karen, *Machine Applique,* (21 Birch Dr., Walnut Creek, CA), 1978.

Bunker, Marie, *New Sewing Thrills from Your Zig-Zag Machine,* self-published, 1954.

Butler, Anne, *Machine Stitches,* BT Batsford, Ltd., 1976.

Clucas, Joy, *Your Machine for Embroidery,* G. Bell & Sons, 1975.

Cody, Pat, *Continuous Line Quilting Designs,* Chilton Book Co., 1984.

Coleman, Anne, *The Creative Sewing Machine,* BT Batsford, 1979.

DMC, *Machine Embroidery,* 1976.

DMC, *Decorating with Machine Embroidery.*

Devlin, Nancy, *Guide to Machine Quilting,* Starshine Stitchery Press, 1976.

Drexler, Joyce, *Thread Painting,* Speed Stitch, 1983.

Embroidery Design, Search Press, 1980.

Ericson, Lois, *Fabrics...Reconstructed,* (Box 1680, Tahoe City, CA 95730, 1985.

Fanning, Robbie and Tony Fanning, *The Complete Book of Machine Quilting,* Chilton Book Co., 1980 (or autographed from PO Box 2634, Menlo Park, CA 94026).

Gale Research, *Catalog of Museum Publications and Media,* 1980.

Graham, Lucille Merrell, *Creative Machine Embroidery,* vol. 1 & 2, 1964.

Gray, Jennifer, *Machine Embroidery/Technique and Design,* Van Nostrand Reinhold, 1973.

Greger, Margaret, *Kites for Everyone,* (1425 Marshall, Richland, WA 99352), 1984.

Haight, Ernest B., *Practical Machine-Quilting for the Homemaker.* (David City, NE 68632), 1974.

Hall, Carolyn Vosburg, *Stitched and Stuffed Art,* Doubleday, 1974.

Hall, Carolyn, *The Sewing Machine Craft Book,* Van Nostrand Reinhold, 1980.

Happ, Theta, *English Smocking on the Sewing Machine*, Delmar Creative Publications (2209 NW 46th St., Oklahoma City, OK 73112), 1985.

———, *Charted Needle Design*, Delmar Creative Publications (address above), 1984.

Haywood, Dixie, *The Contemporary Crazy Quilt Project Book*, Dover, 1977.

Hogue, Refa D., *Machine Edgings*, (c/o Treadleart, 25834 Narbonne Ave., Lomita, CA 90717).

Holt, Verna, *Verna's Machine Embroidery Series*, (3221 Joanne Way #B, Las Vegas, NV 89108), 1983.

———, *Yarn Stitchery on the Sewing Machine*, (address above), 1973.

———, *Classic Cutwork*, (address above), 1985.

Howard, Constance, *Twentieth Century Embroidery in Great Britain to 1939*, BT Batsford Co., London, 1981.

Johanson, Robert, *All About Sewing Machines*, (PO Box 8097, Portland, OR 97207), 1970.

Johnson, Beryl, *Advanced Embroidery Techniques*, BT Batsford, 1983.

Katalin, Kardos, *Kalocsai gephimzes*, (c/o Aardvark Adventures, PO Box 2449, Livermore, CA 94550), 1984.

Kenzle, Linda Fry, *Smocking by Machine*, (PO Box 358, Cary, IL 60013), 1984.

———, *Cutwork by Machine*, (address above).

———, *Hemstitching by Machine*, (address above).

Kinser, Charleen, *Sewing Sculpture*, M. Evans and Co., 1977.

Ladies' Home Journal Creative Sewing, Mason/Charter, 1977.

Lee, Barbara, *Successful Machine Applique*, Yours Truly/Burdett, 1978.

Lillow, Ira, *Designs for Machine Embroidery*, Charles T. Branford, 1975.

Machine Embroidery, Search Press, 1980.

Mason, Enid, *Ideas for Machine Embroidery*, Mills & Boon Ltd., 1961.

McCall's Needle-Art Machine Embroidery, McCall's Needlework & Crafts, 1977.

Murwin, Susan, et al, *Quick and Easy Patchwork on the Sewing Machine*, Dover, 1979.

Needlework School, Chartwell Books, 1984.

Newman, Thelma, et al, *Sewing Machine Embroidery and Stitchery*, Crown, 1980.

Nicholas, Annwen, *Embroidery in Fashion*, Watson-Guptill, 1975.

O'Connor, Kaori, *Creative Dressing*, Routledge & Kegan Paul, 1980.

Paque, Joan Michaels, *A Creative and Conceptual Analysis of Textiles*, (4455 N. Frederick Ave., Milwaukee, WI 53211), 1979.

Pascone, Barbara Lee, *Machine Applique Teacher's Kit*, (895 N. Calle Circulo, Camarillo, CA 93010).

Pullen, Martha, *French Hand Sewing by Machine*, (518 Madison St., Huntsville, AL 35801), 1985.

Quilting, Search Press, 1978.

Redovian, Martin, *Stitch Length Stitch Width*, (Lafayette Sewing Center, 1048 Brown Ave., Lafayette, CA 94549), 1974.

Reeder, S. Gail, *Creative Applique*, Willcraft Publishers (5093 Williamsport Dr., Norcross, GE 30071), 1983.

Ripley, Shirley R., *Decorate a Shirt, Creative Machine Embroidery* (2127 N. Sossaman, Mesa, AZ 85207), 1980.

Risley, Christine, *The Technique of Creative Embroidery*, Studio Vista, 1969.

———, *Machine Embroidery, A Complete Guide*, Studio Vista, 1973.

Robinson, Charlotte, ed., *The Artist & The Quilt*, Alfred A. Knopf, 1983.

Sewing Machine Blue Book (yearly), Bobette Industries Inc. (2401 S. Hill St., Los Angeles, CA 90007).

Short, Eirian, *Embroidery and Fabric Collage*, Sir Isaac Pitman & Sons Ltd., 1967.

Singer Sewing Machine Company, *Instructions for Art Embroidery and Lace Work*, 1911.

Skjerseth, Douglas Neil, *Stitchology*, Seth Publications (PO Box 1606, Novato, CA 94947), 1979.

Swift, Gay, *Machine Stitchery*, Charles T. Branford, 1974.

Thompson, Sue, *Decorative Dressmaking*, Rodale Press, 1985.

Timmons, Alice, *Introducing Patchwork*, Watson Guptill, 1968.

———, *Making Fabric Wall Hangings*, Chas. T. Branford, 1970.

Tower, Libby, et al, *Elegant Way to Applique*, (PO Box 16800, Ste. 180, Mesa, AZ 85202), 1984.

Wagner, Deb, and Esther Wagner, *Wagner's Sewing Machine Artistry*, (774 S. Dale St., Hutchinson, MN 55350), 1984.

Weiss, Rita, *The Patchworker's Sewing Machine Quilt*, American School of Needlework, Northbrook, IL, 1982.

Wood, Kaye, *Turn Me Over...I'm Reversible*, ESP, 1984.

Good Books on Lettering

Hornung, Clarence P., *Lettering from A to Z*, Wm. Penn Publishing, 1946.

Larcher, Jean, *Allover Patterns with Letter Forms*, Dover, 1985.

Priscilla Publishing Co., *Old-Fashioned Monogramming for Needleworkers,* Dover, 1985.

Russell, Pat, *Lettering for Embroidery,* Van Nostrand Reinhold, 1971.

Smith, Jini, *Alphagraphics and Alphabetrics* and *Applique Addict,* (633 Breakers Pt., Schaumburg, IL 60194), 1974, 1978, 1983.

Zieman, Nancy, *"Monogramming by Machine"* (video tape for rent or purchase), PO Box 683, Beaver Dam, WI 53916.

Index

282

HANDY ALL-AT-ONE-GLANCE MACHINE EMBROIDERY CHART

	chapter	stitch		tensions		foot	feed dog	hoop	backing	needle	thread
		width	length	top	bobbin						
applique	3	v*	v	loosen	normal	applique	up	no	stabilizer	12 (80)	extra-fine
automatic	7	v	v	v	v	embroidery	up	no	stabilizer	v	v
beading	3	v	fine	tighten	loosen	embroidery	up	no	no	10/11(70)	extra-fine
cable	6	0	0	v	bypass	darning	lower	no	no	16/18(100/110)	heavy on top
circular embroidery	8	v	v	universal		embroidery	in place	yes	stabilizer	10/11(70)	extra-fine
couching-by-piercing	5	0	0	universal		darning	lower	no	stabilizer	v	invisible
couching, topside	4	0	0	normal	loosen	darning	lower	no	no	v	v
couching, underside	6	0–4	10–12	loosen	bypass	regular	in place	no	no	vv	heavy under
crosshatching	2	0	0	universal		regular	up	no	no	v	v
crosshatching, zigzag	3	v	10–12	universal		regular	up	no	no	v	v
cross stitch	10	v	v	universal		regular	up	no	no	v	v
cut work	3	medium	fine	loosen	loosen	embroidery	up	yes	no	v	v
detached whip stitch	5	0	0	tighten	bypass	darning	lower	yes	interfacing	v	v
edges, special	10	v	v	universal		embroidery	in place	yes	stabilizer	v	v
encroaching zigzag	5	v	0	loosen	normal	darning	lower	yes	stabilizer	10/11(70)	extra-fine
eyelets	8	v	0	universal		none	e. plate	yes	no	v	v
fagoting	7	wide	10–12	loosen	normal	embroidery	in place	no	paper	v	v
free machine embroidery	4	0	0	loosen	normal	darning	lower	yes	stabilizer	v	v
hemstitching	9		10–12	universal		regular	in place	no	no	wing	extra-fine
monograms	10	v	0	loosen	normal	darning	lower	yes	stabilizer	10/11(70)	extra-fine
needlelace	9	0	0	universal		darning	lower	yes	no	10/11(70)	extra-fine
openwork	9	0	0	universal		darning	lower	no	no	v	v
quilting, presser foot	2	0	10–12	loosen	loosen	walking	up	no	stabilizer	v	v
quilting, free	12	0	0	loosen	normal	darning	lower	yes	no	v	v
picot	8	0	10–12	universal		regular	in place	no	no	wing	extra-fine
pintucking	8	0	10–12	tighten	normal	pintuck	in place	no	no	v	v
reverse applique	9	v	fine	loosen	normal	embroidery	in place	no	no	v	v
rugmaking	7	v	10–12	universal		regular	in place	no	no	v	v
satin stitch	3	v	fine	loosen	regular	embroidery	in place	no	no	10/11(70)	extra-fine
satin stitch spots	5	v	0	loosen	normal	darning	lower	no	no	v	v
smocking	8	v	10–12	universal		regular	in place	no	no	twin	v
stocking face dolls	9	0	0	universal		darning	lower	no	organza	10/11(70)	extra-fine
straight stitch	2	0	any	universal		regular	up	no	no	v	v
topstitching	2	0	8–10	universal		regular	up	no	no	v	v
trapunto	2	0	10–12	universal		regular	up	no	organza	v	v
vari-width zigzag	3	v	fine	universal		embroidery	up	no	stabilizer	v	v
whip stitch	4	0	0	tighten	bypass	darning	lower	yes	no	v	v
zigzag, open	3	v	10–12	universal		regular	up	no	stabilizer	v	v
zigzag shading	5	v	0	loosen	tighten	darning	lower	yes	stabilizer	10/11(70)	extra-fine

*varies

This duplicate chart can be readily removed and posted by your sewing machine